TROY CITY, HOMER AND TURKEY

TR**O**Y

CITY
HOMER
TURKEY

CHIEF EDITORS
Jorrit Kelder, Günay Uslu, Ömer Faruk Şerifoğlu

EDITORIAL TEAM
René van Beek, Floris van den Eijnde,
Gert Jan van Wijngaarden

WITH CONTRIBUTIONS BY
Willem J. Aerts, Rüstem Aslan, Mithat Atabay,
Beşir Ayvazoğlu, Mathieu de Bakker, Pim den Boer,
Diederik Burgersdijk, Christiaan Caspers, Hein van Eekert,
Floris van den Eijnde, Laurien de Gelder, Rudolph Glitz,
Irene J.F. de Jong, Jorrit Kelder, Alwin Kloekhorst,
Jacqueline Klooster, Marco Poelwijk, Winfred van de Put,
Wendy Rigter, David Rijser, Ömer Faruk Şerifoğlu,
Ali Sönmez, Şükrü Tül, Günay Uslu, Herbert Verreth,
Willemijn Waal, Gert Jan van Wijngaarden

COORDINATION
Paulien Retèl

W BOOKS

This joint publication by the Allard Pierson Museum and Sezer Tansuğ Sanat Vakfi in cooperation with the Zenobia Foundation is published alongside the exhibition *Troy. City, Homer and Turkey* from 7 December 2012 to 5 May 2013 in the Allard Pierson Museum in Amsterdam.

ORGANISING COMMITTEE MINISTRY OF CULTURE AND TOURISM OF THE REPUBLIC OF TURKEY

Ertuğrul Günay, *Minister of Culture and Tourism*
Özgür Özaslan, *Undersecretary, Ministry of Culture and Tourism*
O. Murat Süslü, *Director General for Cultural Heritage and Museums*
Abdullah Kocapınar, *Deputy Director General for Cultural Heritage and Museums*
Zülküf Yılmaz, *Head of Museums Department, Cultural Heritage and Museums*
Nilüfer Ertan, *Head of Cultural Activities Section, Cultural Heritage and Museums*
Hanife Çırak, *Archaeologist, Cultural Heritage and Museums*

BOARD OF RECOMMENDATION

Jan Paul Dirkse, *Dutch Ambassador to Turkey*
Eberhard van der Laan, *Mayor of Amsterdam and honorary chairman of the Association of Friends of the Allard Pierson Museum*
Özgür Özaslan, *States Secretary for Culture and Tourism of the Republic of Turkey*
Enis Tataroğlu, *Director Turkish Tourist Office, The Hague*

SPONSORS AND FUNDS

The exhibition, book and symposium received the generous support of the Turkish Tourist Office as main sponsor, Turkey-Netherlands 400 years, Corendon Touristic, Sezer Tansuğ Sanat Vakfi, Mondriaan Fonds, Prins Bernhard Cultuurfonds, SNS REAAL Fonds, VSBfonds, Labrys Reizen, Stichting Charema – Fonds voor Geschiedenis en Kunst, the research priority Heritage and digital culture of the University of Amsterdam, and the Friends of the Allard Pierson Museum.

WITH THE SUPPORT OF

NWO Mosaic

WITH SPECIAL THANKS TO

Rüstem Aslan, *Projekt Troia, Çanakkale*
Mustafa Küçük, *Ottoman Archives of the Prime Ministry, Istanbul*
Havva Koç, *Library of the Archaeological Museum in Istanbul*
Mithat Atabay, *University of Çanakkale*

WORKS LOANED BY

Ministry of Culture and Tourism (Ankara), Çanakkale Arkeoloji Müzesi (Çanakkale), Çorum Arkeoloji Müzesi (Çorum), İstanbul Arkeoloji Müzeleri (Istanbul), Gülbün Mesara Koleksiyonu (Istanbul), Special Collections of the University of Amsterdam, EYE Film Institute the Netherlands, Hoogsteder & Hoogsteder (The Hague), Koninklijke Musea voor Kunst en Geschiedenis (Brussels), Rijksmuseum van Oudheden (Leiden), Staatliche Museen zu Berlin, Vorderasiatisches Museum and Museum für Vor- und Frühgeschichte (Berlin), Turkish Consulate (Rotterdam), Cevdet Serbest (Istanbul), Günay Uslu (Amsterdam), Ömer Faruk Şerifoğlu (Istanbul), and private collections.

CONTENTS

MINISTRY OF CULTURE AND TOURISM OF THE REPUBLIC OF TURKEY

To mark the occasion of 400 years of diplomatic relations between the Netherlands and Turkey, the Allard Pierson Museum, the archaeological museum of the University of Amsterdam, is organising the exhibition *Troy. City, Homer and Turkey*, which also displays artefacts from the Archaeological Museum of Istanbul and from museums in Çanakkale and Çorum.

Troy lies in Turkey on the eastern shores of the Dardanelles, at the most important crossing point linking north and south, east and west. With the start of excavations in the 1870s, Troy became one of the world's most important archaeological regions. All the remains and the finds made there reflect the typically Anatolian characteristics of Trojan culture.

The story told in the 8th century BC by the great poet Homer, who originated from Western Anatolia, in his *Iliad* about the Trojan War is of an artistic and literary worth that continues to have an impact into our era in a wide range of artistic fields, including literature, film, theatre, painting and sculpture. The war in the epic was between the Achaeans from the other side of the Aegean and the indigenous Anatolian Trojans. For this reason Troy continued to live on in the memory down the centuries, on account of the conflict between West and East and between Europe and Asia. The Persian King Xerxes visited Priam's citadel during his campaign against Greece, while the Macedonian Alexander the Great paid a visit to the tomb of Achilles during his conquest of Asia. The region's significance was underlined once more by the events and occurrences following the conquests of the great Ottoman Sultan Mehmed II in 1462 and those of the great leader Atatürk, founder of the Republic of Turkey, in the Battle of the Dardanelles. For this reason it is significant that Troy, where the culture of the world has its roots, was declared a 'National Peace Park' by the Republic of Turkey on 30 October 1996.

This exhibition includes important finds from the excavations conducted by Heinrich Schliemann between 1870 and 1890 and by Carl Blegen between 1932 and 1939: from the Bronze Age axes, a gold nugget and gold rod, pottery, weaving weights, drinking cups (*depas*), necklaces and a stone idol; from the Hellenic Period heads of terracotta figurines; and from the Roman era Ilion coins referring back to ancient Troy. Alongside all this, there are tablets on which the kings of Ahhiyawa are referred to, as well as a treaty between Troy and Hattuša.

I am confident that the current close ties of friendship binding the Netherlands and Turkey will be strengthened even further by this exhibition. I would like to take the opportunity to express my thanks to all those who have contributed to making this exhibition possible.

O. Murat Süslü, *director-General Cultural Heritage and Museums*
Ministry of Culture and Tourism of the Republic of Turkey

FOREWORD

EMBASSY OF THE REPUBLIC OF TURKEY TO THE NETHERLANDS

The exhibition *Troy. City, Homer and Turkey* is being held in Amsterdam at a most propitious time, as we are celebrating the 400th anniversary of the establishment of diplomatic relations between Turkey and the Netherlands. As Troy connects our rich and diverse cultures hailing from almost 3,000 years back, the unique relationship between our two countries, based on mutual respect and cooperation, has been reinforced by 400 years of unblemished history.

Now, the exhibition at the prestigious Allard Pearson Museum of Amsterdam will undoubtedly act as an excellent conduit to project our deeply rooted common bonds into the future.

The name "Troy" conjures up many different images to one's mind – wars, fascinating historical figures, the Trojan Horse, human tragedies and so on. While reminding us of the destructive effects of rivalry, war and deception, it also inspires us to value human interactions and to respect one another's cultures and common historical heritage. I believe we should concentrate more on this positive side, as we need understanding and tolerance to flourish more than ever today.

It is my firm belief that this exhibition will further enhance recognition and tolerance between identities and cultures that are different but also very similar. Therefore, I owe an immense amount of thanks and appreciation to all those distinguished scholars, curators and others who brought these truly unique works of art and relics together to the benefit of the discerning public in the Netherlands.

Uğur Doğan, *ambassador to the Netherlands of the Republic of Turkey*

FOREWORD

ALLARD PIERSON MUSEUM AND SEZER TANSUĞ SANAT VAKFI

Troy. City, Homer and Turkey is a collaborative project with many dimensions and perspectives. It rounds off the celebrations marking 400 years of diplomatic relations between Turkey and the Netherlands in 2012 and provides a good launching pad and powerful impetus to a wide range of new initiatives between the two countries. New finds and recent research have provided fresh perspectives to *Troy. City, Homer and Turkey* - in cooperation with Sezer Tansuğ Sanat Vakfı- as may be seen from this publication accompanying the exhibition of the same name in the Allard Pierson Museum, the archaeology museum of the University of Amsterdam.

Those who think about Troy and Homer do not automatically think of Turkey. But this will certainly change after reading this publication and seeing the accompanying exhibition. This is thanks primarily to Günay Uslu, the initiator of the project. Her initial programme, along with the ground-breaking research she conducted for her doctoral thesis at the European Cultural History Department of the University of Amsterdam, provided powerful and essential stimulus for this project. Collaboration between the Allard Pierson Museum and Sezer Tansuğ Sanat Vakfı was key to its success and finds expression in this publication, the exhibition and the symposia.

The exceptional loans from Turkish collections were made possible only with the generous agreement of the Ministry of Culture and Tourism in Ankara. We would in particular like to express our heartfelt thanks to the Minister of Culture and Tourism of the Republic of Turkey, Ertuğrul Günay, the Secretary of State of the Ministry of Culture and Tourism, Özgür Özaslan, and to O. Murat Süslü, Director General for Cultural Heritage and Museums at the Ministry of Culture and Tourism, for the confidence that they have shown in us. We greatly appreciate their generous agreement and the efforts of their staff at the Ministry of Culture and Tourism, at the İstanbul Arkeoloji Müzeleri (Istanbul Archaeology Museums), the Çanakkale Arkeoloji Müzesi and at the Çorum Arkeoloji Müzesi (Çorum Archaeology Museum). The same applies to the support we have received through the Turkish Embassy in the person of Uğur Doğan, Turkish ambassador to the Netherlands, along with the members of his staff, Cem Utkan, M. Hakan Cengiz and Enis Tataroğlu, director of the Turkish Tourist Office in the Netherlands.

The exhibition was put together by a team of curators comprising Günay Uslu, René van Beek and Gert Jan van Wijngaarden. Marian Schilder was project leader, and the management group was chaired by Steph Scholten, director of the Heritage Collections of the University of Amsterdam. We would also like to thank others who loaned artefacts to the exhibition: Alix Hänsel of the Museum für Vor- und Frühgeschichte (Museum for Prehistory and Early History), Berlin, Joachim Marzahn of the Vorderasiatisches Museum (Near East Museum), Berlin, Michel Draguet of the Koninklijke Musea voor Kunst en Geschiedenis (Royal Museums of Art and History), Brussels, Wim Weijland of the Rijksmuseum van Oudheden (National Museum of Antiquities), Leiden, Garrelt Verhoeven of the Special Collections of the University of Amsterdam, John Hoogsteder and Willem Jan Hoogsteder of Hoogsteder & Hoogsteder, The Hague, Cevdet Serbest, Gunay Uslu, Ömer Faruk Şerifoğlu, and private collections.

A group of Turkish and Dutch specialists were asked to publish their most recent insights into Troy for the purposes of this publication. We wish to express our gratitude to these authors and the Zenobia Foundation. This publication was coordinated by Paulien Retèl, and the senior editors included Günay Uslu, Ömer Faruk Şerifoğlu and Jorrit Kelder, with an editing team consisting of René van Beek, Floris van den Eijnde and Gert Jan van Wijngaarden. We would particularly like to thank our translators Cem Yavuz, Kutse Altın, Rohan Minogue, Corinna Vermeulen and Ilia Neudecker and everyone who contributed to creating this publication.

The project has been supported by J.P. Dirkse, the Dutch ambassador to Turkey, Filiz Güneş, the cultural attaché in Ankara and Fokke Gerritsen of the Netherlands Institute in Istanbul, Turkey.

The project could not have been realised without the generous support of many donors and sponsors, including the Turkish Tourist Office as main sponsor, 400 years Netherlands Turkey, Corendon International Travel, Sezer Tansuğ Sanat Vakfı Foundation, the Mondriaan Fund, the Prince Bernhard Culture Fund, the SNS REAAL Fund, the VSB Fund, Stichting Charema – Fonds voor Geschiedenis en Kunst, the research priority Heritage and digital culture of the University of Amsterdam and the Friends of the Allard Pierson Museum.

Ilion, the immortal city of Homer, remains a nonpareil source of inspiration to all humanity for 3,000 years. We hope, through this project, once again it will be realised that European cultural history is inextricably bound up with Troy, the major heritage site in Turkey.

Wim Hupperetz, director, *Allard Pierson Museum*
Ömer Taşdelen, *Sezer Tansuğ Sanat Vakfı*

1 THE STORY OF TROY

HOMER: POET, POETRY AND THE PROMISE OF ETERNAL RENOWN

IRENE J.F. DE JONG

Whoever thinks of Troy thinks of Homer. In the *Iliad* this poet evokes the city of Troy and above all the fate of its inhabitants so vividly that European cultural history is unimaginable without them. Troy lay in ruins after the 12th century BC and only modest attempts at rebuilding were ever made, but in Homer's poetry the city lives on in all its glory with its 'strong walls', 'high gates' and 'wide streets'. A later Greek epigrammist puts the following words into the mouth of the city of Troy itself – referred to here as Ilion:

> Strangers, time's ashes have completely devoured me,
> the renowned city, holy Ilion,
> once famed for its walls with their strong bulwarks, but in
> Homer I still exist, protected by bronze gates. The spears of
> the destroying Greeks shall not again dig me up, but I shall
> be on the lips of all Greeks.
> (Euenus *Anthologia Palatina* 9.62)

Who was this poet Homer, who created such influential works of art with his *Iliad* and *Odyssey*? Unfortunately here we are groping about in the dark. The ancient Greeks themselves knew nothing with certainty about their greatest poet, and today we have not progressed much further. His identity, date of birth and where he lived are shrouded in mist. His dates range from the 9th to the 7th century BC, and even in antiquity many cities laid claim to his place of birth. Linguistic indications point to Smyrna (currently Izmir), the island of Chios or to Cyme in the west of Asia Minor. These are regions where the territories of the Ionians and Aeolians overlapped, and the idiom of the *Iliad* and the *Odyssey* reveals a mixture of precisely the dialects of these peoples. There are biographies from the Roman era, but these lack all value as evidence. They are, as so often in antiquity, constructed from elements taken from the poems themselves. For example, one such biography relates how a certain Melesigenes (= Homer), who is taught by

Phemius (a name suspiciously like that of the famous singer in the *Odyssey*), is convinced one day by a certain Mentes (again a protagonist in the *Odyssey*) to set out on a journey, during which they call at Ithaca, among other places, etc. etc.

Given these uncertainties, it is not surprising that it was suggested in the 19th century – and again more recently – that Homer never existed. Singers performing the *Iliad* and the *Odyssey* were said to have invented the legend of a mythical predecessor 'Homer' in order to lend greater status to their poems.

This may perhaps go too far, but what is certain is that Homer stands in a long tradition of oral singing. This tradition arose in the Mycenaean era (1600-1200 BC), was taken to Asia Minor by singers following the fall of the Mycenaean palaces (1200 BC), and ultimately flourished along the border of Aeolia with Ionia. It is entirely possible that Homer was an exceptionally talented singer and that his epic poems were written down, or at least permanently fixed, on account of their exceptional quality, abetted perhaps by special circumstances. These circumstances could have been the introduction of writing. Another possible factor was the rise of the great Pan-Hellenic festivals in the 7th century BC. During a festival of this kind, the public had the time to listen to long poems like the *Iliad* – the roughly 15,000 lines need 24 hours to recite. Greek tragedy likewise later developed in the context of a festival, the Panathenaea.

The oral origins of the *Iliad* and the *Odyssey* in any event explain why Homer never says anything about himself in his poems. He does not even mention his own name, but is rather an anonymous 'I' that says at the beginning of the *Odyssey*: 'Muse, sing to me...'. The poet was simultaneously singer and composer of his own poems on the spot (although certainly after extended training). As the poet-singer appeared live in front of his public, he did not need to identify himself. They saw him and knew precisely who he was.

There is but a single small detail that the poet reveals about himself: he lived much later than the events he is describing. This is clear from his reference to 'the people of today' by contrast with the heroes of days gone by, whom he at one point even calls 'demigods' (*Iliad* 12.23). He also once looks back on the Trojan War from his own temporal vantage point, in an impressive passage. Once the war has been fought and won, Troy razed and the Greeks departed, the gods clear the Trojan plain

Homer, the poet-singer to whom the *Iliad* and the *Odyssey* are attributed. Where and when he lived are not known with certainty. Later biographies suggest that Homer was blind, and the staring gaze of this bust, a plaster cast from a 1st century BC original, draws on this tradition.

and flush all remains of human activity into the sea, in particular the walls that the Greeks had built around their ships. After the gods have done their work, there is nothing left on the plain to recall the battle in which so many heroes had perished. This passage has been interpreted as a sign that the poet is erasing the traces of his own poetic imagination (in his time there were no walls to be seen on the plain) but it also well suits the tragic undertone of the *Iliad*: the heroes' efforts are in vain, certainly by contrast with those of the eternal gods.

Only one thing can make the life of a hero worthwhile: eternal renown. And this is where the art of poetry makes its entrance. Because for the heroes' fame to endure, it must be stored in poems. Heroes themselves utter words of triumph after they have slain an opponent:

The Trojan War is famous primarily for the Trojan Horse, even if this tale is not mentioned in Homer's *Iliad*. The horse is possibly a reference to a siege engine like a battering ram, but it could also be linked to the god Poseidon. This Greek god was associated with horses and earthquakes, and possibly a devastating earthquake in Troy served as inspiration for the Trojan Horse in later epics, such as the *Aeneid* by Virgil. The Trojan Horse used in the 2004 Hollywood film *Troy* now stands in Çanakkale in Turkey.

But Achilles, his heart filled with courage, gave his dreadful war-cry and sprang among the Trojans. First he killed a general, Iphition, mighty son of Otrynteus and a Naiad, who, beneath snowy Tmolus in the fertile land of Hyde, bore him to that sacker of cities. Noble Achilles struck the man, who charged straight towards him, striking him smack on the head with a cast of his spear, splitting his skull in two. He fell with a thud, and noble Achilles triumphed: 'Lie there, son of Otrynteus, most redoubtable of men. Though you were born by the Gygaean Lake, where your father holds the land, by Hyllus teeming with fish, and the swirling eddies of Hermus, here is the place where you must die.' (Iliad 20.388-393)

But these are only 'winged words' that fade with time. Heroes are also allowed to relate their own adventures. We see Odysseus do this over four books in the *Odyssey*, but after his death he is no longer able to proclaim his own renown. Only poems sung by professional singers are able to keep alive the *klea androon*, the famous deeds of the heroes, down the generations and even for all time. Homer would never say it out loud, but subtly he permits one of his heroes to reveal this truth: Achilles relates that he has the choice of returning home to live out a long but inglorious life there, or of remaining in Troy to die young and to achieve *kleos afthiton*, everlasting fame (*Iliad* 9.410-416). He remains in Troy and we, the audience and the readers, realise that it is the *Iliad* itself that makes the prophecy of eternal renown come true. For good reason Alexander the Great, arriving at Troy on his march eastward, expresses the wish that he will have a Homer to immortalise his deeds.

The important role played by poetry also explains Odysseus's deep emotion when washed up at the Phaiakians as a destitute castaway after wandering for 10 years, he hears the poet Demodocus sing a poem about the Wooden Horse and the fall of Troy, containing a leading role for... Odysseus. He has lost everything, his clothes, his comrades and the booty taken from Troy, but he still has his renown.

Singers are able not only to preserve the glorious past by fixing it in poems, but also to guarantee a *reliable* picture of the past through collaboration with the muses. As goddesses, the muses are immortal and witnesses to all of history (*Iliad* 2.485). In a society lacking the written word, epic poets like Homer fill the role played later by historians.

Thus, singer and hero need each other: the singer is not himself able to perform the heroic deeds of Odysseus or Achilles and needs these heroes as material for his tale; while the heroes may perform the bravest or most evil deeds, but without the poet no one would know of them. In later times the poet Pindar will tell his successful aristocratic clients that there is no better way of spending their money than on an ode from

Papyrus fragment (22 x 14 cm) from Egypt, dating from the beginning of the era, with text from the *Iliad* (4.340-365). The epic probably had a long oral history, during which generations of singers performed tales about Troy, altering and embellishing them. The *Iliad* was set down in writing only subsequently. According to Greek historians, the story refers to events in the 13th or 12th century BC.

Plaster copy of a Greek marble relief from around 125 BC. The apotheosis of Homer is shown. At the bottom left Homer is seated, being crowned and receiving gifts. Other characters on this relief, that is shaped as a mountain, are the god Apollo and the nine Muses and a poet, probably the maker of this relief, Archelaus of Priene.

Pindar. One could opt for a statue but it would always remain on its pedestal, while poems will be sung throughout Greece.

For the Greeks, literature always was more than just entertainment or art; it was an essential part of life. When Homer reveals in his *Odyssey* that a poem about the fall of Troy has within a decade become a hit with the Phaiakians (8.499-520), people that live at the very edge of the civilised world, he is implicitly saying something about the extended impact of his own work. The idea that singers were able to ensure eternal renown is probably a traditional one, typical of all of Indo-European literature. For example, Sanskrit has the term *srávas áksitam* that expresses precisely what the Greek *kleos aphthiton* does. In the case of Homer, however, this advertising slogan has become reality, as this book on Troy published in 2012 demonstrates!

THE ORIGINS OF THE TROJAN CYCLE

JORRIT KELDER

Homer's *Iliad* is without doubt one of the most influential literary works in the history of Western civilisation. Homer describes only a brief episode, a number of days in the 10th (and last) year of the siege of Troy. His tale fits into a much broader cycle of stories about Troy and the Trojan war, which includes another work that is attributed to Homer: the *Odyssey* – the story of the arduous return voyage of one of the Greek heroes, Odysseus, after Troy has fallen to the Greeks. Since their composition in (probably) the early 8th century BC, the *Iliad* and the *Odyssey* have been read, sung, reworked, adapted and studied by numerous scholars, poets and artists. Despite the early fame of these Epics, however, much is uncertain about their author, Homer. We believe that he probably lived in the early 8th century BC and created the *Iliad* at that time. But whether Homer truly created the *Iliad*, or whether he was the talented heir to a long tradition of stories about the Trojan War, remains uncertain. His origins are also unknown. Various cities in the world of the ancient Greeks have laid claim to being the birthplace of the great poet, including the city of Smyrna, now Izmir in western Turkey, and the island of Chios, which is Greek to this day. Although various later 'biographies' of Homer – the so-called *vitae* indicate that all of these cities played a prominent role in Homer's life, it remains unclear where, exactly, the great poet was born and where he composed his great works.

Little is known of the broader story of Troy and the origins of the tale of *'the'* war. The famous Trojan horse, for example, Odysseus' ruse by means of which Troy was ultimately taken, is not mentioned in the *Iliad* and there is only a brief reference to it in the *Odyssey* (Book VIII). We know of the wooden horse and many other episodes from the 10-year siege of the city from a wide range of later compositions, such as the famous *Aeneïd* of the Roman poet Vergil (see 5.3), or the *Posthomerica* of the 4th century poet Quintus of Smyrna. It is likely that many of these later authors based their work on earlier texts, such as the *Ilioupersis (The Sack of Troy)* by Arctinus of Miletus, that are now lost, but there are also indications that new story lines and elements were added – in the mediaeval period in particular – by both western and Byzantine authors (see 5.4).

ORIGINS

The *Iliad* enjoyed a special status as early as the classical period that may perhaps best be compared with the status of the Bible in later times. On account of this special position in Greek - and later Roman – culture, the *Iliad* was subjected to critical analysis at a relatively early stage. One of these early debates, which already raged during the Classical period, concerned the exact date for the war for Troy. Most ancient Greek 'scholars' argued for a date in the early 12th century BC. Regardless of the exact date, the historicity of the War was never questioned.

Recent research has demonstrated that the *Iliad* is the product of a long oral – that is to say spoken – tradition. Stories about the Trojan War must literally have been sung long before Homer's time. It now seems that, as late as the 8th century BC, 5 these various stories were unified into a single work of

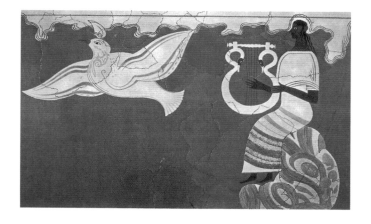

Fresco of a lyre player on the wall of the throne room in the palace at Pylos, Greece. Although elements from the *Iliad* and the *Odyssey* originate from later periods, it is possible that (early versions of) both epics were already known in the Mycenaean period. Possibly an 'ur-Iliad' was being recited in the Mycenaean courts to the accompaniment of a lyre. The singer in this fresco is playing a magnificent instrument embellished with ducks heads.

The landscape around Pylos where Homer's *Iliad* locates the palace of Nestor, the mythological old king. The ruins of a Mycenaean palace have in fact been found at Pylos.

genius, the *Iliad*, that focused on 'Achilles' baneful wrath that imposed infinite sorrows on the Greeks'. It is doubtful that the *Iliad* was put down in writing as early as this stage. There are indications that this took place only in the 6th century, on the orders of the Athenian tyrant Peisistratus. It is extremely likely that the person responsible for ultimately committing the *Iliad* to the written word had motives of his own. A number of conspicuous references to Athens – the house of Erechteus, king of Athens – and to Ionian cities – with which Athens had close links as the 'metropolis' of the Ionian colonies – lend force to the conjecture that the *Iliad* was in fact put down in writing in Athens, or in a centre linked to this city.

The fact that the *Iliad*'s ultimate form owes more than a little to relations within the Greek world of the day is scarcely a surprise. The same may be assumed for earlier variations of the story. For example, it has been noted that the iron objects mentioned in the *Iliad*, such as the iron weight that Achilles puts up as prize in the games to commemorate the death of his fallen comrade-in-arms, Patroclus, does not fit well into the Bronze Age context of the story (see box 'Iron in the Bronze Age'). References to alien peoples, such as the Phoenicians from north-west Syria, also betray Iron Age influence. It has also been suggested that Achilles' famous shield, with its manifold elaborate and realistic scenes from everyday life, is a reflection of precious Phoenician bowls of gold and silver that also showed scenes of this kind and would certainly have been known in the Greece of the 8th and 7th centuries BC.

IRON IN THE BRONZE AGE

The period following the 'Bronze Age' is generally known as the 'Iron Age'. These terms are slightly deceptive, for recent research has shown that iron was already worked in the late Bronze Age, even if only sporadically. The use of iron increased following the collapse of the 'Bronze Age World System', with all kinds of specialists, including smiths, tanners and writers that were funded by the palaces, and the rise of a system based on the *oikos* (household), in which each household aimed to be (to a large extent) self-sufficient. Given that iron ore is relatively abundant, the step was soon taken to manufacture an increasing number of items from iron, in particular objects for daily use. The first larger objects that were used for everyday purposes, such as a large (22 cm) iron sickle from 12th century BC Tiryns (in the Peloponnese), appear fairly soon after the collapse of the Mycenaean palaces.

The question is when the first stories about Troy and the Greek war against Troy began to appear. Linguistic research by, amongst others, the renowned Amsterdam scholar Cornelis Ruijgh (1930-2004) has shown that a significant part of the vocabulary that was used by Homer does not belong to the 8th century, but rather to a much earlier period; that of the Mycenaean palaces (roughly 1400 to 1200 BC). Greek was already being spoken by then, but in a very early, Mycenaean, form that differed considerably from later Greek dialects, such as Ionic and Doric. For example, the Mycenaeans still used the digamma (also known as the 'wau' and nowadays often written as a sort of 'F'): this sound disappeared from the Greek language during the Iron Age. Certain 'gaps' in the *metrum* of the *Iliad* are best explained by the disappearance of this digamma. A well-known example of the disappearance of the digamma is the Homeric word *anax* for prince (or king), which in Mycenaean is *wanax* (spelled *wa-na-ka* in Linear B).

Archaeology also suggests that significant elements in the *Iliad* originate in the Mycenaean period. The geography of Greece, for example, as described by Homer in Book II of the *Iliad* (the famous Catalogue of Ships) corresponds relatively well to the situation in the Mycenaean period, but not to the Iron Age (when several of the important cities of the *Iliad* were deserted). Moreover, a number of objects that are described in the *Iliad*, such as the 'boar's tusk helmet', clearly indicate Bronze Age origins. The picture of political unity between the various Mycenaean kingdoms, with Agamemnon, king of Mycenae, as supreme leader does not fit well into either the Iron Age or the Classical Period, but it is an entirely plausible reflection of the situation in the late Bronze Age. On the basis of all these considerations, it seems reasonable to assume that the origins of the *Iliad* should be sought in the Mycenaean period.

Naturally this is not to say that actual events form the basis of the stories in the *Iliad*, although this can certainly not be excluded. What is certain is that the *Iliad* – and all its precursors – were always in the first instance a *work of art* performed for entertainment – and instruction. It can safely be assumed that this occurred as early as the Mycenaean period: the court culture of the great palaces of Mycenaean Greece does certainly offer a perfect background for Mycenaean bards, reciting epic poems during drinking bouts. An image on the wall of the throne room of the palace at Pylos seems to show a Mycenaean bard like this, complete with ingeniously shaped lyre. It is by no means surprising that the Mycenaean aristocracy liked heroic stories. Elsewhere in the eastern Mediterranean region, such as with the Hittites of Anatolia or in pharaonic Egypt, feasts were given added lustre by recitals from celebrated bards who sang of heroic exploits in a legendary past.

AN ANATOLIAN *ILIAD*?

It is possible that there was not only a Greek, but also an Anatolian epic tradition centred on the Trojan War. A description of a ritual, recorded on a clay tablet that has been found in the Hittite capital of Hattusa and which dates to the 13th century BC, cites the opening line of a Luwian (a Bronze Age Anatolian language) song to be performed at a libation to the goddess Šuwašuna. The opening line runs as follows:

ahhatata alati awita wilusati
When they came from steep(?) Troy.

This could be the opening sentence of a Luwian epic about Wilusa (= Troy), the more so as the line can be read as two verses of seven partially alliterative groups of letters:

ahha=ta=tta alati
awita wilusati

Unfortunately the meaning of the sentence is not entirely clear. The word 'alati' appears only in this text and the translation 'steep' is tentative. In addition, only the opening verse has been preserved. For this reason, some caution is certainly advised. One line of course does not make an Anatolian *Iliad*, but who knows the second line may turn up one day.

Willemijn Waal

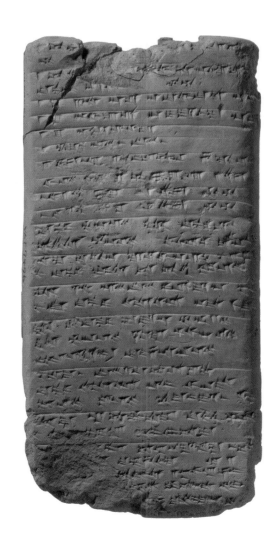

A BROADER PERSPECTIVE:
AN OVERVIEW OF THE EAST

WILLEMIJN WAAL

The story of how the *Iliad* and the *Odyssey* came into being is long and complex. Although both epics are generally regarded as skilfully constructed, powerful poems, they are the result of centuries of oral tradition. In this, the Homeric epics are not alone, nor are they (as has often been posited) exclusively 'Greek', for similar, but far older poems – with similar heroes,

Greek vase from 480-470 BC with a scene from the *Iliad*: as his mother Thetis brings him a helmet, Achilles, shown with his brother Antilochus, mourns Patroclus. Achilles' sorrow at the death of his best friend has a parallel in the *Gilgamesh* epic.

A clay tablet from Hattuša with the opening line of perhaps an Anatolian *Iliad*. The *Iliad* is frequently regarded as the starting point of Western literature, but many elements of its style and themes were known previously in the ancient Middle East. We know of poems from Mesopotamia and Anatolia that reveal similarities with the *Iliad* and the *Odyssey*.

heroic exploits and style elements- are known from the ancient Near East. The *Epic of Gilgamesh*, an epic that originates from ancient Mesopotamia, is one of the more famous of these Near Eastern parallels.

THE *ILIAD* AND THE *EPIC OF GILGAMESH*

Despite their 'unique' status, the *Iliad* and the *Odyssey* are certainly not the first great epics to have been committed to writing. The *Epic of Gilgamesh*, a poem whose essence originated in late 3rd millennium BC Mesopotamia, in many ways can be seen as a precursor to the works of Homer: with respect both to its themes and style, and to the history of how it came into being.

The *Epic of Gilgamesh* – or 'He who Saw the Deep', as the original title ran – tells of the journeys and misfortunes of Gilgamesh, the legendary king of Uruk, and his friend Enkidu. The epic covers a total of 12 clay tablets with around 3,000 lines in cuneiform script.

It is impossible to outline the story in a few sentences without doing a disservice to the enormous wealth, beauty and multi-layered nature of this epic, that is often described as the first humanist document in the history of the world. The epic's overarching theme may perhaps best be described as 'making sense of life', along with the perception and acceptance of the limitations of the human condition.

There are a number of similarities between the *Epic of Gilgamesh* and the *Iliad*. Consider, for example, the two main protagonists, Gilgamesh and Achilles. Both are sons of a mortal father and a divine mother. They share a strong attachment to the latter. The two men also have similar characters: strong, proud, impulsive and emotional. The friendship between Gilgamesh and Enkdiu, moreover, is comparable to that between Achilles and Patroclus. The two heroes are inconsolable when their respective friends die, and this event forms a significant turning point in both their lives. The passages in which the deaths of their close friends are described reveal remarkable similarities:

> *Gilgamesh touched him on the heart,*
> *But the heart beats no more.*
> *Then he covered up his friend like a bride.*
> *Like as a lion, Gilgamesh raised his voice,*
> *Like as a lioness, he roared out.*

19

Cylinder seal made of lapis lazuli from Babylonia, 2200 BC, height 3 cm. Gilgamesh and Enkidu are shown fighting with a bull and a lion on this cylinder seal (depicted here with a modern impression). The Mesopotamian *Epic of Gilgamesh* may in many respects be seen as a precursor of Homer's works.

He turns round to his friend,
He tears his hair and strews it forth. . .
(*Epic of Gilgamesh*, tablet 8, v. 57- 61, translated
by William Ellery Leonard)

And the son of Peleus led them in their lament. He laid his mur-
derous hands upon the breast of his comrade, groaning again
and again as a bearded lion when a man who was chasing deer
has robbed him of his young in some dense forest; when the lion
comes back he is furious, and searches dingle and dell to track the
hunter if he can find him, for he is mad with rage.
(*Iliad* 18.316-323, translated by Samuel Butler)

In both the *Iliad* and the *Epic of Gilgamesh*, the hero lays his hand on the breast of his fallen comrade, and both heroes are compared to a distraught lioness robbed of her cubs.

There are also various similarities between the *Epic of Gilgamesh* and the *Odyssey*: for example, the wanderings and adventures of Gilgamesh recall Odysseus' journey as he returns home from the Trojan War. For this reason, the *Epic of Gilgamesh* has been described as the '*Odyssey* of Achilles'.

How should we explain these similarities? They certainly do not indicate that the *Epic of Gilgamesh* (when it was set down in written form in the 2nd millennium BC) had a direct influence on the *Iliad*. The thematic parallels and similarities in certain metaphors and motifs suggest rather that both epics are rooted in the same oral tradition. During the late Bronze Age, Greece was very much a part of the old Near East, and thus of an extensive cultural continuum, which involved the exchange of ideas and stories. The authors of the *Epic of Gilgamesh* and the *Iliad* and the *Odyssey* drew from the same reservoir of stories and metaphors. Using these stories and metaphors, they cre-

ated their own, original and majestic epics in their own mould and using their own imaginative powers.

GENESIS OF AN EPIC

The origins of the *Iliad* remain shrouded in darkness. The parallel of the *Epic of Gilgamesh* may, however, shed some light on the processes that led to the creation of these famous epics.

We are able to track the development of the *Epic of Gilgamesh* over around two millennia reasonably well. We know from the Sumerian King List (cuneiform inscriptions showing the names of the kings of Sumer) that a king of Uruk called Gilgamesh probably ruled halfway through the third millennium BC. It is generally assumed that a number of legends arose surrounding this king and that these legends were orally transmitted through the ages. From around 2100 BC various stories about this hero were set down in writing. These stories were not merely the committing to written form of an oral tradition already in cir-

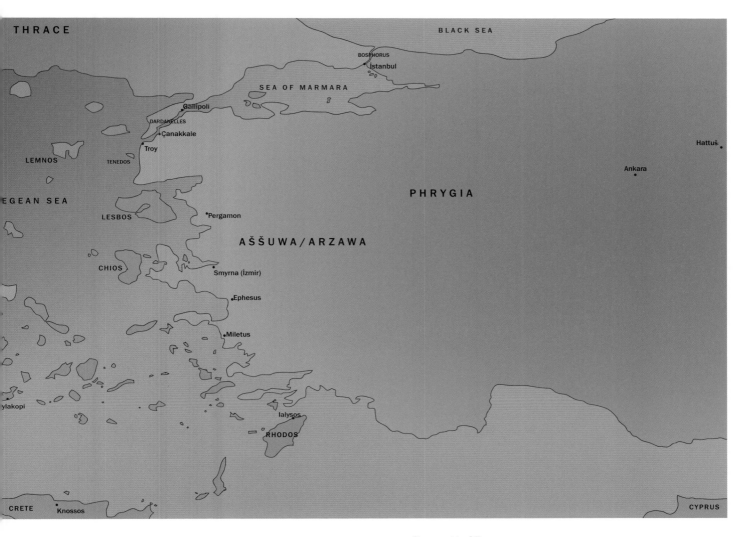

The world of Troy.

culation; for that they have been too carefully edited: they were part of the school curriculum. A unified version of these existing traditional stories arose around 1800 BC, in which several stories were combined. This compilation was not yet standard, since various versions of the epic, unfortunately poorly transmitted, differ from one another. Finally the standard version of the epic was set down on 12 tablets presumably around 1200 BC. This standard version was subsequently attributed to the man of letters Sîn-lēqi-unnini. However, we do not know how big a role he really played in the composition of this final 'canonical' version of the epic. Possibly he was merely the final editor. This standard version was copied over the centuries up to the 2nd century BC. Here it is important to keep in mind that in all probability a lively and much more extensive oral tradition centred on Gilgamesh, which has not survived, continued to exist alongside this written version. We have only these texts that often represent merely the tip of the iceberg.

It is certainly conceivable that the *Iliad* and the *Odyssey* had a comparable history of origin and evolution, and are also the result of a longer tradition of stories based on historical facts and persons. At a given point, a selection of these stories could have been woven into a great epic that was set down in writing. How big a role Homer played in composing this 'standard version' of the *Iliad* is unclear, just as it is with Sîn-lēqi-unnini. Both epics stand rooted in oral tradition, but are simultaneously original literary creations revealing a thematic and dramatic unity.

This scenario corresponds with the fact that 'Homeric society' in the *Iliad* contains elements from the Mycenaean period, the subsequent so-called 'Dark Age' and the Iron Age (see also chapter 4). These inconsistencies support the notion of a dynamic oral tradition, in which certain original elements continue to exist, while others are adapted to reflect contemporary customs and practices.

2 THE ARCHAEOLOGY OF TROY

THE ARCHAEOLOGY OF TROY IN PREHISTORY

GERT JAN VAN WIJNGAARDEN

The name of Troy is famous, and those visiting the site of Troy at Hıssarlik or the Trojan collections at the museums of Istanbul and Çanakkale have high expectations. But many feel confused after their visit and wonder "Was that it?" There are highlights, of course, including a few sculptures and Priam's Treasure, the gold smuggled out of Turkey by the archaeologist Heinrich Schliemann that ended up in Russia at the end of the Second World War after being taken from Berlin (see chapter 7). But most of the finds consist of rather unspectacular pottery and other mundane objects. There are many other archaeological sites in Turkey that are more impressive, for example Ephesus and Hattuša. By comparison with these, Troy appears small and chaotic. Visitors are confronted with the remains of numerous walls; an archaeological maze in the midst of an agricultural landscape. It is difficult to imagine that these are the remains of a city that was described so impressively by Homer, and that has been the subject of films by several Hollywood directors.

It is obvious that the myth of the Trojan War, and not the archaeology, lend particular significance to the remains. The war is said to have lasted 10 years, a long time for a war. However, the archaeological remains at Troy span a period of more than 4,000 years. And this helps to explain part of the confusion. The city has a particularly long history of settlement, and most of the archaeological remains have nothing to do with the war described by Homer. There is no one single Troy; there are at least 10, lying in layers on top of each other.

The sea, visible in the distance from the excavation site, also causes confusion. In the *Iliad* the heroes advance and retreat between Troy and the Greek camp on the beach, and there are even indications that the Greeks could be seen clearly from the walls of Troy. But from the hill of the citadel the distance to the coast appears to be too great for frequent encounters of this kind between the Greeks and Trojans.

A reconstruction of Troy VI-VIIa: Homeric Troy? Recent excavations under the direction of the German archaeologist Manfred Korfmann have shown that there was human habitation outside the walls of the citadel. On the basis of sporadic finds, Korfmann reconstructed a crowded, densely inhabited Lower City, as shown here. However, Korfmann's reconstruction of the Lower City remain extremely controversial.

LOCATION

Troy lies on the edge of a plateau to the east of the course of the Scamander River. The hill rises around 30 metres above a fertile plain consisting of sediment from the Scamander and Simoeis rivers that flow together here. Recent geological research has shown that the coast has changed dramatically through the ages, and that Troy lay at the edge of a deep bay containing a number of good harbours. The coast is now far away, but the city once lay more or less on it.

Geological research around the citadel of Troy has also shown that the city was much larger than the part excavated by Schliemann and his successors, and that there was more than just a citadel. From the second phase of habitation onwards, important parts of the city lay to the south and south-east of it. This lower city, which saw long and changing patterns of settlement, like the citadel itself, was fortified by a ditch and in certain periods a wooden palisade. The lower city features prominently in the discussion over the historical veracity of the Trojan War. Troy looks much more like the city so impressively described by Homer with a large and fortified lower city. However, it is debated whether all parts of the lower city were inhabited at the same time, and there is also no agreement on its extent in the various periods. Following the abandonment of Troy, the lower city became completely invisible, partly because its remains were used by the area's later inhabitants. It has only recently been possible to make the lower city visible with the aid of modern geophysical methods.

Troy's current location in the landscape is thus deceptive. The city's size fluctuated through time, and the sea much was closer to the city than it is today. However, it is difficult to determine the precise chronological evolution of the natural and urban landscapes, and there is no consensus among archaeologists and other experts on the appearance of the city and the landscape in the various periods.

LAYER ON LAYER

Troy is a so-called tell (*höyük* in Turkish), an artificial mound created by thousands of years of habitation. This is a normal phenomenon in south-eastern Europe and the Middle East, where sun-dried mud bricks (blocks of clay mixed with finely chopped straw) were long the most important building material. Bricks of this kind are easy to make and plentiful, but they cannot readily be reused, and for this reason, a new city was built on the ruins of the old every time that the city was destroyed by earthquake or war. The same happened whenever new inhabitants rebuilt the city following a period in which the hill had been deserted. As a result of this continuous process of destruction and rebuilding, desertion and renovation, the Hıssarlik rises more than 15 metres, holding the remains of more than 4,000 years of history.

Within this mound, archaeologists distinguish multiple layers, with the most recent construction phases uppermost, and the bottom layers corresponding to the earliest traces of habitation. Nine major phases of construction have been identified. These are numbered using Latin numerals as Troy I to Troy X. The first seven construction phases (Troy I-VII) refer to continuous prehistoric settlement from around 3000-900 BC. Within these seven main construction phases, less significant construction phases have subsequently been identified that are indicated by letters: Troy IIa, IIb, IIc etc. More than 50 different construction phases of prehistoric habitation can be identified in this way. The interpretation of the multiple layers is not always straightforward, and archaeologists frequently differ on ascribing complexes of finds to particular layers.

The remains of Greek and Roman periods of habitation, Troy VIII and IX respectively, which existed from around 700 BC to 450 AD lie above the prehistoric settlements. Troy X (12th-14th century AD) consists solely of a Byzantine church. After it was abandoned, the site was uninhabited until Schliemann and his companion Frank Calvert began their excavations at the end of the 19th century. The current tourist infrastructure erected at the site could be seen as Troy XI.

Apart from the long and layered history of habitation, it is also significant that the site was deserted over three long periods: in the Early Iron Age from around 900-700 BC, from the Roman period to the building of the Byzantine church (ca. 600 years) and from the Middle Ages to the arrival of Schliemann (ca. 500 years). Troy's first period of abandonment is noteworthy as it corresponds precisely to the time that the Homeric epics are given form and orally transmitted. At the same time that the verses were set down in writing, or shortly thereafter, a Greek shrine was established in Troy around which a city later developed. How the literary and physical construction of Greek Troy were related to each other is an important but still unsolved question (see 2.3 and chapter 4).

ORIGINS: TROY I (CA. 2920-2550 BC)

The oldest settlement remains in Troy can be investigated only with difficulty. They lie at the bottom of the tell, and archaeologists have reached this level in only a few places. The investigations reveal a small city surrounded by a defensive wall of unworked stone. The wall included several towers and at

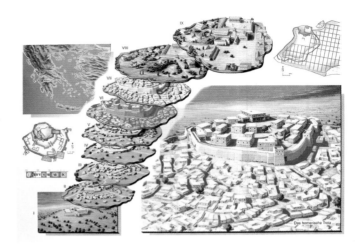

Hisarlık, the current name for Troy, has a long history of human habitation that may be roughly subdivided into 9 significant phases starting in the early 3rd Millennium BC. The cross-section shown here provides an outline of the city's citadel, comparable in its extent with, for example, Dam Square in Amsterdam.

least three gates. Outside the southern and largest gate stood a monumental stone into which a face had been roughly hewn. It is impossible now to determine the precise significance of this stone. It was possibly a god to welcome visitors, or a protective deity. Erecting carved stones of this kind (*orthostates*) at gates was to become a longstanding custom in the history of Troy.

Remains of houses from this period of Troy may only be seen in the deep trench that Schliemann dug right through Troy. The foundations of a number of houses lying next to each other were found, each of which consists of a single elongated room. One house standing slightly apart is noteworthy. It has a large open forecourt, and traces of a hearth were found in the main chamber. This is the earliest example of the *megaron* house; a type of building that played a significant role during the Bronze Age in Greece and Turkey. It is possibly the precursor of Mycenaean palaces and ultimately Greek temples.

The finds from Troy I suggest a relatively simple society, in which people engaged in agriculture, animal husbandry and fishing. The pottery was simple and handmade. There is considerable evidence for crafts like spinning and weaving. The inhabitants of early Troy had, at the same time, contact with the world abroad. Finds, such as moulds for bronze knives and chisels, indicate that bronze-working (a relatively new technology at that time) was adopted early on in Troy's existence.

TROY'S FLOWERING IN THE EARLY BRONZE AGE: TROY II AND III (CA. 2550-2200 BC)

A clear break may be seen between Troy I and Troy II: Troy II developed slowly from the previous phase. After being devastated by fire on a number of occasions, the city was considerably enlarged and furnished with a massive defensive wall made of cut blocks of stone and rectangular clay bricks. The wall contained a number of towers, a monumental drive and ingenious gate structures that led visitors immediately into the city centre. The first habitation immediately to the south of the citadel itself began in this period. This lower city was surrounded by a wooden palisade and had a cistern for storing water.

The kind of habitation can best be reconstructed on the basis of the houses in the citadel itself. There a large number of buildings are to be found of the *megaron* type mentioned above: an elongated room with a hearth and an open forecourt. It is worth mentioning that these *megaron* houses are larger and more massively built than the other buildings in the citadel. This is an indication of increased social difference in Trojan society and of the expression of power. During the last building phase in Troy II, a large central building of the *megaron* type was built in the middle of the citadel itself. The surrounding houses had several square rooms and communal walls of a type that occurs elsewhere in the Aegean, on the Cyclades, on Crete and on the Greek mainland.

The increase in social differences, and the wealth of Troy's 'upper class' are possibly reflected in 'Priam's Treasure' (see 7.2). According to Schliemann, this Treasure was found in a kind of

A reconstruction of the topography around Troy in the Late Bronze Age. Troy's surroundings have changed a great deal over the course of time. The city now lies far from the sea. The coastline previously took a completely different course, and Troy lay on the edge of a deep bay.

An *orthostat* from Troy I. Stones of this kind, also referred to as stelae, were erected at important gates in other parts of Anatolia. It is possible that this stele, which was found at the citadel's southern gate, represented a deity and that offerings were made here on entering the citadel.

Part of 'Priam's Treasure' – a golden diadem, a wine cup and hair rings – copies from the originals in the Pushkin Museum in Moscow. According to Schliemann the items were found together in a kind of box in the fire layer of Troy II. He regarded the opulence of the treasure as proof that Troy II was Homer's Troy: while the Greek soldiers were slaughtering their way through his city, Priam, or one of his servants, was thought to have quickly hidden the valuables before himself falling victim to the Greeks. It is now clear that Troy II was at least 1,000 years older than the Troy of the Trojan War.

chest that had been buried outside the south-eastern gate. Priam's Treasure, as Schliemann dubbed it, includes bronze chisels, gold and silver goblets and gold jewellery. One of the items in the treasure was a two-handled cup, according to Schliemann the depas cup mentioned by Homer (*depas amphikypellon, Iliad* 1.584; 6.220). This in particular was the find that convinced Schliemann that Troy II was Homer's Troy. Close examination of the finds reveals however that the cup and the other finds

may be dated to the period around 2700 BC, long before any Trojan War. Schliemann himself acknowledged this shortly before his death. There is now widespread scepticism whether the objects were found together in the earth. Schliemann is thought to have combined objects from various parts of the city, possibly supplementing these with finds from other digs and perhaps even with forgeries. We will probably never know the precise details. Later excavators have, in any event, found gold objects at various points in the city that in style resemble Schliemann's finds. Taken with Priam's Treasure, they provide an impression of Troy's wealth in the Early Bronze Age.

Troy's increased wealth and social stratification in any event finds expression in the other finds. Earthenware pots in the shape of the human body or head are characteristic. These possibly had a ritual function, although we know nothing of the religion of the time. Some of the pottery from Troy II is of a type that was in use elsewhere as well, in the Aegean region in particular. This indicates that at this time Troy maintained foreign contacts over a broad region. It is worth noting that a large proportion of this pottery consists of drinking cups of a new two-handled type without a base, the depas cups. Another innovation was the introduction of the potter's wheel. Some of the pottery was made using this new technique, especially plates and bowls for eating with. The attention paid to eating and drinking reflected in the range of pottery found in Troy II indicates that feasts played an important role in the social relations of the time.

Troy II was destroyed by a huge fire. The surviving inhabitants continued to live in the same location and made use of the same defensive walls. It is noticeable that the houses of Troy III were much smaller, and that the finds are less opulent than those from the previous phase. Troy's flowering in the Early Bronze Age was clearly at an end.

TROY AS ANATOLIAN CITY:
TROY IV AND V (2200-1700 BC)

It seems that no new inhabitants went to live in the city following the destruction of Troy III. The finds from the earliest layers of Troy IV are a continuation of the Early Bronze Age culture. There are signs that new fortification walls were built,

and the lower city also continued to be used, but it is clear that a major change took place over the course of time. While Troy maintained important ties with the Aegean region in the Early Bronze Age, the city appears to have oriented itself primarily towards the Anatolian interior in the Middle Bronze Age.

This Anatolian orientation is evident from the houses of the period among other things. Just as in the Early Bronze Age they are constructed completely of clay bricks, without stone foundations. These are noticeably long and narrow houses adjoining each other and having walls in common. The houses all consist of at least four adjoining rooms that may be divided into main and subsidiary rooms. This type of building was also used in a number of locations elsewhere in Turkey during this period. Apart from the building type, the fact that each building has its own dome-shaped oven is another noticeable innovation, indicating that new ways of preparing food had been introduced.

The pottery range of Troy IV and V is largely a continuation of that from the previous periods. This emerges for example from the anthropomorphic pots and depas cups that are still

Depas cup. Cups of this sort have been found mainly in Troy II and III, but they have also turned up at excavations elsewhere along Turkey's western littoral and on islands in the Aegean. The popularity of drinking cups of this kind indicates the presence of an aristocracy enjoying a lifestyle in which drinking formed a significant aspect.

Minoan jug with spirals. Its strategic location meant that Troy was at a junction of trade routes from an early date. This Minoan jug from Crete, found in the grave of a child in Troy V, is evidence of Troy's contacts with the Aegean region.

found at the beginning of this period. Many drinking cups and dishes are still being turned on the potter's wheel. Bowls decorated with a red cross are characteristic of the period. In addition there were pottery shapes with clear signs of Anatolian origin, such as large decorated lids. Some of these were imported, but others appear to have been made locally.

Several graves found on the edge of the citadel date from the last phase of Troy V. One of these graves contained the body of a six-year-old child. On the skeleton lay a ceramic jug that had been adorned with spirals. It is a Minoan libation jug of Cretan origin. Similar vases have been found in Knossos and elsewhere on the island. The presence of this vase in a grave dating from the end of Troy V indicates that contact with the Aegean world continued. These contacts were to become much stronger in Troy's subsequent period of flowering: Late Bronze Age Troy VI.

TROY VI AND VIIA IN THE LATE BRONZE AGE

WENDY RIGTER AND GERT JAN VAN WIJNGAARDEN

Troy VI is without doubt the most monumental of the seven prehistoric cities found on the settlement hill of Hisarlık (the current Turkish name for Troy). This phase of habitation dates to the Middle and Late Bronze Age, around 1700 to 1300 BC. This settlement surpasses all previous habitation at Hisarlık in its extent and monumentality, and Troy VI is also larger than other well-known excavation sites in North-Western Anatolia from the same period.

The transition between Troy V, the previous settlement, and Troy VI is not undisputed. The American Carl Blegen, who excavated here between 1932 and 1938, was of the opinon that there were large differences between Troy V and VI in architecture, in pottery and in other objects. According to him the break was complete and the result of a new people, who settled here and brought their own customs and traditions. There may even have been a gap in habitation. The German archaeologist Kurt Bittel expressed a different opinion in his review of Blegen's publication on Troy. According to him, changes did take place, but not to the extent that Blegen believed. Recent excavations support Bittel's view. The transition between the two settlements is so smooth that we cannot always be certain whether a particular find should be dated to Troy V or early Troy VI.

THE ARCHITECTURE
Blegen subdivided Troy VI into eight building phases on the basis of the architectural remains found: Troy VIa up to Troy VIh. On the basis of changes to the defence works around the citadel, these eight phases may be grouped into three main phases; Troy VI-early (VIa-c), Troy VI-middle (VId-e) and Troy VI-late (VIf-h). Each of these main phases of Troy VI are characterised by the construction of a city wall that grew constantly in height and width. Parts of the bottom of the wall are still visible, measuring four to five metres in width and eight metres in height. These impressive walls were a significant argument for Wilhelm Dörpfeld, the German archaeologist who succeeded Heinrich Schliemann, to see Homeric Troy in Troy VI.

There are three towers in the citadel wall and five entrances. Among them are impressive gates in the eastern and southern walls. The citadel wall is reinforced at both gates. The most important gate appears to be that in the southern wall. It is flanked by a tower, at the base of which a number of monolithic stones (two and possibly more) were erected, which, possibly, once were decorated. Erecting stelae of this kind is characteristic of Troy and has its origins in Troy I more than a thousand years earlier (see 2.1). The precise function of these stelae is unknown, but they can probably be linked to the cult and worship of a deity.

A large section of Troy VI was destroyed as a result of building during the Hellenistic-Roman period (Troy VIII and IX). In particular the highest part of the citadel in the northern section was destroyed at the time, and habitation remains of Troy VI were later found only on the southern edge of the hill, in the intervening zone between the city walls of Troy II and VI.

Nevertheless a typical type of urban planning may be deduced from the limited remains of Troy VI. The houses were built on three terraces around the highest point of the citadel. They did not have a parallel orientation, but were laid out along imaginary axes to the centre. The houses were completely different to those of Troy V. They were freestanding and extensive

The defensive walls of Troy VI. The city walls were constructed in an interesting way, at a slightly inclined angle, and with various sections that end in distinctive offsets, the function of which is unclear. During the course of the 13th century BC the walls were reinforced several times. During the period of Troy VII the walls of Troy VI were partially restored and put to use once more.

with several rooms, and a number of the houses probably had a second floor. At least three houses had a *megaron* structure with a forecourt and a central room with a hearth. The largest building was the double-storeyed so-called 'Pillar House' immediately behind the southern gate. No palace has been found in Troy VI. If a palace did in fact exist, which is by no means certain, the destroyed northern and central part of the citadel would be the most logical site for it.

LOWER CITY OR NOT?

Just as in the previous phases, habitation in Troy VI appears not to be restricted to the citadel, but there were also dwellings to the south in an area that is referred to as the lower city.

As the dating of many parts of the lower city is exceptionally difficult (see also 2.1), this lower city has become part of the debate over whether the Trojan War actually took place. After all, with an extensive lower city, Troy VI (or VIIa, for which the same reasoning applies) resembles much more the impressive city described by Homer.

The remains of a few houses that belonged to Troy VI have been found close to the walls of the citadel. Geophysical research and archaeological excavation have revealed a ditch that could have formed part of an impressive line of defence, along with the wall remains and a wooden palisade. However, the problem is that the date of these defence works is extremely uncertain. Parts of them could also belong to earlier or later phases of Troy. Certain experts, including the Germans Manfred Korfmann – head of excavations at Troy from 1988 until his death in 2005 – and the historian and philologist Joachim Latacz, consider the remains to be sufficient evidence for the existence of a large lower city. Others, with the German historian F. Kolb as the most outspoken critic, point out that the evidence for a lower city of this kind is very scanty and may primarily be the result of wishful thinking.

BURIAL

One of Troy's greatest puzzles is locating where the dead were buried. No extensive burial ground is known from any one of the phases of lasting habitation. The fact that the landscape has been radically changed by shifts in the courses of the Scamander and Simoeis rivers perhaps plays a role here; some of the graves could have been washed away by the rivers or covered over by sediment.

There is one exception. Burial sites for cremation urns from the very last habitation phase of Troy VI have been found just to the south of the presumed lower city, and traces of similar burial sites have been found here and there on the plateau. In total 182 urns have been found, but only 19 were lying in their original position as a result of later disturbances of the area. The urns had been placed in shallow holes, and the majority of them contained the cremated remains of several people. Men, women and children have been identified among the dead. The graves and urns revealed very few burial goods, usually not more than one or a few ceramic pots. For Blegen, who exposed the burial site, this lack of funeral gifts was reason to believe that this was where the city's poorest inhabitants were buried. However, another theory is that this was a mass burial site laid out in great haste, perhaps following the destruction of Troy VI.

Recent excavations at Beşik Tepe, which lies around eight kilometres south-west of Troy, indicate that cremation burial sites of this kind were intended not only for poor city dwellers. This spot is often seen as a harbour where seafarers waited for

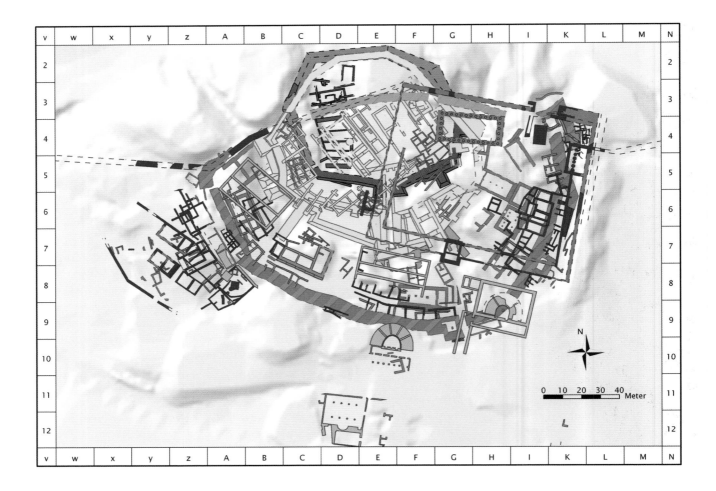

Map of Troy, showing the nine significant phases in the city's history. The walls of Troy VI-VIIa are shown in red and green. In yellow Troy II is depicted, the city that Schliemann identified as Homeric Troy. The buildings from the Greek and Roman periods are marked in blue.

favourable winds. There are 102 graves that have been found for men, women and children, of which 58 are pithos graves, comparable with the urn burials in Troy itself. One of the graves is that of a warrior who was buried with his sword, with a large ceramic basin placed on the grave.

TROY VIIA

The reinforcing of the city wall of Troy VI indicates that the inhabitants were expecting an attack. Nevertheless, the city appears to have been destroyed by an earthquake at the beginning of the 13th century BC. At least that is what large vertical cracks in the city walls indicate. There are also some indications of fire, and slingstones in the destruction layer suggest the possibility that there might have been some fighting. Nevertheless, an earthquake appears to have caused the worst damage.

After the destruction of Troy VI the population hastily erected small houses on the rubble. The city was occupied by the same population groups as before, as is made clear by the pottery used in Troy VIIa, which continued the traditions of the previous phase. The walls were repaired, which is clearly visible especially at the large north-eastern towers, which were restored. In general it may be said, however, that the city had lost its monumental character. This is also clear from the houses on the citadel, which were extremely small and differed little from each other. Larger houses from Troy VI that were reused were subdivided into smaller units. We see an increase in the storage of goods from the large number of huge buried *pithoi* (storage jars). This may be an indication that the inhabitants did not feel secure and laid in supplies. Remains of houses to the south of the citadel reveal that there were also houses in the area of the supposed lower city during the period of Troy VIIa. On the basis of the dates of Troy VIIa (ca. 1300-1180 BC) this is possibly the Troy referred to as *Wilusa* in Hittite tablets (see chapter 3) during a phase when the city was extremely poor.

Troy VIIa was destroyed by war between 1230 and 1180 BC. This is evident from the skeletons, arrowheads and catapult projectiles found. A good example is a skull found in a house just inside the southern gate. It belonged to someone who was never buried. The same applies to a skeleton found outside the fortifications. What is remarkable about skeleton remains like these is that human remains have not been found in any of the previous devastations of the city. There was evidently no time for the survivors to bury all the victims when Troy VIIa was destroyed. These clues suggesting the devastation of war formed the main reason for Carl Blegen to link the end of Troy VII to the Trojan War in the *Iliad*.

EXTERNAL CONTACTS

Day-to-day life in Troy VI may best be studied through the pottery (see page 34-36). Ceramics are also important in revealing cultural links with other regions. Owing to Troy's strategic location on various routes by sea and by land, the city probably had links at the least with other cultures to the east and west, which is confirmed by the pottery that was imported into the city.

The pottery of Troy VI initially showed hardly any differences from that of the previous phases, although Anatolian Grey Ware was something new. This type of pottery is also found elsewhere in North-Western Anatolia. But only at Troy and a number of other locations along the coast does this pottery class include pot shapes inspired by Greek ceramics from the same period. This indicates that by the Middle Bronze Age there were contacts between the Greek mainland and Troy. In addition there were also local pottery shapes in Anatolian Grey Ware, such as a bead rim bowl.

Pottery imported from other regions has also been found in Troy VI and VIIa. Of interest are two Minoan pots indicating contact with Crete. A Minoan stone lamp has also been found in an early phase of Troy VI. In the Middle phases of Troy VI, so-called "matt-painted wares" occur, which are reminiscent of mainland Greece. Most remarkable is the Mycenaean pottery that has been found at Troy, as this is an indication of contact with the Greek mainland. Mycenaean pottery was imported to Troy in later phases. Particularly noteworthy is that Mycenaean pottery was also made locally and influenced local pottery production. This indicates close contact between Greek and Trojan craftsmen.

The north-eastern towers of Troy VI. These large towers dominated the plains in front of Troy and protected the adjacent north-eastern bastion. The towers contained a large cistern that provided the citadel with water during times of emergency.

The contacts between Troy and Mycenaean Greece were certainly not brief, but extended over several centuries. The Mycenaean contacts should not be seen in isolation from a much larger international network that Troy was part of. For example, shards of a total of 61 Cypriot pots have been found at Troy, and Anatolian Grey Ware has been found at various locations in the Mediterranean area, including Syria, Lebanon and Israel. Troy's international character also emerges from the burial ground at Beşik Tepe mentioned above. Some of the 102 graves there contained expensive and exotic funeral gifts, such as bronze ankle rings, collars of costly carnelian and a Mycenaean seal with a stylised face.

Influences from both the Anatolian and the Aegean regions are thus to be found in Troy VI and VIIa. At an architectural level, Troy as a settlement with a lower city, matches other locations in Anatolia and the Middle East. The pottery also emphasises a clear Anatolian background: thousands of kilograms of mainly Anatolian Grey Ware and Tan Ware have been found – pots and above all fragments. In contrast there are only a couple of hundred shards of Mycenaean pottery, a significant portion of which was made locally.

The significance of Mycenaean finds at Troy has been exaggerated somewhat over the years; firstly because of the important place in mythology and research that Troy occupies as a matter of course, and secondly because Blegen has published on the Mycenaean pottery extensively and in detail. However, he neglected to treat the local Trojan pottery with the same respect, even though it is much more numerous and diverse. Moreover, Troy at this time was part of an extensive international trading network made up of many regions. Despite the contact with the Greek world during the period of Troy VI, the Mycenaeans did not play an important role in Troy's material culture.

TROY VIIB (1190-900 BC)

Troy was not deserted following the devastation of Troy VIIa. Parts of the city's defences were even restored once more. What is remarkable is that a new construction method was introduced, with part of the city wall being reinforced with low walls of stone at the bottom.

Much of the pottery from this period appears similar to that from previous phases, although one difference is that, after the potter's wheel had been used for a thousand years (see 2.1), handmade ceramics, comparable with pottery in south-eastern Europe, re-emerged in Troy. A couple of bronze axes from this period that were found by Schliemann are of types known from Hungary. It is unclear whether the pottery and axes point to very close contact with the Balkans, or whether new inhabitants arrived in Troy from this region.

The sole textual indication from prehistoric Troy is a bronze seal found in a layer of Troy VIIb (1190-900 BC). The seal probably dates to the 13th century BC and was possibly the property of a Luwian married couple. It is not known when the seal came to Troy; in the 13th century when it was made, in the 11th century to which the context it was found in belongs, or in the two intervening centuries. The seal plays an important role in the debate on the language that was spoken in Troy (see 3.2 and chapter 4). But it is impossible to reach a verdict on this issue on the basis of this seal, as we do not know when it came to Troy.

Indications are that Troy VIIb was devastated by war on a number of occasions. The city was finally abandoned in around 900 BC following another period of destruction, although there are indications of scattered habitation in the area. These include a few imports from Greece in the Geometric Period, which constitute evidence that the inhabitants maintained international contacts. But Troy would only begin to flourish again after the founding of a Greek city around 200 years later.

HOMERIC TROY?

Shortly before his death Heinrich Schliemann acknowledged that his hypothesis that Troy II represented Homer's city could not be sustained. His colleague and successor Dörpfeld, who had better knowledge of the Mycenaean world, proposed Troy VI as Homeric Troy. The impressive walls of the citadel that had been excavated bore comparison with the walls of Troy as described in the *Iliad*. In addition, the later phases of Troy VI

A so-called *bead rim bowl*. Although many new Mycenaean-like shapes were introduced into the Trojan pottery repertoire during the Late Bronze Age, there are also clear Anatolian influences. The bowl shown in this photograph is an example.

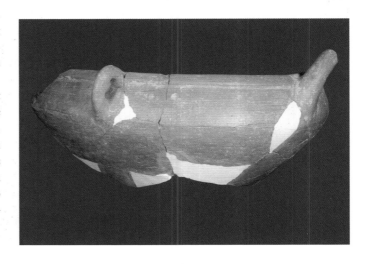

Imported Protogeometric pottery from Troy. Although Troy's significance, and thus also its population, went into steep decline following the destruction of Troy VIIa, its inhabitants continued to maintain contact with regions overseas, including Greece.

Troy VIIa was definitely destroyed by war, and this is the reason that Blegen surmised that this phase represented Homeric Troy. The destruction here must be seen in the context of many other devastating events in the eastern Mediterranean. For example, the Mycenaean palaces and the centres of the Hittite Kingdom were also razed. But this raises a problem in the chronology. The destruction of Troy VIIa took place around 1190 BC. By this point the Mycenaean palaces had been ruined for several decades. Greece was a society with a low level of organisation and scarcely any international focus. If Troy VIIa is to be seen as Homeric Troy then the heroes of the *Iliad* lived after the collapse of the Mycenaean palaces. And if this is the case, one of the devastations of Troy VIIb could just as well have provided inspiration for Homer.

It is thus impossible to determine incontrovertibly which of the archaeological layers in Troy is to be linked to the Troy of literature. Archaeology and poetry are in a difficult relationship. The archaeology of Troy VI and VII provides no concrete leads to life in Troy over several centuries in the Middle and Late Bronze Age, while the poetry of the *Iliad* allows us a literary glimpse into what might have occurred during a very brief episode within this timespan.

were contemporaneous with the flowering of Mycenaean culture in Greece (see 3.3). The pottery found is also evidence of contact with the Mycenaeans, and for this reason at the end of the 20th century the theory was again advanced that contacts between the inhabitants of Troy VI and Mycenaen Greece provided the basis for the myth of a Trojan war.

But there are also finds that contradict the identification of Troy VI with Homeric Troy. For example the extent of the lower city is extremely controversial, and the citadel of Troy VI is fairly small. In addition, relations with the Mycenaeans appear to have been of long duration and in general amicable, given the possible exchange of craftsmen. The most significant objection is however that Troy VI was destroyed by an earthquake and there is in fact no evidence pointing to a war.

THE ARCHAEOLOGY OF EVERYDAY LIFE: THE POTTERY OF TROY VI AND VII

The name Troy conjures up images of Greek myths and Homeric heroes. But there are no texts extant that may be linked directly to Troy's archaeology, which consists of the remains of walls and more particularly a great deal of pottery for the periods in which some experts place the Trojan War – Troy VI and VII. Pottery is important for archaeologists, partly because so much of it has survived. It is virtually indestructible and may be regarded as the 'plastic of antiquity': it was used by all social groups in earlier societies. The study of pottery thus has a prominent position in the archaeology of Troy.
Pottery changes under the influence of fashion, and for this reason particular buildings or find complexes may be dated on the basis of the pottery found in them. Detailed study of pottery provides us not only with greater insight into the nature of household utensils and how they were used, but also clear evidence of the function of an excavated building or house. Ceramics are also useful for demonstrating important cultural links with other regions. Given Troy's location not far from the Aegean it is clear that this contact occurred by sea as well. The pottery from Troy VI-early (ca. 1700-1300 BC) consists primarily of pots and bowls made on a potter's wheel (*Red Coated Ware, Plain Ware and Anatolian Grey Ware*). New pot shapes that appeared in this phase are mainly related to eating and drinking. A significant part of this pottery has its origins on the Greek mainland, but, as we saw above, a local style was also introduced in the form of Anatolian Grey Ware – the so-called bead rim bowl (see page 32).

Tan Ware krater from Troy with decorations on the handle that look like rivets. Undulating patterns applied with a comb and red colouring may be seen.

The American archaeologist Carl Blegen holding a pilgrim's flask from Troy. Blegen believed that Troy VIIa was Homer's Troy and that Troy VI – thought by his predecessor Dörpfeld to be the Troy Homer – had been destroyed by an earthquake, rather than by human hand. A continuing discussion rages over which habitation layer should be associated with Homeric Troy. Traces of fire are possibly evidence of war and suggest that Troy VI was destroyed not only by an earthquake but by other factors as well.

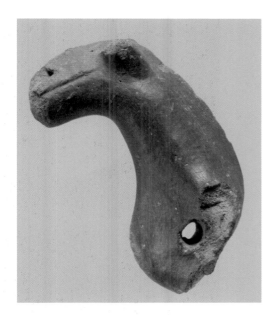

Handle in the form of a horse's hoof. In the *Iliad* 'horse tamer' is one of Hector's many sobriquets. And there is in fact increasing evidence that Troy was an important 'horse city' during the Late Bronze Age, mainly because of the horse bones and chariot remains found.

Tan Ware krater from Troy, inspired by Mycenaean pottery. A lion is to be seen above the spiral on the right, and to the left a human figure next to the spiral.

The appearance of the first imported fine wares painted in the Mycenaean style of the Greek mainland is significant. Two Minoan stirrup jars similarly attest to contacts across the sea. By far the most part of the pottery of Troy was produced locally, such as Tan Ware, a variant of Anatolian Grey Ware, which is kiln-fired under oxidising conditions, the addition of oxygen resulting in an orange-brown colour. The earliest Tan Ware consists typically of plates and small bowls.

Towards the end of Troy VI a large number of new pottery styles arose. The various carinated cups, or cups on a raised stem, slowly evolved into a shape comparable to a Mycenaean *kylix*. Mycenaean influence becomes increasingly visible in the style repertoire. Decorations on the pottery include imitation rivets that recall metal examples. Metal pots occur only extremely rarely in Late Bronze Age Western Anatolia and are probably only for use by the elite. The most important pottery shapes from the Troy VI layer are plates, drinking bowls and a large number of kraters (mixing vases). One special shape is the pilgrim flask with a shape that is Anatolian, but that is also to be found on the Greek mainland. Chemical analysis reveals that a flask of this kind once contained dairy produce. A number of terracotta animal figures has also been found, often a horse's head attached to the pot as a handle or ornament. These horse protomes are often associated with the arrival of the domesticated horse at the start of the Troy VI period.

The pottery of Troy VIIa (ca. 1300-1180 BC) corresponds in many aspects to that of the previous period, even if several new shapes are introduced, such as the kylix without a rim. The Mycenaean *skyphos* (two-handled drinking bowl) is often found, as well as an Anatolian variant.

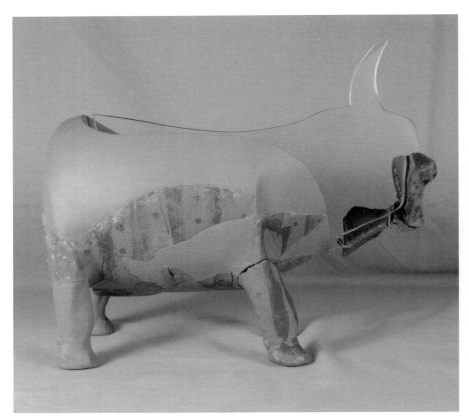

Earthenware bull found in Troy's Lower City near the defensive wall of Troy VI. Bulls played an important role in the Hittite pantheon, being associated with Tarhunt, the god of the sky and storm. The Trojans possibly shared this god with their neighbours to the east.

Bronze human figure, possibly representing a deity, although it could also be a priest or a worshipper. The lack of extant texts from Troy means that we know little of the how its inhabitants perceived the world.

This period also reveals that the Trojan population allowed itself to be influenced by Mycenaean culture. Mycenaean pottery was increasingly
imitated locally. An example is a local Tan Ware krater with a human figure, a bird and part of a lion painted on it in red. Cypriot pottery found at Troy reveals contact with Cyprus and the Levant. These contacts were not one-sided, as Anatolian Grey Ware from Troy has also been found on Cyprus and in the Levant.

An exceptional find is a figure of a bull found in fragments in a house outside the citadel. The stylistic characteristics of this bull reveal influences not only from the Aegean, but also from the Hittite world. Interestingly a bronze figurine was found in the same house, possibly representing a deity. Comparable figurines have been found in central Anatolia and northern Syria.

Wendy Rigter

FROM ACHILLES TO ALEXANDER

FLORIS VAN DEN EIJNDE

Who has not heard that Troy was uninhabited after
it was once razed to the ground by the Greeks
(Strabo, *Lycurgus of Athens* 13.1.41)

The history of Hisarlık knows many gaps: earthquakes, fires and wilful destruction by enemies have left their mark on the city's history and archaeology. One such devastation, that of Troy VIIa around 1180 BC, is exceptionally important however, as it meant the end of a golden era lasting centuries. This event heralded in the end of the Bronze Age for northeastern Anatolia, where the fall of this important citadel spelled the end of dominance for the once all-powerful Hittite Kingdom. By contrast with the destruction of the earlier Troy VI, which archaeologists attribute to an earthquake, Troy VIIa appears to have been deliberately razed. The demise of Troy VIIa is thus a logical candidate for scholars such as Latacz and Korfmann (see 2.2), who seek an historical core to the *Iliad* and the *Odyssey*, epics that came into being much later than the destruction of Bronze Age Troy. According to common – though not universally accepted understanding – these works were composed in the second half of the 8th century BC, almost five centuries later.

What happened to the city during these crucial centuries in which the story of the Trojan War literally acquired epic proportions? And what happened to the city in the centuries following Homer, when his works evolved into the touchstone of ancient – and indeed Western – literature? These questions are of major importance, as the 'mythical' Troy of Homer had already in antiquity been identified with the Bronze Age ruins we know today as "Troy". At this spot, Greek Ilion, and later Roman Ilium, evolved into a major historical and religious monument, a place of pilgrimage for the tourists of antiquity, which in turn had a marked influence on the Homeric tradition. The city played a major role as a *lieu de memoir* in later antiquity, providing inspiration not only for Homer but also for generations of poets and artists to come.

THE EARLY IRON AGE

Little is known of the first centuries after the Fall of Troy VIIa, but it is clear that with the demise of this Troy a period of decline set in for this mighty fortress. The virtually simultaneous collapse of the Hittite power structures and the general decay of international trading relations caused a sharp decline in the population of the entire Aegean region. Troy VII, which depended on its strategic location overlooking the Dardanelles and the Aegean, was hit especially hard. There is, furthermore, evidence that the area saw migrations during this period. Archaeological research has revealed that the material culture of subsequent Troy VIIb was heavily influenced by foreign factors. While pottery from Troy VIIa reveals a clear relationship with other cities on the western littoral of Asia Minor, the later material is evidently linked to styles that had previously been seen only in the Balkans.

Here we are able to pull together a number of interesting conclusions. If Troy VIIa was indeed destroyed by a Greek/Mycenaean coalition, as Homer suggests, this event did not lead the victors to occupy the citadel permanently. Insofar as Mycenaean pottery has been found in Troy, it originates from the period before the destruction, and thus from a time when Greeks certainly did not control of the citadel. The pottery originating from Greece therefore seems to have arrived at Troy through trade. No Mycenaean pottery dating from after the destruction has been found on the site. Ironically, the Fall of Troy seems to have been precipitated by one of its main trading partners, causing the end of Mycenaean-Trojan exchange.

The material culture that we encounter in Troy VIIb, after the disastrous destruction of ca. 1180 BC may rather be compared to ceramics from Europe, in particular from the region of Thrace to the north of the Dardanelles and the Sea of Marmara. Apart from the Anatolian Grey Ware that had been manufactured in Troy for well over a millennium, handmade pottery manufactured without using the pottery wheel, is attested during this period. Recent research has shown that this material, referred to as knobbed ware, was made locally, indicating that a new population, originating from the eastern Balkans, settled in Troy during this period, probably alongside the original inhabitants. In this phase the population withdrew to the safety of the old citadel, and the much larger lower city was abandoned. In the citadel itself, houses from the previous phase were repaired and reoccupied.

Balkan influence has been associated with the influx of the Phrygians, a civilization that reached its zenith in the 8th century BC. They seem to have taken advantage of the power vacuum left by the Fall of Troy and the collapse of the

The settlement mound of Troy is comprised of the remains of innumerable phases of habitation. More than a century of archaeological research has turned the original sloping mound into a crater landscape. The walls of the oldest phase are in the middle of the mound and at considerable depth. Later phases may be found further towards the outside of the mound. The maze of ruins resulting from more than three millennia of habitation and construction remains just as confusing to today's visitor as it was to the first archaeologists who excavated the site.

Hittite Kingdom. These early Phrygians occupied a major part of North-Western Anatolia, including Gordion – well-known from the "Gordian Knot" episode in the Alexander legend – a former Hittite citadel in Central Anatolia that the intruders chose as their capital. The European origin of the Phrygians is supported by the fact that their language is closely related to Greek (see Plato, *Cratylus*, 410a).

The fact that Phrygia is referred to in the *Iliad* as among Troy's allies (*Iliad* 2.862-863) is put forward as a counter-argument to this historical reconstruction. The area is usually associated with Ascania, a region that stretched along the Sangarios (Sakarya) River from the Black Sea to the Phrygian heartland around Gordion. According to the Homeric epic, a young King Priam marched at the head of an army to support the Phrygians to fight off an attack by the Amazons (*Iliad* 3.184-189) and even took a Phrygian princess, Hecuba, as his wife (*Iliad* 16.715-719). How are we to explain this tradition if the Phrygians were not even present in Anatolia at the time of the Trojan War?

In this regard it is important to remember that the Troy of the *Iliad* is in the first instance a reinvention by Homer. In the 8th century BC Phrygia was a powerful state, ruled by a king that we know as Mi-ta-a from Assyrian clay tablets, and from Greek historiography as the legendary King Midas who turned everything he touched to gold. It is not improbable that Homer, or one of the bards that preceded him, did not want to omit this powerful state from the epic and included a Phrygian princess in his poem to bestow it with "historical accuracy".

Whatever the truth is, this proto-Phrygian phase of the settlement at Troy also came to an end, around 950 BC. Over the two subsequent centuries there is scarcely any evidence of human activity in and around the citadel.

THE RETURN OF THE GREEKS

One of the many paradoxes linked to the saga of the Greek conquest of Troy, is the fact that the Mycenaean Greeks did not permanently occupy the city they had expended so much blood, sweat and tears on conquering. The story of the city's destruction was evidently taken back to the Greek mainland along with the legendary treasure, where it was handed down from generation to generation five centuries. The idiom of the Homeric epic suggests that this tradition was transmitted within the Aeolic-Greek speaking region in Northern Greece and on the Northern Aegean islands of Lesbos and Tenedos. Only after around 1000 BC did cautious colonisation of the northeastern littoral of the Anatolian mainland by Aeolic speaking Greeks get underway. This influx of Greeks into the Troad – the region surrounding Troy, between the Dardanelles and the Mytilini Strait that separates Lesbos from the mainland – corresponds with the virtual disappearance of proto-Phrygian influence in Hisarlık, and it is natural to assume that the entire region was occupied by Greeks. The Aeolians did not settle in Troy itself, however, but at points closer to the coast, such as Sigeion and Assos.

The Greek colonists of the Troad also imported their memories of the legendary war for Troy. Seeing the proud ruins of Troy must have made an overwhelming impression on the Greeks, who had no cities of their own anywhere near this size. This undoubtedly played a decisive role in the continued existence of the Trojan epic in its extended Homeric version. Although they did not settle in Troy itself, two important sanctuaries arose on top of the still clearly visible ruins from the end of the 8th century BC. On the western slopes of the citadel traces have been found of a sanctuary that, based on the type of votive offerings, appears to have been in use from the 8th century BC. Three successive buildings offered visitors a space for ritual meals and sleeping quarters for those who came from afar. In the Archaic Period (700-500 BC) wild animals were kept in the sanctuary, possibly dedicated to a mother goddess resembling Cybele.

A shrine to Athena was built on the former citadel. According to post-Homeric tradition, Odysseus and Diomedes stole the wooden statue (*palladion*) of Athena from her temple in the hope of advancing a Greek victory. The same tradition reports how the famous Trojan Horse, filled with Greek soldiers, was borne by the Trojans to the shrine of the goddess as a gift. Contrary to the prevailing opinion, the origins of the shrine to Athena probably do not lie in the Bronze Age, but rather in the 8th century BC, when shrines to Athena were erected on many Bronze Age ruins, such as Athens and Mycenae. As protectress of citadels she is intimately associated with the impressive fortifications of the legendary past. The fact that Homer does not mention the shrine to Athena suggests as well that it was not erected in Troy until the 8th century, when the first votive remains appear. Unfortunately, the excavations of the 19th century have largely destroyed the shrine itself, and a passage from Herodotus (7.43.2) dating to the 5th century BC is our

earliest attestation of the sanctuary. The stories about the theft of the *palladion* and the soldiers hidden in the Wooden Horse derive from Vergil's *Aeneid* (2.1-452), written at the end of the 1st century BC, by when Troy had become a magnet for tourism and the shrine was enjoying international renown (see also chapter 7).

Troy – or Ilion as it was now called – was a holy site for the Aeolian Greeks in the Troad. It probably did not belong to any one city but rather served as a cult site shared by the Aeolian colonists on the north-western littoral of Asia Minor. The open-air museum that Troy had become, with its ruins and shrines, enabled the Greeks to reflect on their own past and to create a common identity. Here they found legitimation for their territorial claims in Asia Minor as they traced their complex genealogies back to the Greek heroes of the *Iliad*. The Trojan cycle was thus born of an historic core and fleshed out by mythological imagination, inspired by the city's archaeological remains.

ILION AS PROPAGANDA

From the 6th century BC onwards the Greek *poleis* gradually lost their independence. Lydia, Persia, Athens, Macedonia, Pergamon and Rome successively ruled the Aeolian cities in Asia Minor, resulting in Ilion's, international acclaim. Independently, the *Iliad* and the *Odyssey* spread the city's fame throughout Greece and even abroad, as is shown by this passage from Herodotus:

Hand formed pottery with knob-decoration. Following the severe destruction of Troy VIIa around 1180 BC, a number of new forms of earthenware turn up that are reminiscent of Balkan pottery. Some experts suspect that there was an influx of different peoples into the region at the time. However, existing pottery traditions were continued.

When the army had come to the river Scamander (...) Xerxes ascended to the citadel of Priam, having a desire to see it. After he saw it and asked about everything there, he sacrificed a thousand cattle to Athena of Ilium, and the Magi offered libations to the heroes.
(Herodotus, *Histories* 7.43.2)

In this passage the Persian King Xerxes halts to inspect the city of Troy during his expedition to Greece (483-479 BC). Although Herodotus does not relate why Xerxes sacrifices a thousand cattle, or to which heroes (Greek or Trojan) the magi offer libations, it is not difficult to reconstruct the underlying motives. As Herodotus writes earlier in his *Histories* (Book I), the Trojan War was regarded as part of a centuries-long struggle between 'Asia' and 'Europe'. For Xerxes Troy was the ideal spot to bestow symbolic significance on his invasion of Greece. By honouring Athena and the heroes of Troy he underlined the expedition's aim: to avenge the Fall of Troy and to punish the Greeks.

One and a half centuries later Alexander the Great visited Troy at the start of his great campaign through Asia. Just before the first major battle (334 BC), which was fought at the River Granicus (Biga), he halted his army to pay his respects to the city. He swapped his armour for a suit that was kept in the temple of Athena and that was said to originate from the time of the Trojan War. He then organised a race for himself and his comrades at a spot which had been identified as the Grave of Achilles on the coast, close to where the Greek army was believed to have camped. The symbolism of Alexander's actions mirrors that of Xerxes'.

By honouring the Greek hero Achilles with games, Alexander was undoubtedly recalling the funeral games of Patroclus described in the *Iliad*. Analogous to the vengeance wreaked by Achilles for the death of his beloved brother-in-arms Patroclus, Alexander, as avenger of Achilles, would accomplish the conquest of the Persian Empire.

Although Alexander died before making good his promise to turn Troy into a prosperous city once more, his successors, the Diadochi, dedicated themselves to embellishing the city.

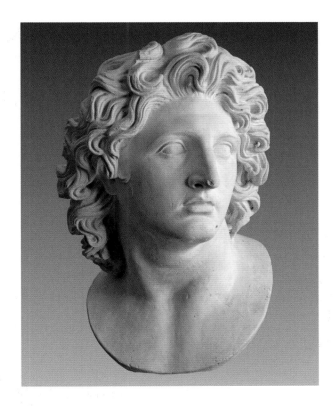

Alexander the Great (356-323 BC) is one of the greatest conquerors in world history. He visited Troy at the start of his campaign of conquest through Asia with the aim paying tribute to the famous city and his great hero Achilles. Plaster, after an original from 1st century BC.

A new temple to Athena was built, along with a theatre accommodating some 8,000 spectators. In addition a 'Panathenaic' festival was established following the example of Athens. The newly built shrine became the centre of a newly formed political league in the Troad, a federation of around 10 Aeolian-Greek cities that celebrated their common festivals in Ilion and held political meetings there.

Greek vase from 530-520 BC with a depiction of Cassandra, who has sought refuge from an approaching Greek hero under the shield of a statue of the goddess Athena. Cassandra was able to see into the future and had predicted Troy's demise, although she was not believed.

41

3 TROY AND ITS NEIGHBOURS

THE HITTITES

WILLEMIJN WAAL

The Late Bronze Age – the period between around 1600 and 1180 BC – may be seen as the golden age of Troy. This may be deduced from archaeological finds and the monumental scale of the building during this period on the citadel, both fortifications and dwellings. Many details of what Troy looked like that are to be found in the Iliad seem to correspond closely with what archaeological work has exposed so far, although there are also considerable differences. The Homeric epics suggest the city was the centre of a large empire, able to call on allies from distant regions, but in reality it was one of a number of relatively important centres along the western Anatolian littoral. The city was certainly not the centre of a large empire, and for a large part of its history was subject to rule by other more powerful neighbours.

Troy was certainly an important centre for trade in north-western Anatolia – the German director of the excavation around Troy, Manfred Korfmann, has for example put forward the idea that the city controlled trade through the Bosporus towards the Black Sea – but it always had to pay close heed to its neighbours. The Hittites were without doubt the most important of these. Cuneiform texts from the Hittite capital at Hattuša even indicate that the king of Wiluša – as Troy was presumably called – was a vassal of the king of the Hittites. The neighbours to the west – the Mycenaean Greeks – were active in Troy, probably primarily for purposes of trade, but on occasion also out for plunder or conquest. Then there were various peoples on the western coast of Anatolia, who appear to have united from time to time to defend themselves against the Hittites, if the Hittite texts are to be believed, but who usually operated as independent statelets.

During the late Bronze Age, Troy was certainly a prosperous city, but it also lay in the border region between the Hittites and the Mycenaeans. The city's rulers needed to be politically skilful in order to maintain a measure of autonomy.

A photographic overview of Hattuša, the capital of the Hittite Empire. The city's fortification walls were constructed as a sort of outer 'cassette' that was filled with rubble and earth and thus formed a sound buffer against earthquake. The upper structure of the walls, which no longer exists, was made of unbaked clay brick.

THE HITTITE KINGDOM

The Hittite Kingdom (ca. 1650-1180 BC) was one of the great powers of the old Middle East in the Late Bronze Age, along with Babylonia, Assyria, Egypt and others. Its capital, Hattuša, lay on the central Anatolian plateau, around 150 kilometres to the east of Ankara, near modern-day Boghazköy or Boğazkale. The borders of the kingdom fluctuated considerably over the 500 years of its existence. At the peak of its power it occupied a large part of modern Turkey and parts of northern Syria.

The core of the kingdom, the region around the capital, was under direct Hittite control. The rest, referred to by the Hittites themselves as the 'land of Hatti', consisted primarily of a network of vassal states under the rule of local kings. These vassals were bound to the Hittite Great King through personal treaty and an oath of honour. They enjoyed a measure of freedom in running their internal affairs, but matters like foreign affairs were for the Hittite king to decide.

SOURCES

A number of collections of clay tablets have been found in Hattuša and in smaller Hittite cities. These tablets are inscribed in the Old Babylonian cuneiform that the Hittites had adopted from Mesopotamia. This cuneiform script is mainly syllabic but also uses logograms. Estimates put the number of clay tablets, and more particularly tablet fragments, dug up in the capital at 25,000-30,000.

Most of the compositions were in Hittite, the official language of the empire, although texts written in Sumerian, Akkadian, Hurrian, Hattian and Luwian have also been found. Hittite is an Indo-European language and the oldest member of this group that has survived in written form. Apart from cuneiform, an indigenous hieroglyphic script existed that was used for Luwian. Luwian was closely related to Hittite and was presumably spoken in a large part of the empire (see 3.2). This hieroglyphic script has survived primarily in stone rock inscriptions and seals, but it was probably also used for wooden documents that have not come down to us. Anatolian hieroglyphic script continued to be used after the fall of the Hittite Kingdom until around 700 BC.

Anatolian hieroglyphic script in the capital Hattuša. This script was probably used not only on stone but also on wood, although nothing remains of the latter. This is also the case with Linear B: the shape of Linear B signs indicate that the script was probably primarily designed for inscriptions on materials other than clay.

TEXT GENRES

The surviving texts date to all phases of the empire, although the vast majority were written in the final period. All the tablets are state documents that were found in the tablet collections in the storerooms of the temple and in the palace. No private Hittite texts have yet been found. The contents of these tablets are extremely varied; apart from religious themes like festival and ritual protocols, oracle reports, cult inventories and prayers, there are also annals, legal texts, mythological and literary texts, treaties and letters.

The last category includes international correspondence with the other kings of the era with whom the Hittite king was on an equal footing. There are for example letters to his peers in Babylonia, Assyria and Mitanni (the kingdom of the Hurrians) and to the pharaohs of Egypt. The Hittite king also corresponded with the king of Ahhiyawa, a kingdom to the west of Hatti that may be identified as Mycenaean Greece.

ALAKŠANDU OF WILUŠA

In the 1920s a treaty between the Hittite King Muwatalli II (1295-1272 BC) and a vassal king of Wiluša, called Alakšandu, was found in Hattuša, capital of the Hittite Kingdom. Researchers immediately saw a remarkable resemblance between the names Alakšandu and Alexander. In the *Iliad*, Alexander is the Greek name of Paris, the Trojan prince who carried off the beautiful Helen from Sparta – the cause of the Trojan War. The name Wiluša strongly recalls the city (W)Ilios (accusative case (W)Ilion). In the Homeric era, the name of this city began with the letter *Wau*, which was later dropped. Initially this identification was received with some hesitation, particularly as the site of Wiluša, which was first mentioned in the annals of King Tudhaliya I (ca. 1400 BC), was uncertain. Since then it has been established on the basis of subsequent evidence that the Hittite Wiluša lay in the Troad region, just as did Homeric Troy. Wiluša is also named alongside Taruiša/Truiša (both readings are possible in cuneiform), which may very well reflect the name of Troy.

The feminine form of the name Alexander (a-re-ka-sa-da-ra) has been found on Mycenaean Linear B tablets from the late Bronze Age, indicating that this Mycenaean name was in use at the time. It is virtually certain that Alakšandu is the Hittite masculine form of this name, and the fact that the prince of Wiluša bore a Greek name confirms that there was contact between the Mycenaean Greeks and the inhabitants of Troy. While Alakšandu may well be a Greek name, the name of

King Priam is probably Luwian. The latter is certainly identified with the name P(a)riyamuwas that occurs in Hittite texts. The name Paris is also possibly Luwian.

The Treaty

The treaty between Alakšandu and Muwatalli indicates that there had been contact between Hatti and Wiluša for some time. The Hittite king refers to this in the opening lines:

Thus speaks my sun, Muwatalli, great king, king of Hatti, beloved of the storm-god of lightning, son of Mursili, great king, hero:
Once my forefather Labarna went to war with the Arzawa lands [region in western Anatolia] and the land of Wiluša and defeated them. Thereafter Arzawa began war, and Wilusa defected, but because it is long past, I do not know from which king of Hatti Wiluša defected. But even if Wiluša was separated from Hattuša, they remained on friendly terms with the kings of Hatti and regularly sent envoys.

On the evidence of this fragment, relations had always been good, even when Wiluša was separated from Hatti as a result of war – it was so far in the past that Muwatalli no longer knows which of his forefathers it took place under. It should be noted here that the historical prologues of Hittite treaties are not always completely reliable: they usually serve to justify the treaty and may represent matters in a better light than was actually the case. The treaty with Alakšandu was moreover a standard vassal treaty, in which the Hittite king clearly had the final say, as is shown by the following passage:

Furthermore, this tablet that I have drawn up for you, Alakšandu, will be read out to you three times a year, so that you, Alakšandu, shall know it. These words are in no way reciprocal: they issue from Hatti!

In conclusion it is interesting to note that the god 'A-ap-pa-li-u-na-aš' is included among the gods of Wiluša in the list of gods that are invoked at the end of the treaty. This god may possibly be identified as Apollo, who backed the Trojan side in Homer's *Iliad*. Unfortunately there is a break in the clay tablet just before this point, so that we cannot completely rule out the possibility that there might have been another syllable in front of the name.

Conclusions

What conclusions may be drawn from the treaty? Is the Alakšandu mentioned here really to be identified with Alexander/Paris in the *Iliad*? The similarity in names is striking, but there are also elements that do not correspond with the *Iliad*. For example, the treaty between Muwatalli and Alakšandu is a standard vassal treaty: Alakšandu is clearly subject to the Hittite king. This differs from Homer's legendary Troy, where Priam was king of a large and independent kingdom.

The Alakšandu treaty: a treaty between Hittite Great King Muwatalli II (1295 -1272 BC) and his vassal Alakšandu of Wiluša. The text of the treaty indicates that Wiluša was subordinate to the Hittite king. If Wiluša may be identified with Troy, then the political situation in the treaty (showing Wiluša as a 'regular' Hittite dependency) diverges from the Homeric picture of Troy as a great and independent city with a large number of allies.

Moreover, the Hittites are not mentioned in the *Iliad*, and in the *Odyssey* they play only a minor role that does not match their prominent position in the late Bronze Age.
It is clear that we should not read Homer as a reliable historical source. We should bear in mind that the Trojan War is actually of subordinate significance in the *Iliad*. The war serves as a backdrop for conveying human emotions and motivations. It is certainly not inconceivable, and is even plausible, that for the purposes of this background, use is made of one or more historical events and/or personalities that the audience was familiar with (see also 1.3). The underlying historical facts are in the end of little or no significance to the epic. The events and protagonists of the *Iliad* have taken on a life of their own, and the Alexander in the *Iliad* no longer has anything to do with the historical Alakšandu of Wiluša.

THE LANGUAGE OF TROY

ALWIN KLOEKHORST

In the second millennium BC Troy was an extremely prosperous city, a bustling trading centre where traders from all corners of the world gathered and where a multitude of languages was to be heard on the street. However, the question which language the inhabitants of Troy themselves spoke during this period is not easy to answer. There is simply no conclusive evidence. No texts have been dug up in Troy it self, apart from a single seal with a Luwian inscription (see page 59), nor do the historical sources on Troy provide a clear answer. We will thus have to focus on indirect clues to the possible origins of the language of the Trojans.

WESTERN ANATOLIA IN THE SECOND MILLENNIUM BC

In the second millennium BC, Anatolia was dominated by the Hittite Kingdom (see 3.1). All the information we have available from this period about Troy and the rest of western Anatolia is derived from the royal archives of the Hittites. On the basis of these texts we know that around the 13th century BC, western Anatolia consisted of various small kingdoms or statelets. The most important of these, from north to south, were Māša, Wiluša, Šēha, Arzawa, Mirā and Lukkā.

The area where Troy lies belongs to the region referred to by the Hittites as Wiluša, and it is now generally accepted that this name corresponds to the Greek name for Troy, Ilios. The Hittite name Wiluša may be analysed linguistically as *wilw-ša*, in which *-ša* is a suffix used in many country names, while the *-w-* automatically becomes a *-u-* when placed between two consonants. And the Greek Ilios, with its older variant Wilios, may derive from the older *Wilwios. (The star indicates that we are dealing with a reconstructed form that has not been found as such, but which may be assumed to have existed on linguistic grounds.) Given that *–ios* is a well-known suffix in Greek for country names, *Wilwios may be analysed as *wilw-ios*. Clearly, both names have the same root *wilw-*.

A land called Trūiša also comes up a few times in the Hittite texts. It lay close to Wiluša or was perhaps even part of Wiluša. It is now generally believed that this name corresponds to the Greek name Troiē. In Hittite *-iša* is a suffix, which means that Trūiša may be analysed as *trū-iša*, while the Greek word Troiē presumably derives from the older *Trōē, which we may analyse as *trō-ē*. As Hittite did not have the *ō*sound, we may assume that the Hittite *trū-* and the Greek *trō-* are the same.

WILUŠA

The Hittite texts referring to Wiluša provide no convincing evidence for the language was spoken in Troy, although we may make a number of assumptions on the basis of indirect evidence.

Firstly, a treaty between the Hittite and Wilušan kings that has been found in the Hittite archives at Boghazköy (see page 45), indicates that Wiluša was a vassal state under Hittite suzerainty. As the Hittite king corresponded with his vassals in Hittite (the relevant treaty was drawn up in Hittite), there must at the very least have been scribes working at the Wiluša court who were competent in Hittite. We could even imagine that there must have been Hittite diplomats living in Wiluša who discussed affairs with the Wilušan court in Hittite.

Secondly, we know the names of two Wilušan kings from the Hittite texts. It has not been possible thus far to convincingly link the name of one of these kings, Walmu, to any specific language. The name of the other king, with whom the treaty mentioned above was concluded, is Alakšandu, which has a much more familiar ring to it. In the 1920s, when the tablet that mentions it was dug up, Alakšandu was immediately linked to the Greek Aleksandros, the name used in Homer's *Iliad* for the Trojan prince Paris. The use of a Greek name by the royal family of Wiluša indicates that the Wilušans must at the very least have had close links to the Greeks, and possibly even that Greeks had married into the royal family (which could possibly be compared to the legend of the Greek Helen who fell in love with Paris and left Sparta for Troy, causing the Greeks to launch an attack on Troy to get her back).

We know from archaeological and Hittite sources that from around 1400 BC, Greeks (that is to say Mycenaeans, referred to by the Hittites as the people of Ahhiyawa, or rather 'Achaeans'), settled at certain points in western Anatolia, primarily in Millawanda (Miletus) and on the island Lazpa (Lesbos). A great deal of Mycenaean pottery has also been found in Troy, especially from phases of habitation in the 13th century BC, suggesting the presence of – or in any event acquaintance with – Greeks. This presence evidently left its mark on the Wilušan royal family. Nevertheless it is unlikely that the Wilušans were originally Greeks themselves. The Hittite texts reveal that Wiluša was certainly under the influence of Ahhiyawa, but not part of it.

OTHER WESTERN ANATOLIAN STATES
AND THE LUWIAN HYPOTHESIS

The language or languages that were spoken in other western Anatolian states cannot be determined conclusively from
sources dating back to the second millennium BC. There is
certainly indirect evidence that some of these states must have
used Luwian as their language. Luwian is an Indo-European
language closely related to Hittite that we know from a number
of texts contained in the royal archive of Hattuša, and more especially from later hieroglyphic inscriptions from south-eastern
Anatolia and Syria that date to around 1100-700 BC. The most
important indications that Luwian was used are the following:

1. Old Hittite texts dating to around 1600 BC refer to a land
   called Luwiya that may possibly be located in western Anatolia, and more specifically in the vicinity of the state Ar-
   zawa/Mirā. If the language is called Luwian (*luwili* in Hittite) after the land of Luwiya, it is also probable that Luwian
   was spoken in this region, in any event around 1600 BC.

2. The names of various kings from western Anatolian states,
   in the form that we know them from Hittite texts, appear to
   be of Luwian origin.

3. The only texts found in western Anatolia itself are a number
   of rock inscriptions written in Luwian hieroglyphs. Some
   of these inscriptions consist solely of the names of people,
   which do not really have to be 'in a specific language'. How-

A typical Aegean landscape: view from Keros towards
Koufonisi in the Cyclades. In the background the mountains
of Naxos are visible. On that island, there was an important
Mycenaean settlement. Naxos and other smaller islands in
the Aegean formed a convenient springboard for shipping
between Anatolia and the Greek mainland.

ever, a recently found inscription includes several Luwian
words, thus conclusively proving the use of Luwian. As may
be seen on the language map, these inscriptions are found
primarily in the region of Arzawa/Mirā and the southern
part of Šēha.

We may assume on the basis of these arguments that Luwian
was spoken in any event in Arzawa/Mirā and possibly also in
part of Šēha in the second millennium BC. Some experts have
for this reason argued that it is certainly possible that Troy also
used Luwian as its language. One expert (Calvert Watkins)
has even attempted to identify Luwian etymologies for Trojan
names as they occur in Homer's *Iliad*. For example, the name
of the Trojan king, Priam, is analysed as *priya-muwa-*, which
in Luwian would mean something like 'pre-eminent in power'.
The hypothesis that Luwian was spoken in Troy received
support in 1995, with the discovery at Troy of a second millennium BC seal, bearing the name of a scribe and his wife written

in Luwian hieroglyphs (see chapter 4). Unfortunately, this seal does not conclusively prove that Luwian was used in Troy. The seal itself dates to the 13th century BC, but it was found in a layer of destruction from around a century and a half later. However, as many 'foreign' traders were present in second millennium BC Troy, the possibility that this seal belonged to a non-Trojan cannot be excluded.

The 'Luwian analysis' of names like Priam is also inconclusive, as it is simply impossible to prove that the Homeric names did indeed originate in second millennium BC Troy. And even if the name is authentic and should be interpreted as Luwian, this does not of itself say anything about the language situation in Troy. Just as in the case of Alakšandu/Aleksandros, it does not necessarily suggest more than the fact that the Trojan royal house had links with Luwian-speaking states (an extremely likely possibility given the proximity of Arzawa/Mirā, which was as we have seen probably Luwian-speaking).

Taking everything into account, we may conclude that it is entirely possible that there were Luwian speakers in Troy, with the seal as evidence, but that it cannot be proven that the city as a whole was Luwian-speaking. It should be borne in mind that Luwian-speaking Arzawa/Mirā and surroundings, despite its relative proximity still lies at the considerable distance from Troy of around 200 kilometres to the south. Moreover, the language situation in a single western Anatolian state cannot be projected across the whole of western Anatolia without further evidence. As we will see below, other languages must have been spoken alongside Luwian in the western Anatolia of the second millennium BC.

AROUND 1200 BC: CRISIS

Around 1200 BC, the entire eastern Mediterranean region descended into crisis: Mycenaean civilisation collapsed and Troy VIIa was destroyed, while the Hittite Kingdom also disappeared during this period. With the collapse of Hittite supremacy the cuneiform tradition disappears from Anatolia. We have no clear view of what happened in western Anatolia between ca. 1700 and 800 BC.

Greek authors form an important source of information on western Anatolia in the first millennium BC. Following the fall of the Hittite Kingdom Greek peoples settled in this region in increasing numbers, and halfway through the first millennium the largest part of the western Anatolian littoral had become Greek-speaking. On the basis of works by Greek authors originating from that area (for example Herodotus, who was from Halicarnassus), we know a lot about the political situation in the region. We are able to make out the following small kingdoms: Mysia, Lydia, Caria, Lycia, Bithynia, Phrygia and Pisidia. The city of Troy and its surroundings fell under Mysia, which is also known as Phrygia-on-the-Hellespont.

From around 800 BC, alphabetic script came into use in the western Anatolian region, and most of the small kingdoms referred to above used their own variant of the alphabet to communicate in the local language. Texts written on perishable materials have unfortunately been lost, but we certainly have many rock inscriptions and inscriptions on stone monuments. On the basis of these texts we are able to draw up a language map of western Anatolia in the first millennium BC (Greek and Roman inscriptions have for the sake of convenience been ignored). Each dot indicates the spot where one or more inscriptions were found. On this basis we have a relatively good idea of the languages of Lydia, Caria, Lycia and Phrygia. We have only a single inscription from Mysia, and the inscriptions from Pisidia, in two differing languages, Pisidian and Sidetic, are also extremely scanty. We have no inscriptions at all from Bithynia.

POPULATION MOVEMENTS AROUND 1200 BC

Of course, one cannot simply project the language map of the first millennium BC backwards to the second millennium. The crisis that took place in 1200 BC was so extensive that it is likely that various population movements took place at this time. This is also what the Greek authors tell us. According to these authors, the Mysians, Phrygians and Bithynians originated from Thrace, the region to the north of the Sea of Marmara.

From a linguistic point of view these tales may well be true. The language of the Phrygians (of these three languages the one we know best) is certainly an Indo-European language, but it does not belong to the same branch as Hittite and Luwian, the Indo-European languages spoken in Anatolia in the second millennium. Phrygian appears rather to be closely related to Greek. Given that Phrygian could not have come from Greece itself, which was already Greek-speaking, it is extremely likely that it was originally spoken to the north-east of Greece, for example in modern Bulgaria. The Phrygians must have migrated to Anatolia at a certain point, as the Greek sources relate, taking their language with them. The fact that a memory of this Phrygian invasion continued to exist suggests that it could not have taken place too far in the past. A date around 1200 BC could well fit with these facts. It appears safe to assume that the Phrygians invaded Anatolia via Thrace following the collapse of the Hittite Kingdom, or more probably after indications of its pending collapse. The sole Mysian inscription that we know suggests an extremely close relationship with Phrygian, and we may perhaps assume that the Mysians and Phrygians spoke different dialects of one and the same language. (Compare also the alternative name for Mysia: Phrygia-on-the-Hellespont.) We know nothing about Bithynian, but as the story about the Mysian and Phrygian invasion of Anatolia appears to be true, this may also apply to the Bithynians.

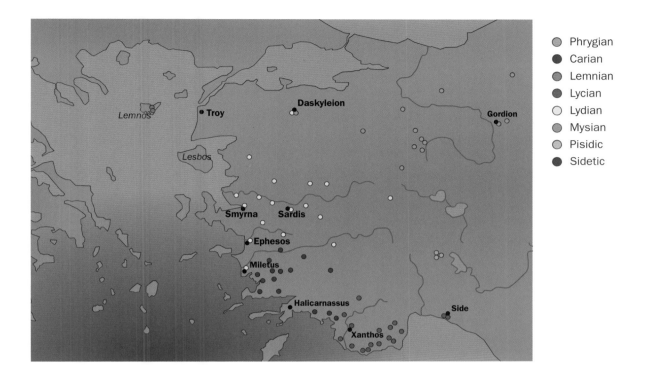

Linguistic map of Anatolia in the 1st millennium BC.

The other languages found in western Anatolia – Lydian, Carian, Lycian, Pisidian and Sidetic – are also Indo European languages but belong to the same branch as Hittite and Luwian. They are so closely related to Luwian that we regard this group of languages as a sub-branch, the Luwian branch. It is thus very probable that these languages are completely indigenous, and it is generally assumed that they or their precursors were spoken in western Anatolia as early as the second millennium BC. However, this does not mean that at the time these languages were spoken in precisely the same places as in the first millennium. As we have noted, the collapse of the Hittite kingdom allowed various population groups to invade the region from northern Anatolia, and it is entirely possible that groups within Anatolia were also forced to move. For example a convincing case has been made (by the Leiden language expert Beekes) that the Lydians must have lived further to the north of Lydia in the second millennium BC, in the region called Māša during this period. They would then have been forced to migrate further to the south following the invasion of the Phrygians, Mysians and Bithynians.

THE LANGUAGE OF TROY: LYDIAN?
Whenever we zoom in on Troy and view its immediate surroundings, we observe the following situation. No inscriptions from the first millennium BC have been found in the vicinity of Troy itself. The closest languages are Phrygian, Mysian and Lydian. We have seen that the Phrygians and Mysians invaded Anatolia only after the fall of the Hittite kingdom. Thus, neither Phrygian nor Mysian could have been the original language spoken in Troy. However, this does not apply to Lydian. This language, which belongs to the same linguistic branch as Hittite and Luwian, which was very probably spoken in Anatolia in the second millennium BC, is the language found closest to Troy during the first millennium (in the Lydian capital at Daskyleion), and is thus a candidate for having been the language of Troy. A number of experts advocate this view, including the eminent linguist Günter Neumann, but there is another – and in my view better – candidate.

THE LANGUAGE OF TROY: LEMNIAN/ETRUSCAN?
Alongside Phrygian, Mysian and Lydian, there is yet another language found in the vicinity of Troy, namely Lemnian. This language is named for Lemnos, the Aegean island that lies immediately west of Troy. Two stelae and a few pottery shards with inscriptions in Lemnian have been found on the island. An interesting point is that Lemnian reveals extensive similarities with Etruscan. These similarities are so significant that we

49

may regard the two languages as closely related dialects. How are these facts to be interpreted historically?

The origin of the Etruscans has long been one of history's great unsolved puzzles. As already in antiquity the Etruscans were thought not to be native to Italy, but to have originated elsewhere, namely in Lydia. This was long dismissed as a myth with little historical basis, but the realization that the Etruscan language is closely related to the language of Lemnos has again sparked the debate. Professor Beekes of Leiden University recently published a lengthy article in which he listed 24 arguments that provide strong evidence that the Etruscans did in fact come from Lydia. However, according to Beekes, this does not refer to classical Lydia (as per Herodotus), but rather to the region the Lydians inhabited in the second millennium BC, that is to say the region that was then called Māša. The Etruscans are thought to have left there by ship in response to the crisis of 1200 BC and ended up in Italy.

I almost completely share Beekes' conclusion that the Etruscans must have originated in western Anatolia. I propose to alter his hypothesis in just one respect. Classical sources mention various locations in western Anatolia and the northern Aegean region where Etruscans, referred to in Greek as Tursenoi, lived at the time or had previously lived. In his article Beekes provides a summary of these locations. We see that some of these locations do in fact lie in the region where Māša was situated, but the majority of them are in the region around Troy/Wiluša and on islands to the west. I would like to conclude on the basis of this information that the Etruscans/Tursenoi inhabited Troy/Wiluša and the islands to the west as their core territory with an offshoot to the southern coast of the Sea of Marmara. To the east this region overlaps the region where the Lydians lived in the second millennium BC, and that could very well be the reason why in classical antiquity it was believed that the Etruscans originated in Lydia.

Apart from Beekes' 24 arguments in favour of why the origins of the Etruscans must have lain in this region, two additional arguments may be adduced to support the link between the Etruscans and Troy. Firstly, the root of the name Troy in Hittite, *trū-* (Trūiša), and in Greek, **trō-* (Troíe), appears to be identical to that in the name for the Etruscans, which is *tru-*. (The *e-* in 'Etrusc' is a vowel prefixed to facilitate articulating the initial consonant cluster *tr-*. Compare the e-less variant *tur-* in the Greek word Tursenoi, and the Latin Tuscia derived from the earlier **Turskia*.) Secondly, the myth that Aeneas, a Trojan prince, ends up in Italy by way of extended wandering after the fall of Troy, and settles down after fighting a battle with the indigenous people there, as described in Virgil's *Aeneid*, may have its origins in a migration from the region of Troy to central Italy. Without doubt many names and events have been added to this tale over the course of time, just as with the Iliad, but the 'core' of this tale may well relate to real (Bronze Age) events.

All in all, it appears to me entirely possible that the original language of Troy was a precursor of Etruscan. It should be emphasized, however, that in the absence of clear textual evidence from Late Bronze Age Troy itself, the language of Troy remains subject of conjecture.

A stele from the 6th century BC. This funerary monument was found on Lemnos in 1885. The Lemnian language was possibly related to that of the Etruscans. After the conquest of Lemnos by Athens in 510 BC, it was replaced by Attic Greek and Lemnian died out.

THE MYCENAEAN GREEKS

JORRIT KELDER

We know from Hittite texts that, from around 1400 to 1220 BC, the western coast of Anatolia was subject to incursions from people from the land of Ahhiyawa. There has been almost a century of debate on whom precisely the Hittites had in mind, but it is now clear that Ahhiyawa must have lain in Greece, although precisely where within Greece remains unclear. Consequently, Ahhiyawa must have been a reference to the Mycenaean Greeks.

The Mycenaean Greeks, or Mycenaeans, are named after the city of Mycenae: an important, and probably the most important, city in Greece during the late Bronze Age, located not far from modern Argos on the Peloponnese. Mycenae is mainly known for the remains of the palace and the nearby royal tomb now known as the 'Treasure of Atreus'. But remains of similar palaces and tombs have been found elsewhere in Greece, although these are more modest in scale. Mycenaean palaces have been found at Pylos (in the south-western Peloponnese), Tiryns and Midea (both, like Mycenae, on the Peloponnesian peninsula of Argolis), Athens, Thebes and Orchomenus (in Boeotia in central Greece), Knossos and probably Chania (on Crete), and probably at Volos and Dimini (in Thessaly). Recent finds suggest that another palace lay on the southern Peloponnese, a little to the south of modern Sparta, although the remains are still very scanty and most of the site is yet unexplored. There must also have been a very important centre to the north of Sparta, at the village of Pellana.

CULTURAL UNIFORMITY

How did these various palaces relate to each other? Were they, as Homer suggests, part of a unified realm under the leadership of the King of Mycenae? There are some indications that this was, indeed, the case.

The material culture of Greece in the 13th and 14th centuries BC is remarkably homogenous: throughout Greece, palaces were constructed in the same way, walls were painted in the same way, pottery (such as the famed Mycenaean stirrup jars, that found a receptive market throughout the eastern Mediterranean) was used in the same way, and the same script was used on the same types of clay tablets.

This cultural uniformity is remarkable and would not recur after the late Bronze Age. Even in the Classical Period, there were major cultural differences between the different Greek

The Lion Gate, the entrance to the citadel of Mycenae, dating from ca. 1250 BC. The design might have been borrowed from Hittite precursors, such as the Lion Gate in Hattuša. The two lionesses could have been the coat of arms of the ruling Mycenaean dynasty, while the pillar on the altar represents the palace of Mycenae. The heads of the lionesses – now lost – were probably made of a different type of stone and stared directly at the visitor.

states, among other aspects in language, script, customs and pottery. The fact that the Hittites in the 13th century BC refer to a great king of Ahhiyawa suggests that this cultural uniformity was paralleled by (and, indeed, may have been the result of), a certain degree of political unity. The problem when establishing political structures in Mycenaean Greece, however, is that there is very little evidence to go by. Various texts, inscribed on clay tablets that were found in the palaces at Pylos, Knossos and Thebes, are useful when it comes to reconstructing modes of taxation, the use of land and the variety and scope of Mycenaean industries, but they say little about political structures. An additional problem is that the texts, known to us as 'Linear B texts', only refer to areas in the (more or less) immediate vicinity of the respective palaces. They inform us on things like harvests, the distribution of goods and artisans, such as smiths and fullers, and occasionally the movements of small groups of soldiers in the immediate environs of the palaces: they scarcely

Michael Ventris, the British architect who deciphered Linear B. This script was found on clay tablets in the ruined palace of Knossos on Crete. Ventris initially thought that it was related to Etruscan, but came to the conclusion in 1952 that it was an extremely old variant of Greek.

A Linear B tablet. The majority of the Linear B tablets extant date to the late 13th century, shortly before the destruction of the Mycenaean palaces. There has been considerable debate on dating the tablets from Knossos: it has traditionally been assumed that Knossos was finally destroyed around 1400 BC and for this reason that the tablets from the palace also originated at the time. However, texts from other Mycenaean centres, which are dated to around 1200 BC, appear sometimes to have been composed by the same scribes.

refer to activities elsewhere in Greece. The rather 'provincial' scope of these Linear B archives caused many experts to believe that the palaces controlled only their immediate surroundings and had no control over other palaces. According to these specialists, the Mycenaean palaces were politically independent states; the remarkable cultural similarities were, according to these scholars, the result of trading and other contacts. I doubt whether this is a correct interpretation. The Linear B archives were only a very small part of the day-to-day administration of the palaces, and were probably never meant to be preserved (they were only baked accidentally in the fire that destroyed the palaces). There are indications that other writing materials, such as wooden tablets, were also used, but these have not survived. The picture presented by the Linear B texts is thus incomplete by definition, and, as a consequence, it is problematic to make any statement about political structures in the Mycenaean world on the sole basis of the Linear B evidence.

Since various Hittite texts refer to a "great king" (i.e. a king that ruled over other kings) of Ahhiyawa, there is a clear indication of political unity within the Greek world. However, there is still discussion over the nature of this 'Greek unity'. Most experts now tend to believe that there was 'something bigger' in Greece, and that the different Mycenaean palaces cooperated in one way or another. For example, the American archaeologist Eric Cline has recently put forward the idea that various Mycenaean palaces, and perhaps all, formed a kind of confederation, which was possibly led by the king of Mycenae. A scenario of this kind is certainly not inconceivable. Consider, for example, the Delian League in classical antiquity, the precursor of the Athenian empire.

A Mycenaean bridge at Kazarma, to the east of the plain of Argos. Mycenaean road builders attained a high level of proficiency, and there is evidence of roads in even the most inhospitable regions. These roads may have been built mainly to allow the Mycenaean elite to travel from palace to palace with ease. Chariots, often depicted on frescos and vases, were used for this purpose.

Picture of a chariot on a vase from 1300-1250 BC, made in Mycenae and found on Cyprus. Chariots were also used in battle: according to a Hittite text from around 1400 BC the Mycenaean ruler Attariššija (possibly the Hittite way of writing the Greek name Atreus) deployed 100 chariots against a Hittite expeditionary force in Western Turkey.

MYCENAEAN GREEK

At the end of the 19th century, a number of extremely old sealstones revealing a script with hieroglyphic signs unknown at the time were acquired by the British archaeologist Sir Arthur Evans. He was able to trace their origin to Crete. In 1900, Evans began excavating the site of Knossos in Central Crete, where remains of a palace had earlier been discovered, with the expectation of uncovering further traces of a lettered culture. A large number of clay tablets came to light in this

Bronze Age palace, revealing texts in an unknown script that Evans had also encountered on a number of vases. It was clear that two script variants from different periods were involved. Evans referred to variants A and B and termed both scripts 'linear', as the symbols were made up of little lines (in contrast with the hieroglyphs on the sealstones). In 1939, the American archaeologist Carl Blegen also found large numbers of tablets on the Greek mainland at Pylos. Evans had meanwhile been working for some time on deciphering the texts, but had made only limited progress. He did however make extremely accurate drawings of all the finds and these were posthumously published in 1952 (Evans died in 1941). In that same year, the English architect Michael Ventris managed to decipher Linear B. He further developed his thoughts on Linear B with a fellow-Englishman, the linguist John Chadwick, and together they published a landmark article in the *Journal of Hellenic Studies*. Linear B could now be read, although the older texts from Crete, referred to by the term Linear A (which are much fewer in number and have in general come down to us in more fragmented form) remain undeciphered to this day. Many archaeologists and linguists, including Ventris himself, were amazed when the Linear B texts yielded a very old form of Greek. The texts now provided proof that the palaces of the Mycenaean era were inhabited by Greek-speaking people. In addition, it was now possible to draw all kinds of historical and linguistic conclusions on the basis of the new material. The texts date from the 14th and 13th centuries BC. The oldest Greek known until then was that of the Homeric epics, the *Iliad* and the *Odyssey*, from the beginning of the 8th century BC. Although a whole new world thus opened up for philological analysis, the contents of the texts turned out to be disappointing. The material consists overwhelmingly of geographic and personal names and of numbers. The texts consist mostly of palace inventories and other administrative records, such as lists of offerings to the gods, furniture, carts and wheels, wool and agricultural yields. Only seldom do the texts include complete sentences. In addition, it should be noted that the clay tablets, which were baked in the fires that destroyed the palaces all date from the final year of the palaces' existence (in the case of Knossos, this may be in the 14th century BC, in the case of Pylos, this was probably during the final decades of the 13th century BC), and thus only present a picture of the final year of the respective palaces. Nevertheless, historians are able to draw a few cautious conclusions regarding the economy and management system of the regions controlled by the palaces. Moreover, the items described can be compared with the archaeological evidence.

Despite the somewhat rudimentary grammatical construction of the texts, the Linear B texts offer a vast amount of material for study, and major progress has been made since 1952 in analysing the phonetics, phonology and morphology of ancient Greek. For example, we now know that Mycenaean still used the *qu*-phoneme (labiovelar) lost in later Greek, and that the *h* was still used within the word. Mycenaean also shares a number of developments with some Greek dialects. This meant that theories about mutual relationships between the historical dialects had to be revised.

Unfortunately, the syllabic nature of the script certainly does not facilitate reading and interpreting the texts, since virtually all the symbols represent either a vowel or a combination of consonant + vowel (*a, pa, ta, na* etc.). As Greek has a fair number of consonant clusters (*pt-, st-, tl-* etc.), and many Greek syllables and words end on a consonant that cannot be enunciated directly, the script is only moderately suited to this language. In addition, there is but a single symbol for the *r-* and *l-* syllables and for the *k-, g-* and *ch-* syllables, and it is also impossible to differentiate between short and long vowels. As a result, not all the words that we are now able to read are easy to understand. For example, the word *ka-ko* may be read as *kakos*, 'bad', or as *chalkos*, 'bronze'. Moreover, the case ending, which is important for understanding the function of the word in the sentence, can in general not be expressed. For example, for a certain class of words, the first case ends in *-os*, the third in *–ooj* and the fourth in *-on*, with all three represented by *-o*. The situation is even more complicated with proper nouns.

Marco Poelwijk

The ruins of Gla in the Copais valley in Boeotia, Greece. This huge fort, with walls running for almost three kilometres and three to five metres thick, was probably the 'command centre' of an extensive drainage project, by means of which the larger part of the valley was drained. The resulting agricultural land provided for good harvests and greater prosperity. Traces of construction have been found in the earth just outside the walls of the fort, and it is possible that Gla had a 'lower city' just like Troy.

MYCENAEANS IN ANATOLIA

In view of the observations presented above, we may assume a significant measure of cooperation between the palaces under the leadership of the king of Mycenae. Consequently, it is entirely possible that Mycenaeans sailed eastwards at his command, to found new cities on the western coast of Anatolia, and to raid or capture existing ones. Archaeological finds in the region around Miletus in particular appear to support the Hittite texts and suggest that Mycenaean Greeks settled there from around 1400 BC. Although this may initially have involved fairly small groups, there are indications that more Mycenaeans soon settled on Anatolian soil. Wolf-Dietrich Niemeier, the German director of the excavations at Miletus, has even argued for a full-blown colonisation. Noting the quantity of Argive pottery at Miletus, Niemeier even suggested that this colonisation may have come from the region around Mycenae.

The 14th and more particularly the early 13th witnessed the *floruit* of the Mycenaean world. The palaces on the Greek mainland became ever grander and more monumental, whilst various Mycenaean infrastructural works of immense scale further attest to the wealth and vigour of Mycenaean society. These works included a network of roads stretching across the whole of the plain of Argos, linking the villages and cities on the plain

Grave circle A, on the citadel of Mycenae. In the mid-13th century BC, the defensive circuit of Mycenae was strengthened and expanded, bringing a large piece of land with a number of elite graves from the 16th century BC within the walls of the citadel. When Schliemann, following his success at Troy, tried his luck at Mycenae and discovered these graves, he believed them to be the last resting place of Agamemnon and his associates. However, Schliemann was out by almost four centuries.

to Mycenae. The high quality of the masonry of several bridges (some of these bridges are still standing) can still be appreciated. There are even indications that this network of roads stretched well beyond the Argolid: traces of Mycenaean roads have been found in Arcadia, the region around Corinth, and in Messenia. But the Mycenaeans were not only skilled in constructing roads: the 13th century BC also witnessed the completion of several huge drainage and irrigation projects. The Nemea valley, which had originally been a swamp, was drained with the aid of dams and drainage channels. The same was done, but on a far larger scale, at Lake Copais, in Boeotia in central Greece. It has been suggested that the necessary manpower for these grand projects was obtained by recruiting, or enslaving, people from western Anatolia.

4 HOMER AND TROY

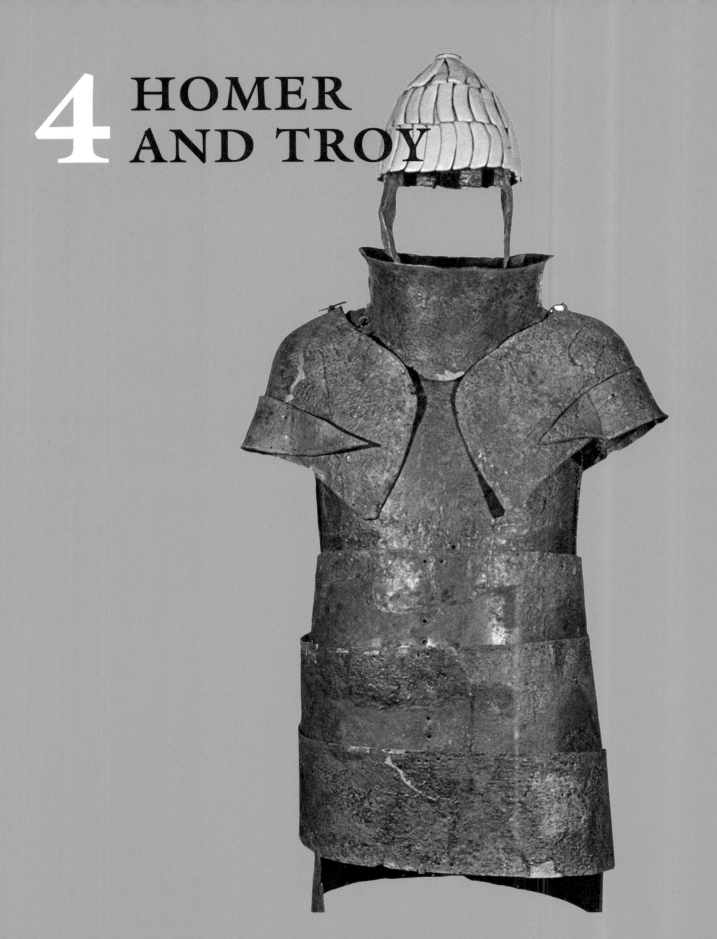

TROY AND THE WAR: ARCHAEOLOGY, DOCUMENTARY SOURCES AND EPIC

JORRIT KELDER

The story of the Trojan War, best known through Homer's *Iliad* and *Odyssey*, is by no means of exclusively Greek pedigree. Many elements in Homer's works betray a strong Near Eastern influence, whilst (as has been discussed in 1.2) a Luwian text with a possible reference to 'high (or steep) Wiluša' could point to an early Anatolian tradition based on a Trojan war. Whether Troy and the war were already the theme of an epic tradition in Greece during the Bronze Age remains uncertain. A number of elements in the *Iliad* suggest that as early as the Late Bronze Age there were songs in Greece about the war for Troy. For example, the metre of certain parts of the *Iliad* seem more compatible with early – Mycenaean – Greek than with later dialects of Homer's own period. Moreover, the description of the geography of the plain in front of Troy in the *Iliad*, as well as Homer's description of Greece itself, with references to numerous cities long deserted by Homer's time, seem to indicate a Late Bronze origin for at least parts of the Trojan epic (this is especially the case in Book II of the *Iliad*, the 'Catalogue of Ships', which lists the Greek contingents sailing for Troy). On top of all this, a number of archaeological items that are mentioned in the *Iliad* and *Odyssey*, such as weapons and suits of armour, including so-called 'boar's tusk helmets' and bronze cuirasses, also point to the Bronze Age origin.

This is not of course to say that the *Iliad* has been copied verbatim from a Late Bronze Age story: there is clear evidence of later changes and additions in the Homeric epics, often on an extensive scale. And it certainly does not mean that a 'Mycenaean *Iliad*', should it already have existed, was directly linked to actual events of the period. The *Iliad* was at all times a work of art, a tale intended to entertain. Nevertheless, at a number of points the epic appears so realistic, and there are now so many archaeological and textual data that fit remarkably well with the era Homer depicts in his works, that it is conceivable, and even probable, that the core of the *Iliad* really does have an historical basis.

MYCENAEANS IN ANATOLIA

The Mycenaean Greeks are archaeologically 'visible' on the Western Anatolian littoral from at least 1400 BC onwards. There are many indications for early Mycenaean (trade) activity throughout that region, whilst at the site of the later (classical Greek) city of Miletus, especially, there are strong indications of/suggesting Mycenaean colonisation. Large quantities of Mycenaean pottery (both imported from Mainland Greece and locally made), kilns and Mycenaean-style burials have been found at Miletus. A number of Hittite texts dating to the 14th and 13th century BC confirm the archaeological data and indicate that 'Millawanda' (the Hittite rendering of Greek Miletus) served as a Mycenaean basis for activity in Anatolia.

These Hittite texts further reveal that around 1400 BC the west of Anatolia, then part of the Hittite Kingdom, was subject to incursions from a certain Attarissiya, referred to by the Hittites as 'the man [or king] of Ahhiya'. Although there has long been heated debate over the identity of Ahhiya (or Ahhiyawa, as it is called in later Hittite texts), in recent years it has become increasingly clear that this is the Hittite name for Mycenaean Greek territory, the home of the Achaeans – one of the names that Homer uses for the Greeks in the *Iliad*. There is some evidence that Attarissiya and his group of Achaeans made a big impression on the Anatolian population: a decorated shard of pottery found in Boghazköy (the current name of the Hittite capital Hattuša) appear to show a Mycenaean warrior, complete with body armour and boar's tusk helmet.

It is evident from Hittite texts that there were Mycenaeans in Western Anatolia and that their presence was not always of a peaceful nature: Attarissiya – possibly the Hittite pronunciation of the heroic Greek name Atreus – is reported to have fielded an unspecified number of foot soldiers and a hundred chariots against a Hittite expeditionary army sent west to restore order. Despite these upheavals, it appears that Troy initially experienced little trouble from Mycenaean incursions. The first contacts between the inhabitants of Troy and the Mycenaeans were probably of an amicable nature. It has been suggested that the two came into contact through fishing, whereby the schools of mackerel and tuna in the Aegean could have served as 'meeting

This suit of armour from the late 15th century BC was found in a *tholos* tomb – a monumental beehive grave – in Dendra, a small village near the Mycenaean citadel Midea. The similarity between this cuirass and the armour of the 'bronze-greaved Achaeans' in Homer's *Iliad* is remarkable. The boar's tusk helmet is also described by Homer.

A graffito on a potshard found in Hattuša, capital of the Hittites. This is probably a depiction of a Mycenaean warrior, complete with boar's tusk helmet and a long decorative plume. Hittite texts refer to Mycenaean incursions into Western Anatolia from the early 14th century BC onwards. Millawanda – the later Miletus – on the western coast appears to have been the most important Mycenaean centre in Anatolia.

TROY AS CONFLICT ZONE BETWEEN TWO MAJOR POWERS

While there is no archaeological evidence for hostile relations between the Mycenaean world and the Trojans, this does not mean that there was never any conflict. Archaeology is particularly well suited to detecting broad outlines and developments: specific events, such as a war over Troy, do not necessarily have to be visible in the archaeological record. A number of Hittite texts reveal that the situation in Troy was not always peaceful. One of these texts (dating to the early 13th century BC and known to experts as the Manapa-Tarhunta letter) mentions internal squabbles and the deposing of King Walmu of Wiluša (almost certainly the Hittite name for Troy). It is not clear precisely what led to Walmu's deposing (the Wilušan King, it should be noted, was supported by the Hittite great king and could thus bank on military assistance), but a certain Piyamaradu, probably an Anatolian noble, appears to have played a major role in the Walmu's expulsion, claiming the throne of Wiluša himself. Although this is not made clear in the Manapa-Tarhunta letter itself, we know from later texts that Piyamaradu was supported in his actions by the king of Ahhiyawa – a king from Mycenaean Greece. Whilst the deposing of Walmu probably was the result of internal Trojan dissatisfaction, Troy's geographical position – sandwiched as it was between the Hittite and Mycenaean spheres of influence – dictated that the city often was subject to power play between its two larger neighbours, Ahhiyawa and Hatti.

That the Mycenaeans sometimes also had a direct influence on political affairs in the region emerges from a later Hittite text that is part of an extensive correspondence (which has survived only in extremely fragmented form) between the Hittite King Hattušili III and his counterpart in Greece, an unnamed king of Ahhiyawa. This text, which is known as the Tawagalawa letter and dates to around 1250 BC, refers not only to a conflict between the Hittites and Ahhiyawa over Troy (possibly a reference to the earlier affair centring on Piyamaradu; see box), but also refers to further Mycenaean activities on the western Anatolian littoral, including continuing support for the rebel Piyamaradu and the 'abduction' of Anatolian people to the Greek mainland. The well-known Hittitologist Trevor Bryce has suggested that these Anatolians were taken to Greece to work on various huge building projects. For example, the famous Lion Gate at Mycenae shows some similarity with Anatolian sculptures, and comparisons may also be made between the so-called 'galleries' in Tiryns and underground passages in the Hittite capital Hattuša. Whether or not Bryce's hypothesis is true, it is certainly clear that the Mycenaeans did in fact put slaves of Anatolian origin to work in Greece: the Tawagalawa letter is not the only source to mention this fact; Linear B texts found

ground' for Trojan and Mycenaean fishing fleets, although trade contacts probably also played a role. When the first contact was made is unclear. There is good evidence for Trojan trade links with the Cyclades in the 3rd millennium BC. However, the first large quantities of Mycenaean pottery found in Troy are to be dated to the early 14th century BC on stylistic grounds, and it may thus be assumed that there was at least sporadic contact between Troy and the Mycenaean world. These contacts increased during the 13th century BC: large quantities of Mycenaean pottery have been found in the Trojan habitation phases VI and VIIa, whereby it should be noted that a large part of this 'Mycenaean' pottery appears to have been made in Troy itself. From a cultural point of view, the western Anatolian littoral, and thus Troy as well, was a real contact zone between Anatolian and Aegean (Mycenaean) civilisations in the 13th century. The British archaeologist Penelope Mountjoy aptly dubbed it, *The East Aegean – West Anatolian Interface*: a period of unprecedentedly close relations and exchanges between the Greek and Anatolian worlds. Although there is no definite proof, it is conceivable that Mycenaeans lived in Troy during this period.

at the palace at Pylos also refer to slaves from various parts of western Anatolia (possibly including Troy).

A WAR OVER TROY IN THE TAWAGALAWA LETTER?

An important piece of evidence for contact between the Mycenaeans and the Hittites is the Tawagalawa letter, a letter from the Hittite king (presumably Hattušili III) to the great king of Ahhiyawa. The name Tawagalawa, a brother of the great king, is presumably the Hittite version of the Greek name Eteocles (shown in Linear B as e-te-wo-ke-le-we). The Greek *epsilon* and *omicron* are usually reproduced as an 'a' in Hittite; the city Miletus is transliterated as Millawa(n)da and Lesbos as Lapza. In the case of Tawagalawa the 'e' at the beginning of the word has been dropped.

The Tawagalawa document deals primarily with the above-mentioned Piyamaradu, a troublemaker who caused the Hittite king a great deal of difficulty in the west of Anatolia. The letter is conciliatory in tone, and the Hittite king, probably Hattušili III (1267-1237), clearly wants to form a united front with his Ahhiyawan counterpart against this troublesome Piyamaradu. The Hittite king asks the great king of Ahhiyawa to make clear to Piyamaradu that they are indeed on the same side and requests him to deliver the following message to Piyamaradu:

> My brother, in any event write this to him [=Piyamaradu] The king of Hatti has convinced me with respect to the Wi[lu]ša question, where we were enemies, and we have made peace. Animosity between us would [now] not be right.

Unfortunately the clay tablet is damaged to some extent, as a result of which the word Wiluša (*Wi-lu-ša*) is not 100% certain, although very plausible. Lower down in the letter there is another reference to a conflict between Ahhiyawa and Hatti, for which the Hittite king appears more or less to be offering his apologies, excuses his behaviour by saying that he was very young at the time. This text thus refers to a conflict over Wiluša in which the Mycenaean Greeks played a role.

Willemijn Waal

Although there is evidence of Mycenaean interference in Trojan affairs (the Greek name of the Trojan king, Alakšandu, already suggests this), the 10-year siege described by Homer seems to be more than a bit far-fetched. In addition to the unlikely length of the duration of Homer's war, there are chronological difficulties when it comes to relating 'historical events' to Homer's songs. The conflict over Troy referred to in the Tawagalawa letter clearly takes place in the past – i.e. before 1250 BC. This does not agree with the traditional date of Homer's

Trojan war. According to the later, classical Greek tradition, Homer's war took place around 1183 (this date is calculated on the basis of other legendary events, such as the 'Return of the Heracleidae'), although Herodotus proposed a date around 1250 BC. As the chronology of Mycenaean Greece is anything but certain (new research regularly leads to small shifts) and that of the Greek legends and traditions is in any case extremely problematic, there are good grounds for caution in identifying the conflict mentioned in the Tawagalawa letter as the Trojan War of the *Iliad*.

The lack of written sources from Troy itself presents us with a major problem in determining the historicity of the Trojan War. There are sporadic references to the city in Hittite texts and there is possibly a reference to women captured from Troy on a Linear B tablet from the Mycenaean palace of Pylos (PY Ep 705.6). But no texts have thus far been found in Troy –

Arrowheads found at Troy VI. The German archaeologist Wilhelm Dörpfeld believed that this must have been the Troy of the Trojan War partly on account of these arrowheads. However, weapons are not proof of a war, and the city's destruction is currently usually attributed to an earthquake.

A seal from Troy. Although this seal was found in Troy VIIb, it originates from the 13th century. It is the only artefact showing 'script' that has been found in Troy to date.

Homer describes in detail the armour of the Achaeans (Greeks) laying siege to Troy. Some of the Greek heroes wear precious armour that was by that the time ancient, including boar's tusk helmets swords inlaid with gold. The huge shields shown on this dagger from Mycenae (a replica of an original from the 16th century BC) are referred to by Homer. At the time of the Trojan War shields of this kind, which protected the bearer virtually completely, were unusual. Smaller round shields were normally used.

whether in Mycenaean Greek, in Hittite or in another Anatolian language – that could provide greater clarity on the links between the city and the Greeks. The sole 'evidence' found to the effect that writing was not unknown in the city is a seal with a Luwian inscription that reveals the name and title of a scribe and his wife, but this seal has been found in a 'late' phase of habitation (Troy VIIb), and it is not clear whether it was in use at Troy during the city's heyday. It is entirely possible that the Trojans conducted their administration on wood or other perishable materials – in all probability this was the case in the rest of Anatolia and possibly also in Mycenaean Greece – that have not withstood the ravages of time.

TROY: RAZED BY WAR OR BY EARTHQUAKE?

No trace of *the* Trojan War is to be found in Troy itself. A layer of destruction that dates to around 1300-1250 BC and spelled the end of 'Troy VI', was long seen as the *smoking gun*. A number of arrowheads, found by the German archaeologist Wilhelm Dörpfeld in the citadel and identified as Mycenaean, were immediately linked to the war as described in the epic. But nothing more has been found in this layer of the city that could be conclusively linked to a Mycenaean destruction. In the final analysis most experts are now convinced that the demise of Troy VI, which must have been a wealthy and thriving palace-city, was caused by an earthquake, like those that occur from time to time in the Aegean. This earthquake must have been extremely powerful, as an entire chunk of the Trojan citadel's wall was shifted out of place.

Although the Homeric Achaeans can thus not be held responsible for this destruction of the city, there certainly appears to be a reference here to a well-known element in the story of Troy, the famous Trojan Horse. In ancient Greece the horse was a prestigious animal associated with the god Poseidon, who ruled not only the seas but was also known as the 'Earth

Shaker', the god of earthquakes. Carl Blegen, who led the excavations at Troy in the 1930s, has for this reason suggested that the Trojan Horse could be a literary allusion to a natural disaster. Another explanation could be that the Horse refers to a siege engine, such as a battering ram. Whether the Horse was in fact an earthquake or a battering ram, the fact remains that there is no evidence that the Mycenaean Greeks were responsible for the final destruction of Troy VI. Moreover there are problems with the chronology. Notwithstanding these 'problems', if it is assumed that an 'historical' war over Troy was fought at some point, and that this war was the inspiration for the *Iliad*, then Troy VI seems a good candidate.

WARS OVER TROY?

Although it is plausible to argue that Troy VI was the city described in Homer, the problems in chronology and the lack of conclusive evidence of man-made destruction have led various experts, in particular the archaeologist Blegen mentioned above, to believe that Troy VIIa, the subsequent habitation phase, must have been the Troy of the Trojan War. From a cultural viewpoint this city was in many respects similar to its predecessor, Troy VI. The inhabitants were almost certainly the same as those of Troy VI, or their descendants, and rebuilt their city following the devastation. Troy VIIa was in all respects a prosperous city, although the nature of the citadel in particular had changed: where previously the spacious, monumental residences of the local elite stood, smaller, more densely packed houses were now erected. For a long time it was assumed that this was a sign of 'fear' and that the Trojans sheltered in numbers behind the restored high walls of the citadel. Results from the recent excavations by the University of Tübingen, however, have challenged this view: traces of human activity have been found at various places on the plain around the citadel, and there are clear indications that the citadel was surrounded by an extensive 'lower city' from the early 13th century (Troy VI) onwards. There has been a great deal of discussion regarding the nature of this lower city. The Tübingen excavation leader, Manfred Korfmann, argued for a densely populated area of around 7,000 inhabitants over an area of 200,000 m² on the basis of the archaeological evidence. This area was surrounded by a wall of unbaked mud bricks (to this day a construction material in frequent use in the Middle East) and possibly even a moat for protection against attack by chariot for example. By the standards of the Late Bronze Age, Troy would thus have been a large and important city. Although many experts agree with this reconstruction, others see Troy VIIa in a completely different light. The best known critic of Korfmann's thesis is Frank Kolb, his Tübingen colleague. Kolb finds no, or in any event inadequate, evidence for an extensive lower city and characterises Troy VIIa as merely a reinforced citadel with sporadic surrounding habitation. In his view, the wall did not exist and the 'moat' was part of a system of irrigation canals. It is true that the excavations have exposed only a tiny part of the lower city, and a measure of caution is required. On the other hand there are good grounds, in my view, for at least considering the possibility of a line of defence of some kind (a wall or palisade), if only because of the structure of the citadel's north-eastern bastion, which has a kind of bulge that is best explained as a link with the lower city's wall. The exact nature of the habitation certainly remains a point for discussion, as long as no extensive parts of the lower town have been excavated. Those parts of the lower town that have been investigated suggest that a number of the buildings in this area were built to a considerable, and almost monumental, scale. On the whole, the archaeological evidence, to my mind, suggests that the lower city of Troy VIIa was a prosperous settlement, although perhaps less densely populated than has been suggested.

Troy VIIa, a prosperous and large city, was destroyed around 1180 BC. This time there is convincing evidence of violence: human remains have been found at various locations within the citadel, but here too it is not clear who was responsible for the evidently violent demise of Troy VIIa. It could have been Mycenaeans, but the problem with that hypothesis is that Mycenaean Greece itself descended into crisis around the same time, between 1200 and 1180 BC. Virtually all the palaces in Greece were destroyed or abandoned during this period. This was not an isolated event; there were major problems elsewhere in the eastern Mediterranean region. Flourishing ports like Ugarit in what is now Northern Syria were destroyed, and even the powerful Hittite Kingdom disappeared around this time. This destruction has often been linked to the Sea Peoples, a term known from Egyptian texts and that appears to refer to a large group, or groups, of various dislocated and heavily armed peoples. These 'Sea Peoples' are also thought to be responsible for a failed attack on Egypt. Who these peoples were remains conjecture, although the Egyptians called one of these groups 'Ekwesh', a name that could be related to the Ahhiyawa. Whatever the case, if Mycenaeans were involved in the fall of Troy VIIa, this did not take place in a 'conventional' war such as those we know from the Late Bronze Age – two kings with their armies drawn up opposite each other. Instead, we could think of *hit and run* tactics, comparable with the Viking incursions into Early Mediaeval Europe.

In sum, both Troy VI and Troy VIIa are plausible candidates as backdrop for the war described in the *Iliad*, although none of these cities conforms exactly to the Homeric city. Perhaps it is not even necessary to choose between Troy VI and VIIa: elements of both cities and their respective destructions could be included in a single story. Moreover, Greek legends refer to at least two wars for Troy: the city was destroyed for the first time by the legendary hero Heracles and, more than a generation later, a second time by Agamemnon and his troops.

The number of stories about Troy in the Greek tradition, the references to Troy in the contemporaneous Hittite sources, and the 'hybrid' culture of Troy VI and VIIa emphasise the significance of Troy as cultural, economic, strategic and ideological centre. Whether or not the Trojan War actually occurred, the story of the *Iliad* is certainly a realistic characterisation of the unstable situation around Troy in the Late Bronze Age, with the city tenuously wedged between the power of the Hittites and that of the Mycenaeans.

The plains around Sparta, see from the Menelaion. There was an important centre here during the Mycenaean period, but it is not clear whether this was the regional capital. However, this site was clearly linked to Helen and her husband Menelaus in the 8th century BC: a shrine was erected on top of the Mycenaean ruins to honour them – the Menelaion.

THE WORLD OF HOMER

FLORIS VAN DEN EIJNDE

Homer is often cited as an historical source for the Greek Early Iron Age (ca. 1100-700 BC), although extreme caution is needed in making use of Homer as a reference for this period. After all Homer is not an historian such as Thucydides, who lived some three centuries later. This causes problems that arise in the historical interpretation of Homer's poetry and which may be subdivided into two categories.

The first is the question of dating the *Iliad* and the *Odyssey*. This is important, as different dating of these two works means that the historical conclusions that we draw from them potentially refer to different periods. It is almost universally accepted that Homer is describing the world of the 8th century BC. Researchers locating the Homeric world in the 9th century BC, such as the eminent Amsterdam professor of Greek linguistics, Cees Ruijgh, or conversely in the 7th century BC, such as the acknowledged Homer expert from Oxford, Martin West, have thus far received little support from historians and archaeologists.

What we understand by 'the world of Homer' thus does not relate at all to the Late Bronze Age, the period that drew to a close around 1200 BC. Of course the story of the Fall of Troy took place in a mythical past that is often associated with this period. But just as with the Medieval literary cycles – for example the Arthurian legends, the legends of Alexander or the *Roman de Troie* – the author of the *Iliad* and the *Odyssey* describes a world that must above all be intelligible to his audience. And that audience had to be able to locate the bard's tale within its own frame of reference. In the case of the description of Priam's palace, we should think rather of the simple, hut-like structures characteristic of the Early Iron Age, and not of the large stone palaces of the Late Bronze Age, simply because neither Homer nor his audience had a clear idea of what these lost palaces looked like.

It is certainly the case that the stories about Troy were handed down by the bards orally for centuries, long before the *Iliad* and the *Odyssey* were set down in writing (see page 69). This means that certain verses in the epic are without doubt much older than the rest of the poem, the so-called "fossilised" verses that have been handed down unchanged over the generations. This may be attributed to the strict dactylic hexameter that often prevented bards from adapting these verses. Accordingly, we are able to date the earliest rules for verse to around 1500 BC,

Greek armour from Argos from the 8th century BC.

Bronze cauldron from 675-650 BC, found in an Etruscan grave in Cerveteri (Italy). From around 800 BC onwards contact between Greece, Italy and the Middle East increased. People liked to see themselves as part of an 'international world': valuable utensils were decorated with oriental elements. This large bronze cauldron, used for cooking, is adorned with artistically shaped griffin's heads.

Wooden throne from Salamis (Cyprus), inlaid with ivory, 8th century BC. In Homer's day the elite were seated on chairs of this kind during banquets.

around seven centuries before the Homeric epics were created. However, these remains are often of a formulaic nature and in general tell us little about the historical context of the poems. In other words, they contain few descriptive elements on the customs of the Homeric heroes and the objects they used.

This brings us to the second major problem we run into when studying the world of Homer: the poetic nature of the language. Just as for example with the Arthurian cycle, we have to ask how we are to distinguish fact from fiction. Because if we decide that the *Iliad* and the *Odyssey* are no more than myth, dreamed up by a bard intent solely on entertaining his audience, then little concrete remains for any historian wishing to use the text as a primary source. The war over Troy itself offers few grounds for optimism. There is certainly a shaky consensus that there was such a war – a war that Greeks did in fact participate in – but few today are convinced of the historical 'facts' provided by the author of the *Iliad* – that the war dragged on for 10 years and was waged over a woman abducted by her

lover. This leads to the following paradox: precisely those passages presented in the *Iliad* as 'historical narrative', or are at any rate seen as such by the modern reading public, contain unreliable information that has strayed well away from any possible historical core as a result of poetic licence and oral transmission.

The situation is different with those elements that the poet had perforce to introduce in a realistic way to be intelligible to his audience. Two fairly divergent aspects are at issue here: the normative aspects of the epic, and the material description of the world in which the Homeric heroes operate. The customs for example that govern religious gatherings, funeral rituals, dealing with strangers and ceremonial gatherings fall into the first category. The behaviour that the Homeric heroes displayed is part of the same normative framework that Homer's audience also conformed to – or at least aimed to reflect. Only by having his heroes function in the same normative framework as his audience, was the poet able to imbue his stories with the desired moral force. The description of the codes and customs that for example applied during a marriage ceremony had to be intelligible to the audience, as these codes had to be recognisable. For example, King Menelaus reprimands one of his comrades in Book IV of the *Odyssey* because he proposes sending Telemachus, an uninvited guest at the wedding of his children, away to another host:

> '*Eteoneus, son of Boethous, you never used to be a fool, but now you talk like a simpleton. Take their horses out, of course, and show the strangers in that they may have supper; you and I have stayed often enough at other people's houses before we got back here, where heaven grant that we may rest in peace henceforward.*'
>
> (*Odyssey* 4.30-36, translated by Samuel Butler)

Menelaus' reprimand may be seen as a normative hint to the audience on how to treat uninvited guests at a party.

MATERIAL OBJECTS IN HOMER

A second element historians use to reconstruct 'the world of Homer' are the material objects described in the *Iliad* and the *Odyssey*. Here too, the description of the buildings and objects may be expected to correspond to the world of Homer's audience, or they would not be understood.

We may take the throne rooms in the palaces of Priam and Alcinous as examples. These great halls (*megara*), which formed the backdrop for ceremonial events, were built with wooden doorposts and rafters, and a sharply inclined saddle roof probably of thatch. In the descriptions of these *megara* we read of a swallow building its nest in the rafters, geese cackling around the building and the ever-present droppings of the animals brought in from the fields to be slaughtered. Weapons and suits of armour adorn the walls to emphasise the host's military prowess. Iron spits, pokers, cauldrons and forks were kept close to the hearth for cooking and tending the fire. Guests are seated on raised chairs (*thronoi* or *klismoi*) with high backrests, armrests and footstools. Expensive fabrics and animal pelts, sometimes painted in purple, are used to decorate the chairs of the heroes. The eating utensils consist of gold or silver kraters, bowls and cups, and may be placed on sideboards inlaid with *lapis lazuli*. The meal is prepared and served by large numbers of female slaves, who are not kept hidden from the visitor's eyes in order to enhance the impression of wealth. Dogs lie sleeping at the feet of their masters. Contemporaneous archaeological show that such descriptions belong to the 8th century BC rather than to the Bronze Age.

FEASTS IN HOMER

In Homer, a central component of a feast, apart from the copious amounts to eat and drink, is the bard who entertains the audience with an episode from the epic cycle. The most famous example of a scene of this kind is the recitation by the blind singer Demodocus, who entertains the guests of King Alcinous in his palace on the island of the Phaeacians by relating the fate of the Greeks fighting at Troy, unwittingly causing Odysseus to weep. It is interesting to note that the scene with Demodocus may be interpreted as a reflection of the poet himself, like a self-portrait, while simultaneously reflecting the context in which the Homeric poems were performed: at the ceremonial meals where the Homeric nobles meet.

Although it is questionable whether the 8thcentury palaces (*megara*) as a rule contained such large quantities of gold, silver, slaves and other luxuries, we cannot escape the general impression of the poem, which in many cases is supported by archaeological finds. Conversely, when we accept the general resemblance of the text to the material culture of the 8th century BC, our analysis of the Homeric *megaron* enables us to reconstruct some of the ruined archaeological remains, such as a house on the Athenian Agora, dated to the 7th century BC. This building is of a suitable scale scale to compare it to the Homeric *megara*, and has been identified as a banqueting hall of a local clan. From this building, we may add a couple of elements to the picture drawn by Homer, such as the prominent burial ground next to the banqueting hall and the potters' workshop.

SMYRNA: THE CITY OF HOMER

The best indication of the urban context in which the *Iliad* and the *Odyssey* were composed, is ancient Smyrna, a city of Aeolian origins on the western coast of Asia Minor. This city was conquered by the Ionian Greeks in the middle of the 8th century, and all indications are that the Homeric epics were largely created within a generation or two of this event. Homer's idiom is largely based on Old Ionic Greek, but contains a relatively large number of even older Aeolisms, indicating that the poet himself spoke Ionic Greek but was telling a tale originating in an older Aeolic tradition.

The city of Smyrna is in a certain sense unique within the Greek world, as it had a strong city wall (of a kind not found on the Greek mainland) and was large by 8th century standards. The houses are mostly oval or have a semi-circular extension (apsis) and look more like the Homeric mud brick hut-palaces than the large stone palaces of the late Bronze Age. Grain silos have been found in the city that, in combination with the city wall, create the impression of a well-defended town.

HOMER AS TRAVEL GUIDE?

Although Smyrna may well have been a major source of inspiration for what Troy once looked like, it is also important to take into consideration the ruins of Troy itself. Homer's description of Troy and its physical condition raises the ques-

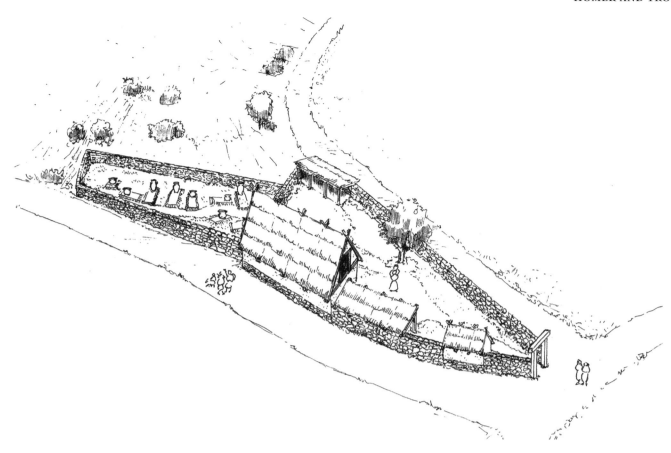

tion whether he had knowledge of the city's topography. Given the long period between the destruction of Troy VIIa and the period when Homer lived (around five centuries), it seems exceedingly unlikely that reliable information about the appearance of the Bronze Age city should have survived during the long period of oral transmission. On the other hand, it is not improbable that Homer possessed specific knowledge of ancient Troy, perhaps because he visited the ruins and saw them at first hand, or else through an informant who reported back to him in detail. According to the German archaeologist of Troy, Manfred Korfmann, the archaeological context of the city has been sufficiently well preserved to indicate that Homer knew the general topography of the city. The German

The so-called 'House A' excavated on the Athenian agora. This house was probably used by an eminent Athenian family for ceremonial occasions. The most prominent members of the family were buried to the left of the house, and to the right there was a potter's workshop.

The city of Smyrna (Izmir in modern Turkey) was one of the cities that laid claim to being Homer's birthplace. In the 8th century BC Smyrna possessed a strong defensive wall, a harbour and houses with an apsis (semi-circular extension). It was an important Greek centre in the Geometric Period (1050 to 720 BC, so called for the decorations on the pottery made at the time). The city was conquered by the king of Lydia in the 6th century and subsequently abandoned.

archaeologist cogently argues that the walls of Troy, reaching up to eight metres high, must still have been clearly visible in the 8th century and would have made a great impression on any visitor (see also 2.3). Korfmann even identified a large city gate as the most logical candidate for the departure of the Trojan Prince Hector and Andromache in the *Iliad*. She begs her husband to defend the city from there, rather than do battle below on the plain:

'as for the host, place them near the fig-tree, where the city can be best scaled, and the wall is weakest. Thrice have the bravest of them come thither and assailed it, under the two Ajaxes, Idomeneus, the sons of Atreus, and the brave son of Tydeus'
(*Iliad* 6.433-436, translated by Samuel Butler)

In Korfmann's view, this spot is the most obvious candidate for an attack on the city, given that it is the natural approach to the city from the plain. Recognizing this fact, Homer may well have had the gate in mind when he wrote these verses. The gate offers a good view out over the plain right up to the Beşik Bay, believed in antiquity to have been the site of the Greek army's camp. The monumental city gate thus was a suitable place for King Priam and Helen to inspect the troops in Book III of the *Iliad*, as well as the place where the powerless Trojans watched as Achilles dragged the lifeless body of Hector behind his chariot back and forth in front of the city. The plain, with its flat salt surface, is, moreover, ideal for conducting the kind of war described in the *Iliad*: the heroes are driven to the front in their chariots in order to engage in hand-to-hand combat there.

It has frequently been noted that many geographic and climatological descriptions in the *Iliad* correspond well to the area around Troy. For example, Homer describes the terrible sea wind, the rivers Scamander and Simoeis, the islands Tenedos and Lesbos, and also a tumulus (burial mound) near the coast, believed in antiquity to be the grave of Achilles and where none less than Alexander the Great came to pay homage to the deceased hero. Also, Homer usually refers to the city in combination with an *epitheton ornans* (an honorary title), like 'steep', 'deep-soiled', 'with high towers' and 'with wide roads', adjectives that correspond well to Troy's archaeological context (see also 4.3).

And finally there are the water sources, also clearly visible from the walls of Troy, that are described in the passage where Achilles pursues Hector around Troy's walls:

'On they flew along the waggon-road that ran hard by under the wall, past the lookout station, and past the weather-beaten wild fig-tree, till they came to two fair springs which feed the river Scamander. One of these two springs is warm, and steam rises from it as smoke from a burning fire, but the other even in summer is as cold as hail or snow, or the ice that forms on water. Here, hard by the springs, are the goodly washing-troughs of stone, where in the time of peace before the coming of the Achaeans the wives and fair daughters of the Trojans used to wash their clothes. Past these did they fly, the one in front and the other giving haste behind him'
(*Iliad* 22.143-157, translated by Samuel Butler)

Archaeologists believe they have found evidence of the existence of beautifully adorned (possibly thermal) water sources close to the city's western wall. These wells must have been visible throughout antiquity, indicated by the fact that they were still in use in the Roman period.

CREATION AND TRANSMISSION OF THE HOMERIC EPIC

An important characteristic of oral tradition is its variability. Every bard is in a position to add elements and make changes at will in line with his own literary agenda and the demands of the audience. The process of transmission or alteration, adaptation and change presumably took place for generations before Homer's time and ensured that the Trojan War, as described by Homer, is far removed from anything that actually took place at the time of Troy VIIa, as the archaeological layer generally associated with Homeric Troy is called (see chapter 2). For this reason we are unable to reach a firm judgement on the relationship between the events on the battlefield of Troy, as described by Homer, and historical reality. We know that some kind of devastation took place in Troy at the end of the Bronze Age and that this was possibly the consequence of war. However, the question whether and to what extent a Greek alliance was responsible for its destruction cannot be answered with any certainty, not to mention the problematic historicity of heroes like Achilles and Hector.

For a long time there was no consensus on the authorship of the Homeric epics. 'Unitarians' believing that the *Iliad* and the *Odyssey* were written by the same author, Homer, argued with 'analysts' who saw two or more authors working on the epics over several generations. There is currently a cautious consensus that main episodes of the two epics were compiled by a single author in the second half of the 8th century BC, although some the elements may date as far back as 1500 BC.

Considerable changes to the fabric of the *Iliad* and the *Odyssey* were carried out not only in the period before Homer's 'definitive' composition, but regular adaptations were also made subsequently. An example of a 'suspect' passage of this nature from the *Iliad* is the lemma in the catalogue of ships about Athens (2.546-556), which contains a number of anomalies that have led to the theory that it was not included into the epic until much later. The 'normal' formulation in the catalogue of ships lists (1) the origins of a particular Greek regiment, (2) the areas subject to 1, (3) the most prominent hero, (4) his most important comrades-in-arms and (5) the number of ships they provided. The lemma on the Argive contingent led by Diomedes may serve as example:

'The men of Argos, again, and those who held the walls of Tiryns, with Hermione, and Asine upon the gulf; Troezene, Eionae, and the vineyard lands of Epidaurus; the Achaean youths, moreover, who came from Aegina and Mases; these were led by Diomed of the loud battle-cry, and Sthenelus son of famed Capaneus. With them in command was Euryalus, son of king Mecisteus, son of Talaus; but Diomed was chief over them all. With these there came eighty ships.'
(*Iliad* 2.559-568, translated by Samuel Butler)

The lemma regarding the Athenian contingent is the only one that deviates significantly from this pattern:

'And they that held the strong city of Athens, the people of great Erechtheus, who was born of the soil itself, but Jove's daughter, Minerva, fostered him, and established him at Athens in her own rich sanctuary. There, year by year, the Athenian youths worship him with sacrifices of bulls and rams. These were commanded by Menestheus, son of Peteos. No man living could equal him in the marshalling of chariots and foot soldiers. Nestor could alone rival him, for he was older. With him there came fifty ships.'
(*Iliad* 2.546-556, translated by Samuel Butler)

Instead of the usual summary of subject cities, there follows a tale about the forefather of the Athenians, Erechtheus, the goddess Athena herself and the votive offerings the Athenians brought her. And instead of the usual list of the central hero's comrades-in-arms, there follows in the Athenian lemma a song of praise to the prowess of the Athenian hero Menestheus. Although the status of this passage is difficult to assess, the general view is that we are dealing here with a later interpolation, possibly from the 6th century BC, when a group of Athenian editors worked on the Homeric texts to make them suitable for performance during the Panathenaic Games.

The absence of the city of Athena and its hero Menestheus in the Homeric narrative has often been noted. Recent research suggests that the toponym Athens arose late (8th/7th century BC), explaining why the city is not mentioned in the *Iliad* or the *Odyssey* and why the Athenians later felt the need to insert their city into the central Greek epic. The divergent form of the Athenian lemma thus reveals that we are dealing with a later insertion, whereby the content was made to fit the contemporaneous context of a religious festival for the goddess Athena at the expense of the original Homeric formula.

Mathieu de Bakker and Floris van den Eijnde

HOMER AND THE ETERNALISING OF TRANSIENT TROY

MATHIEU DE BAKKER

'Ilios with its good horses' (5.551), 'deep-soiled Troy' (e.g. 18.67), the 'indestructible citadel' (21.447) – generations of students have marvelled at the evocative adjectives that Homer uses in his *Iliad* (to which the verse numbers above refer) to describe the city. He calls the Trojans a 'great-souled' (e.g. 11.459), 'proud' (10.299) and 'horse-taming' (e.g. 4.509 and 8.71) people. They wear bronze armour (e.g. 17.485) and their 'deep-bosomed' women wear trailing robes (e.g. 6.442 and 24.215). The descriptions of individuals also reveal splendour and power. The Trojan King Priam is 'furnished with a strong spear' (e.g. 4.47), his son Hector is 'great' (e.g. 8.160), 'brilliant' (e.g. 12.462) and 'adorned with a fluttering helmet crest' (e.g. 18.284), while his brother Paris 'equals the gods' in beauty (e.g. 11.580).

At the start of the *Iliad* the city is in the 10th year of a bitter struggle against an alliance of Greek states, in which the lives, liberty, honour and possessions of its inhabitants are at stake. The conflict originates from the brutal violation of the hospitality of Menelaus, king of Sparta, by Paris, who stole his host's wife Helen along with various treasures during a state visit. The *Iliad* reports a duel between the two rivals that could have ended the conflict, but when this duel is interrupted through divine intervention (3.340-448), settling the quarrel is no longer possible. Yielding to the implacable anger that the goddesses Hera and Athena feel towards the Trojans, Zeus aims to destroy the city (15.69-71). This punishment is disproportionate but ineluctable, and inherent in a war in which the human proportion and moderation is increasingly left aside. The city of splendour and power must fall, like Carthage, Magdeburg, Dresden and Nagasaki in later centuries.

Troy as *lieu de mémoire* of war's atrocities – this is the virtue of the genius of Homer, who in his *Iliad* describes 50 days of the 10-year siege. As the omniscient narrator he remains impartial and only rarely reflects explicitly on the actions of his heroes, whom he depicts as people with ambitions, desires and fears, with great virtues but also with fatal shortcomings. As a result of this story-telling device, we feel sympathy and admiration for both parties. We join Hector and Andromache in laughing at their little boy Astyanax bursting into tears when he sees his father's glittering helmet (6.467-471), and we share in the intense sadness felt by the Greek warrior Achilles on hearing of the death of his bosom friend Patroclus (18.22-35).

Hector and Achilles are the greatest heroes of the Iliad, the former a brave and dutiful defender of his native city, the latter an ambitious prince who knows he will not return alive and aims to make up for this by winning fame. At the end of the

The access road to the Trojan citadel from the Early Bronze Age (Troy II). Schliemann thought that this citadel, with its monumental walls, gates and paved road, was Priam's city. Given the monumental execution of the gate shown here, Schliemann believed he had found the Scaean Gate referred to by Homer. Towards the end of his life Schliemann realised he had made a mistake, and that Troy II was more than a millennium older than the Troy of Homer's war.

Iliad Homer stages these two superheroes in a duel to the death. We experience this confrontation largely through the perspective of Hector, who initially believes he has a good chance of winning, only to discover later that the gods have deserted him and that his end is nigh. At that point he says to himself:

> '(D)eath is now indeed exceedingly near at hand and there is no way out of it- for so Jove and his son Apollo the far-darter have willed it, though heretofore they have been ever ready to protect me. My doom has come upon me; let me not then die ingloriously and without a struggle, but let me first do some great thing that shall be told among men hereafter.'
>
> (*Iliad* 22.300-305, translated by Samuel Butler)

Exactly at the moment when he realises that his demise is imminent, Homer elevates Hector to Achilles' equal: both now know that they will pay the ultimate price to Moira, goddess of fate, with immortal fame as compensation. In the subsequent duel Homer compares Hector to an eagle (22.308-311), demonstrating thereby that the Trojan's heroism is in no way inferior to that of his opponent. Achilles is protected by a large shield made by Hephaestus, god of the forge, showing scenes from

Reconstruction of the walls of Hattuša, built in typical Anatolian stile. The walls of Troy may have had a similar appearance.

many daily aspects of life in a world far away from the Trojan War. Both heroes well know that they will never again take part in that life. Then Achilles fells Hector with a thrust of his spear (22.312-327).

Hector's death scene has rarely been equalled in literature. The lead-up to the duel, Hector's recognition of his own shortcomings and the ultimate price that he pays as a result all serve to expose that the human will to survive is irreconcilable with the heroic code that is focused on winning honour and shunning weakness. Precisely for this reason Plato calls Homer the first tragic poet in his *Politeia* (Plato, *Politeia* 595c1-3). Time and time again heroes die in the *Iliad* because they go too far in pursuing their ambitions in defiance of the counsel of their fellow-warriors or the gods. Hector gains immortal fame but also pays the ultimate price, as he is unable to prevent the fall of Troy, the enslavement of his wife Andromache and the cruel execution of his father Priam and his defenceless son Astyanax.

Homer turns Troy into the backdrop of a gripping war story, while emphasising the city's wealth and the courage of its inhabitants. What else does he teach us about Troy? What are the specific traits that he attributes to the city and its inhabitants? And how do these relate to the historical background of the city as reconstructed on the basis of documentary and archaeological sources?

HOMER'S DESCRIPTION OF TROY AND THE TROJANS

Homer's topography of Troy and its environs corresponds in outline with the city's historical location. This can be derived from the adjectives that the poet uses to describe the city. These 'ornamental epithets' were part of a treasury of fixed formulae that the epic singers knew by heart and used to improvise when composing their poetry. A distinction is made between generic and Troy-specific epithets. The first group contains adjectives like 'well-built' (e.g. 4.33 and 21.516), 'with wide streets' (e.g. 2.141), 'lovely' (5.210) and 'holy' (e.g. 20.216), that point to the city's beauty and the feelings it evokes in its inhabitants and gods. The above mentioned adjective 'deep-soiled' is another member of this category, as it refers to the fertile plain around the city and not to the citadel itself. Troy is further described as 'beetling' (22.411), 'high and steep' (e.g. 13.625) and 'exposed to the wind' (e.g. 12.115), descriptions that match with the citadel on a hill that Schliemann exposed.

Troy-specific epithets primarily emphasise the city's impressive walls and gate structures (e.g. 16.698), built according to Homer by Poseidon and Apollo (7.452-453), and razed after the war by the same gods, when they change the courses of the rivers, undermine the walls and expunge all traces of the battle (12.17-35). It should be observed here that in Homer's day Anatolian settlements could be distinguished from their Greek counterparts by their imposing walls. The epithets that refer to Troy's particularly high or steep walls could thus point to an Anatolian element that had become an inherent part of the formulaic language of the epic.

Homer, however, gives the walls a function at various crucial points in his story. Early in the *Iliad* Helen points out to Priam the Greek heroes from the walls, as Menelaus and Paris fight their duel (3.161-244). A much more emotional sample of such a *teichoscopy* (view from the wall) we meet in the duel between Hector and Achilles. Priam and his wife Hekabe (Hecuba) beseech Hector to come inside and then watch him fleeing around the city thrice before he dares to take on Achilles (22.25-247). His death is occasion for grief and panic. Andromache faints when she, unaware of the duel, climbs the walls to see her husband being dragged through the dust behind Achilles' chariot (22.405-474).

Elsewhere however, Homer depicts Troy as a primarily Greek city with a citadel (4.508) and with shrines to gods from the Olympic Pantheon, such as Apollo (e.g. 7.83) and Athena (e.g. 6.88). Troy is also characterised as a city with fine horses and its inhabitants as horse tamers (see above). In the Archaic Period ownership of horses was seen as evidence of wealth and status. For example, the Greek king Agamemnon seeks to win over Achilles by means of a gift including 12 horses that have proved themselves in the race. Possession of horses ties in with the picture that Homer sketches of Troy as a wealthy city ruling over a vast hinterland until the arrival of the Greeks (e.g. 24.543-546).

Homer's decision to portray Troy as a Greek city can be explained as a result of his impartial storytelling strategy, aimed at enhancing empathy for both sides on the part of his Greek audience. In this way, he is able to indelibly impress upon them the endless suffering caused by this drawn-out war. As an additional advantage he is able to have Greeks and Trojans talk to each other without the need for interpreters. No mention is ever made of differences in language in the many dialogues that take place on and around the battlefield. The Carians, allies of the Trojans, are described as 'barbarous-tongued' (2.867), but other than that, the use of a different language is never made explicit.

Homer notes a small difference between Greeks and Trojans in the way they approach the battlefield. The Trojans march towards the Greeks making a deafening noise, and Homer compares them to a swarm of migrating cranes bringing down doom on the Pygmies living at the edge of the world (3.2-7). By contrast, the Greeks draw up in grim silence like a mist driven by the south wind down over the mountain tops (3.8-12). Another difference is that Priam had several wives, who bore him 50 sons and 12 daughters (e.g. 24.493-497). It is not known whether there is an historical kernel in this cultural difference, but it certainly suited Homer in drawing attention to the suffering caused by the war. Time and again he relates how Priam's sons fall at the hands of the Greeks, and when the old king beseeches Achilles at the end of the *Iliad* for Hector's body, the poet describes with great pathos how he kisses the hands 'that slew so many of his sons' (24.477-479).

That Troy is also referred to as Ilios is less remarkable than it seems. It should be observed that the poet had forms ready for every conceivable change of metre of long, short, open and closed syllables within the dactylic hexameter format. In the same way he refers to the Greeks in turn as Achaeans, Pelasgians, Argives or Danaans, and calls the Trojans also Dardanians. Possibly, Ilios was originally used as a toponym to refer to the city itself, and Troy to the city including its surrounding territory. Paris' alternative name of Alexander is also of interest. According to some experts, Homer distinguishes between Alexander as a name in an international – and thus

A drinking cup (*kylix*) from 575-550 BC, depicting two soldiers (hoplites) in combat. In Homer's *Iliad* duels of this nature between two heavily armed warriors are repeatedly recounted.

Hellenic – context and Paris as a local Trojan name. The possibility that a Greek viceroy was appointed as a non-Trojan to manage the affairs of the city has been offered as an historical explanation for the name Alexander, but a literary reason need not be excluded. Homer relates that Hector refuses to call his little son Astyanax 'master of the city' but prefers the nickname Scamandrius – after the river nearby – because he, Hector, alone is able to protect the city. (6.402-403). Similarly, Paris does his martial appellation Alexander ('defender/protector of men') little justice when, splendidly attired in a panther skin on his first appearance on the battlefield (3.15-20), he runs away at the first sight of his rival Menelaus (3.33-37) and needs the assistance of Aphrodite in the subsequent duel to escape death (3.380-382). It is noteworthy that Hector never calls him 'Alexander', but twice mocks him as *Dysparis*, 'Ill-fated Paris' (3.39 and 13.769).

HOMER AND HISTORICAL TROY

With the aid of his omniscient and impartial narrator's perspective, Homer authenticates his Trojan war story and makes it seem historical. This is further enhanced by other storytelling devices, such as including lists of the peoples participating (see the catalogue of ships, 2.484-877) or of fallen warriors, or the detailed description of the course of the battle. The *Iliad* also avoids the overly frivolous or incredible aspects of the Trojan myth, such as the Judgement of Paris and the story of the Wooden Horse. He attributes all manner of human characteristics and foibles to the gods and makes them resemble the Homeric heroes themselves. Another significant device is the manifold use of direct speech which he ascribes to his characters, thereby allowing them to have their own voices and to be shown as individuals through their own choice of words and style.

Centuries later Greek historians like Herodotus and Thucydides trod in the footsteps of Homer, adopting many of his narrative techniques and considering him the first historian. Significant differences, however, remain. Whereas Herodotus and Thucydides as historiographers claim to rely on autopsy and sources for their research, Homer derives his authority from the Muses and makes clear in his work that he is far removed from the time and place of the story that he is telling. While a historian like Herodotus makes his historical characters resemble prominent contemporary politicians and narrates his story as if he is an eyewitness, for example through the use of the historic present – the stylistic device used to refer to the past using the present tense – Homer distances himself from the story he narrates. His heroes are stronger than the people inhabiting his own world and are able to carry objects that can only be lifted by three men of his own time (e.g. Achilles, 24.453-456). The historic present is conspicuously absent from his epic. Homer contrasts this heroic past with a present that finds its way in his work in his *similes*, in which everyday scenes from nature, agriculture and hunting are used to illustrate the actions on the field of battle. Similar scenes are displayed on the Shield of Achilles (18.468-608) and underscore the unbridgeable difference between the world of the narrator and that of Troy under siege. Homer, it appears, aims at authentication in his storytelling, but, by contrast with later historiographers, deliberately abstains from integrating his own, present world within his narrative.

The success of Homer's authenticating narrative technique is revealed by the reception of his epic. The *Iliad's* presumed historical accuracy caused many later Greeks to derive their origins from the Homeric heroes, and the Trojan past was not in doubt, not even outside Greece. The Persian king Xerxes, instance, sacrificed a thousand head of cattle at Priam's citadel at the start of his Greek campaign (Herodotus, *Histories* 7.43.2; see 2.3), and the Romans saw themselves as descendants of the fleeing Trojans. Such unconditional faith is reflected in the names that Schliemann gave his excavated treasures, like the Mask of Agamemnon in Mycenae and Priam's Treasure – that later turned out to be anachronistic – and in the name of the Mycenaean 'Palace of Nestor' near Pylos excavated by Blegen.

These days the historicity of the Trojan War as narrated by Homer is no longer unquestioningly accepted. There is a vibrant debate about the events that took place in Troy at the end of the Bronze Age and the repercussions of those events on Greek poetry several centuries later. Key to this is the realisation that the Homeric epic is the culmination of a long tradition of poetry that has been orally transmitted (see also the box in 4.2) and had its roots in the Bronze Age. This poetry was not learnt by heart, verse by verse, but improvised by bards who made use of a store of ready-made formulaes that they could insert into their recitations during performance.

Although Homer as historical source confronts us with considerable problems, these may not detract us from the literary qualities of his masterpiece on the Trojan War. He made use of the city, its walls, houses and palaces, as a backdrop to illumine human mortality, the tragedy of the heroic life and the sufferings of war. Hector's death and Homer's description of the Trojans' reaction by means of a simile provide an outstanding example:

> (...)*It was as though the whole of frowning Ilius was being smirched with fire.*
> (*Iliad* 22.410-411, translated by Samuel Butler)

This is the last in a series of *similes* in which the narrator makes use of besieged cities as image. The series begins with Achilles' return to the battlefield following the death of Patroclus to relate the story of a besieged city that succumbs (see 18.207-214, 18.219-212 and 21.522-525). With Hector's death Homer anticipates Troy's pending demise, and we know already that Poseidon and Apollo will expunge the traces. Homer is thereby expressing the transience of human existence, while at the same time erecting an eternal monument to ensure that the deep-soiled city with its beautiful horses will never be forgotten.

Zeus, the supreme god for the Greeks. In the *Iliad* Homer has the gods play a crucial role during the course of the Trojan War. Zeus remains neutral in the struggle between the pro-Greek and pro-Trojan gods. Nevertheless he is the one who pays heed to the decree by the Fates that Troy must fall. This marble head from the 2nd century BC was excavated at Troy by Wilhelm Dörpfeld.

5 TROY IN GRAECO-ROMAN ANTIQUITY

W BOOKS

KUNST
LIFESTYLE
GESCHIEDENIS

—

Bekijk en bestel
onze titels op
WBOOKS.COM

—

Bezoek ook
Artplatform.nl
en schrijf je in voor
de nieuwsbrief

- Dagelijks nieuws over
  kunst en cultuur
- De Tentoonstellingsagenda
- ArtSpots
- Museumtijdschrift

W BOOKS

GESCHIEDENIS

**HET GROTE
JAREN 50 BOEK**
ISBN 978 90 400 0710 1
€ 49,95

HET ORANJE BOEK
ISBN 978 90 400 0746 0
€ 14,95

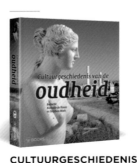

**CULTUURGESCHIEDENIS
VAN DE OUDHEID**
ISBN 978 90 400 7772 2
€ 49,50

'THE VERY RUINS HAVE BEEN DESTROYED'
TROY IN GRAECO-ROMAN LITERATURE

CHRISTIAAN CASPERS

"He walked round the memorable name of burnt-out Troy and searched for the mighty remains of Apollo's wall. Now barren woods and rotting tree-trunks press down on the palace of Assaracus, tired roots strangle the temples of the gods, and Pergama is covered over with thornbushes: the very ruins have been destroyed... Every stone has a name. Without knowing it, he crossed a stream trickling through the dry dust, that was once the Xanthus. He stepped carelessly over the high grass: his Phrygian guide warned him not to walk over the shade of Hector. Scattered stones preserving no trace of sanctity lay before them: the guide asked, "Don't you see the altar of Zeus Herkeios?"
(*De bello civili* 9.964-979)

This is how the Roman poet Lucan, writing in the first century CE, imagines Julius Caesar visiting the city of his ancestors. The poet contrasts the renown of ancient Troy with its present humble condition: the 'mighty remains' of a wall that is apparently hard to recognise; the landmarks that Caesar passes by, oblivious of their significance. Lucan's perverse description emphasises that this city has no physical presence whatsoever beyond the memories that its name evokes.

Anyone who has visited the site of ancient Troy may well recognise something in the experience that Lucan ascribes to Caesar. At the same time, Lucan says something significant about Troy's exceptional status as a symbolic locus of memory, or lieu de mémoire, in antiquity. As we shall see, the Trojan War bequeathed a literary heritage that enabled generations of Greeks and Romans to define their collective identity; but a full-scale depiction of the city that formed the backdrop to these narrative traditions is lacking.

In the 'standard version' of the Trojan myth, Menelaus reclaims his abducted wife Helen after the fall of the city. On being confronted with her great beauty once more, Menelaus relinquishes all intention of punishing her for her infidelity Tondo attributed to the painter Lydos (560-540 BC).

A WEALTH OF STORIES

Even when we take into account the fragmentary transmission of ancient art and literature, we can state with certainty that the Trojan War always played a prominent role in the perceptions of both the Greeks and the Romans. Direct recollections of the war would have disappeared within a few generations, through a natural process enhanced by the decline of palace cultures on the Greek mainland at the end of the 12th century BC. However, this lacuna was filled almost immediately with reconstructed recollections. The assumed continuity with the heroic past played a significant role in Dark Age ancestor worship, and the Trojan War itself readily found a place in the repertoire of professional performers of hexameter poetry.

Soon after the introduction of the Greek alphabet, this orally transmitted poetry was given permanent form in a more or less coherent series of epic poems, the oldest of which, the *Iliad* and the *Odyssey*, were attributed to a singer from Ionia: Homer. This epic 'cycle' influenced the lyric poetry of Sappho, Alcaeus and Stesichorus, as well as the choral songs of Pindar and Bacchylides, without relinquishing its own centrality in the Greeks' literary experience. From the 6th century BC onwards, the poems attributed to Homer in particular gained a key role in Greek education, and their canonical status in classical Athens was assured by the establishment, in around 525 BC, of competitive recitals during the *Panathenaea* festival. In the same period, the war was given permanent visual expression in monumental groups of sculpture, for example on the western pediment of the temple of Aphaia on the island of Aegina.

Alongside Homer's works, other narrative traditions about the war achieved currency, whether derived from critical historical research or from tales and songs that passed from parent to child. We find traces of these alternative traditions in classical-period art and literature, as well as in the mythological handbooks of late Antiquity. One such tradition comprised the well-known story in which the young Achilles spent time on the island of Skyros. Alarmed by a prediction that their son would die in battle at an early age, Peleus and Thetis placed him in the care of Lycomedes, the king of Skyros, and told him to pose as one of his daughters. Odysseus, dispatched to fetch the truant hero, caused Achilles to drop his guise by unexpectedly sounding a battle trumpet and so forced him to go off to war after all. In this tale, which is not part of the epic cycle, Achilles' role is markedly at odds with his Homeric persona.

Themes from the Trojan cycle were presented in theatrical productions that were part of another Athenian festival, the Great Dionysia. The war features prominently in *Ajax* and *Philoctetes* by Sophocles and in *Hecuba, Trojan Women* and *Iphigenia in Aulis* by Euripides, as well as in the insecurely attributed Rhesus. It provides the backdrop to Aeschylus' *Oresteia*, to the Electra tragedies by Sophocles and Euripides, and to Euripides' *Andromache, Iphigeneia in Tauris, Helen, Orestes* and *Cyclops*. And these are just the dramas that have come down to us intact: a mere fraction of the total number of plays (tragedies, satyr dramas and comedies) that were produced for an audience of thousands between around 500 and 150 BC.

These theatrical treatments of the Trojan myth attest to a living creative tradition, in which individual tragedians allowed themselves considerable poetic licence. For example, the premiss of Euripides' *Helen* of 412 BC is that Helen, who is by most accounts eminently responsible for the suffering of both Greeks and Trojans, was not even in Troy for the war's duration: she stayed in Egypt, in chaste anticipation of the arrival of her husband Menelaus. Euripides is not the inventor of this mytheme, but he was the first to carry it through to its ultimate dramatic conclusion, and his treatment evidently caused a literary furore. In the same year, the playwright Aristophanes presented

a comedy that mercilessly parodies Euripides' "new-fangled Helen" (*Thesmophoriazusae*, line 850); while four years later, in his *Orestes*, the tragedian responded by portraying Helen once more as the traditional *femme fatale*. "This is the Helen that we know," one of its characters knowingly confides (*Orestes*, line 129).

For the Greek *poleis* of the Archaic and Classical periods, the Pan-Hellenic expedition against Troy set a benchmark against which military conflicts of the more recent past were measured. This applied in particular to the wars against Persia in the first half of the 5th century BC, in which the Greek poleis once more formed an alliance to stand up against a great eastern power. Measuring the enormity of Xerxes' Persian forces, Herodotus cites 'the legendary expedition by the sons of Atreus against Ilios' as well as the historical campaigns of Xerxes' father Darius, only to conclude that the scope of Xerxes' campaign surpassed them all (*Histories* 7.20). His colleague Thucydides concurs:

The story of the sojourn of the young Achilles on Skyros was not part of the epic cycle, but was nevertheless a theme frequently interpreted and depicted in Antiquity and subsequently. The Roman sarcophagus shown here shows the moment that Achilles was discovered as a result of Odysseus' ruse.

if the differences in scale between the Bronze Age palaces and modern *poleis* are taken into account, he notes, the Trojan campaign was at the time probably the largest ever in scope; but in absolute numbers it does not match the Persian War (*Peloponnesian War*, 1.10).

The other famous conflict of the 5th century, the Peloponnesian War between Sparta and Athens, also invites comparison with the Trojan War. Such a comparison is implicit in Euripides' theatrical production for the Dionysia of 415 BC, a tetralogy on Trojan themes that culminated in the only play still extant, *Trojan Women*. Even without an explanatory booklet, the audience of the day would have had little difficulty in mapping the ruthless machinations of Euripides' Greek military commanders at the end of the war onto the actions of some of their own politicians, who in the months preceding the 415 Dionysia had convinced the Athenian Assembly to ratify the extermination of the entire male population of the rebellious island of Melos.

While the Trojan War set a standard on the tragic stage and in historiography, individual epic warriors like Achilles served as role models for the youth of Athens in everyday life. The story of Achilles' sojourn on Skyros has the classic hallmarks of a *rite de passage* – separation, role reversal and reintegration – and it is conceivable that it had its origins in the *ephebeia*, or 'national service', undergone by many Athenian youths at the age of 15 to 16. The immense popularity of depictions of

The western pediment of the Temple of Aphaia on the island of Aigina (ca. 500 BC) depicts the Trojan War. The slightly more recent eastern pediment contained a group of statues that referred to the mythical 'first' expedition against Troy under the leadership of Heracles. Plaster copy of a dying hero on the western pediment.

an armed Achilles crouching in ambush for the Trojan princess Polyxena and her brother Troilus may also relate to the *ephebeia*, which stimulated individual military exploits rather than adult hoplite warfare.

By the end of the 3rd century BC, the Greek *poleis* became dominated by the Macedonian kingdom. As Alexander the Great swiftly extended the Greek world all the way to the Indus River, the role of the Trojan War in the Greek experience was altered. No longer a benchmark for the military prowess of individual *poleis*, it became a paradigm for a unified Greek identity *vis à vis* the indigenous populations of Egypt, Asia Minor and the Middle East. In the Museum of Alexandria, under royal patronage, the *Iliad* and the *Odyssey* came to be objects of scholarly study, inspiring the likes of Callimachus and Apollonius of Rhodes to write their own poetry in support of the Greek heritage of the Ptolemaic empire.

Achilles' ambush of Troilus and Polyxena was a particularly popular iconographic theme that is found not only in vase painting but also on coins. The version shown here, on a lekythos (oil jug) from ca. 490 BC, shows Achilles crouching behind a fountain house. The fountain house differentiates the assault on Polyxene from the murder of her brother, which is not shown, that took place at a shrine to Apollo, according to the epic cycle.

At around the same time, the idea was born that the nascent Roman superpower owed its founding to the descendants of Aeneas, a Trojan prince who only just escaped the destruction of his city. Roman authors translated the Greek texts about the war into Latin, and created their own versions as well. Their Roman audiences would already have been well versed in the myths about Troy through the import and manufacture of painted pottery in Southern Italy and Etruria and of theatrical performances in Greek. But again, the mythical significance of the war changed: Roman generals like Flaminius and L. Cornelius Scipio expressly put themselves forward as the descendants of Aeneas, stopping at Troy to bring sacrifices and votive offerings while on their way to battle against Alexander's successors in the east. For Julius Caesar, this identification became particularly important: his family reckoned itself to be in direct descent from the Trojan royal house. The high point of Rome's celebration of Troy was the *Aeneid*, the epic that Virgil authored under the patronage of Augustus in order to furnish his imperial rule with an authoritative prehistory. Following in Virgil's footsteps, Ovid devoted the 12th and 13th books of his *Metamorphoses* to Troy's demise and the flight of Aeneas.

A CITY WITHOUT A FACE

As the preceding section demonstrates, the Trojan War continued to fascinate the Greeks and the Romans down the centuries. But what about Troy itself, the location where a significant part of these stories is played out? An audience that delighted year after year in recitals of Homeric verse and theatrical reworking of the Trojan myths; that poured and drank from pottery painted with Trojan scenes; that was surrounded by statues of Trojan heroes: how did such an audience imagine the city for which their heroic ancestors had fought for 10 long years?

In a recent and rather controversial book on the composition of the Iliad, Martin West (see also 4.2) argues that Homer, writing several centuries after the events he is recreating, must have conceived parts of his Trojan epic *in situ*. "The city was in ruins in his time, but the massive walls of the Bronze Age citadel still towered up to a height of twenty feet above the ground: he must have sat on that windy eminence, like the modern visitor, and admired the panorama", West writes. If Homer in fact described the *Iliad's* Troy on the basis of his own observations, then he was one of the few Greek authors to do so: up to the 3rd century BC, we find very few traces of anything like 'Troy tourism'. Herodotus recounts that the Persian king Xerxes, marching on Greece with his army, stopped over at Troy to make a large sacrifice to Athena (*Histories* 7.43; see also 2.3); but the historian, though by his own account a seasoned traveller, nowhere reports that he took the trouble to visit the city him-self – in spite of the fact that the Athenian colony Sigeion (the refuge of the deposed tyrant Hippias, himself one of Herodo-tus' subjects) lay just a few kilometres from Troy.

From the moment that Alexander the Great, visiting Troy in 334 BC, swapped his armour for an ancient Trojan breast-plate and pledged several benefactions, the city (refounded by then as 'Ilion') commanded increasing attention. The Hellenis-tic temple of Athena was furnished with a painting of the Fall of Troy, and the 2nd-century temple of Apollo Smintheus in neighbouring Chryse was adorned with a frieze showing scenes from the Trojan War. In 188 BC, after the end of the Seleucid War, Troy was officially recognised as the mother city of Rome and consequently drew numerous visitors from the Roman elite.

For Greeks of the Archaic and Classical periods, by contrast, Troy existed above all in a world of their own imagination: a world nourished primarily by Homer. It is all the more re-markable, then, that Homer's description of the city and its sur-roundings is extremely succinct: apart from a few conspicuous details (see 4.3), the *Iliad* and the *Odyssey* lack a self-contained depiction of Troy. Greek pictorial art follows the suit of epic: as a rule, vase paintings reveal no more than a few elements of the surroundings to help the viewer assign meaning to the scene. The fountain house in the depiction of Achilles' attack on Polyxena, for example, is not a random piece of landscape painting: for the many artists who depicted this theme, it was a means of distinguishing this scene from the subsequent epi-sode in which Achilles kills Troilus, of motivating the presence of Polyxena and of providing Achilles with something to hide behind. Nor is this iconographic parsimony inspired merely by the limited format in which the vase painter worked. In Poly-gnotus' famous murals of the Fall of Troy for the Cnidian club house at Delphi, the architectural details, placed on vertically arranged planes to suggest perspective, also serve primarily to make the depicted epic tales recognisable.

The role of epic verse and pictorial art in creating an imagi-nary Troy thus remains limited to supplying isolated landmarks around which the action takes place. Neither of the two genres lent itself, as far as can be ascertained, for projecting a synoptic or panoramic view of the city where the war took place. Even more notable, perhaps, is the lack of a description of Troy in the surviving Greek dramas. The backdrop of a classical-period tragic production was extremely sober: the stage floor was bor-dered by a simple back wall with a gate in the middle and doors to either side; and apart from the central altar on the *skene*, no use was made of scenery. The audience gleaned information regarding the setting of the drama exclusively from cues in the play's text and the dramatic action.

However, even in a play wholly dedicated to Troy like Euripi-des' *Trojan Women*, references to the physical Troy are subordi-nated to the course of the dramatic action. The play dramatizes a charged moment before the captured city is consigned to the flames. In a series of encounters, queen Hecuba hears of the fate of her daughters, each of whom has been allocated to one of the Greek conquerors, and that of her grandson Astyanax. Human suffering is portrayed in all its forms, but only a few words are devoted to the city itself. In *Trojan Women*, attention is directed to the fortifications of Troy rather than to the city as a whole or even to its temples, the desecration of which eventually calls down the wrath of the gods on the Greeks:

'Farewell, once prosperous city! Farewell, stone ramparts!
If Pallas, daughter of Zeus, had not engineered your de-
struction, you would still be standing on your foundations.'
(lines 45-47)

This is how Poseidon takes his leave of the city whose fortifica-tions he himself helped to build. Halfway through the play, a choir of distraught Trojan women sings:

'Ah! Love, Love, when once you sought these Dardan halls,
deep-seated in the hearts of heavenly gods, how high did
you make Troy tower in those days, when you married her
with deities!... But all the love the gods once had for Troy is
passed away.'
(lines 841-859)

These references to Troy's walls come to a climax in Hecuba's last speech, delivered after she hears of the death of Astyanax. A messenger brings her the body of her grandson, whom the Greeks have hurled from the battlements 'like a discus' (line 1121). In Hecuba's reaction to the news, Troy's walls built for eternity and the young life that will never reach maturity are poignantly contrasted:

'Poor child! How sad that the walls of your father, those
towers that Loxias raised, have shorn from your head the
locks that your mother fondled and so often caressed ...'
(lines 1173-77)

'BY ITS SMOKE ...'

It seems fair to say that, between the 7th and 4th centuries BC, the Greeks showed a definite lack of interest in Troy's physical appearance. As we have seen, this lack of interest corresponds in part to generic characteristics of Greek literature and art: in most classical genres, narration takes precedence over de-scription. Historiography as practised by Herodotus and

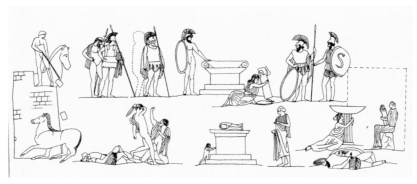

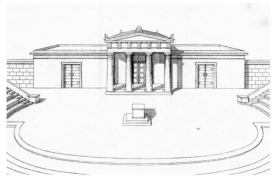

Antique vase paintings of Trojan themes are not the only depictions to show nothing more than a few landscape details. Depictions on a larger scale also confine themselves to recognisable landmarks. This was true of mural paintings in the Cnidian *lesche* (association building) from 550 BC in Delphi, as is clear from the comprehensive descriptions of the travel guide writer Pausanias in the 2th century AD. Reconstructed drawing of the painting on the eastern wall by Martin Stansbury-O'Donnell.

Settings in the classical Greek theatre were exceptionally austere. There was an altar on the stage, and the backdrop was formed by an undifferentiated façade containing three doors. This reconstruction of a 5th century *proskenion* (stage setting) was drawn by the archaeologist Wilhelm Dörpfeld.

Thucydides is an exception, but these authors expressly set the Trojan War aside – perhaps in order to avoid competing with the poets. Generics apart, however, there is another reason for the lack of synoptic presentations of Troy: unlike other cities, Troy was percieved by the Greeks to be synonymous with its own destruction, rather than with its founding or its acme.

This thought is expressed most memorably in the words that the tragedian Aeschylus ascribes to Agamemnon, the architect of Troy's demise. In the *Agamemnon*, the king's homecoming is the occasion for a long and triumphant review of the atonement that the Trojan king Priam has had to make for Helen's abduction. But what, ask the play's Chorus, of the city itself and its proverbial treasures? Answers Agamemnon:

'By its the smoke the captured city is even now eminently visible!'
(*Agamemnon*, line 818)

From these words, we can derive the same insight as from Lucan's description of Caesar's visit to the city. What, for a Greek audience, gives meaning to 'Troy' is the contrast between, on the one hand, the lasting renown of the war waged over its territory, and its definitive erasure on the other. What lies contained between these two extremes – a living city with infrastructure, markets, holy places, gymnasiums, etc. – has literally disappeared from view.

The Greek conception of Troy as a city that, paradoxically, derives its significance from its own demise persists in the Roman literary tradition, where the Trojan myth gains a whole new meaning, but the city itself remains invisible. Virgil's epic has space for a city under construction (Carthage: *Aeneid* 1.418-452) and for a city of the future (Rome: *Aeneid* 8.310-369), but not for a description of Troy. Even after the city was granted a new name and a new lease of life in the Hellenistic period, Ilium remained a *lieu de mémoire* without physical attributes.

TROY IN GREEK ART – MORE THAN ILLUSTRATIONS TO HOMER

WINFRED VAN DE PUT

Myths and sagas were an inexhaustible source of inspiration for Greek, Etruscan and Roman artists. Stories about Troy were extremely popular in Antiquity, and it is no surprise that painters and sculptors of the day often fell back on this city's demise and the stories related to it. The way they did this and the episodes the artists depicted changed markedly over the course of history.

HOMER'S OWN ERA
At the time that Homer sang his epics, presumably in the 8th century BC, the Greeks began to make images of animals and people. They did so in stone and bronze (in the form of larger and smaller statues), but especially on earthenware vases. In this early (so-called Geometric) period, however, the depicted scenes had to do with burial, mourning, the heroised life of the deceased; pottery often served as grave-gift or monument., There is a possible reference to mythology on a single example: an interesting vase shows a large ship with two rows of oarsmen. A man, shown larger than the oarsmen, appears to be holding a woman by the arm and leading her to the ship . Is this the first depiction of the abduction of Helen by Paris? This is possible, but it could also be a parting gesture, and the figures are otherwise unrecognisable.

Only in the 7th century BC do recognisable myths make their appearance in the art of vase painting. Homer's influence may readily be discerned: the gruesome blinding of Polyphemus with a burning stake, an episode in the *Odyssey*, is depicted several times. Already in these early depictions, the vase-painter is at liberty to change the story considerably. Homer makes much of the sharpening of the tree branch that Odysseus will use to blind the one-eyed cannibal in his story. In the depictions, the weapon used seems to be a skewer This does not accord with Homer's version, because the poet goes to great lengths to make the point that the Cyclops, as an utter brute, is wont to swallow his food raw, including a few of Odysseus' unfortunate companions. And this is just one of the details that do not agree with Homer.

ILLUSTRATION SOURCES
When we look at Greek illustrations of myths it is important to bear in mind that the extant literary works reflect only a small part of the stories in circulation at the time that inspired the painters and sculptors. Sometimes the illustrations correspond to what we know from the literature, but more often they are references to stories that we know were related in heroic poems or tragedies and that have not survived. But just as today, the material the artists used as source did not have to be limited to the 'official' literature. Songs, orally transmitted fairy tales, stories deriving from specific locations or cults, anything could serve as raw material for their images. And then there was the artistic freedom that the artists themselves enjoyed, whether they were tragedians, epic or lyrical masters, or vase painters. They adapted the stories, dreamed up new details or gave a completely new twist to a well known theme. In Euripides' tragedy *Helen* for example, Zeus' daughter turns out not even to have been in Troy: when Paris arrived in Egypt with Helen, a phantom took her place. There are innumerable examples of variations, in illustrations dealing with the Trojan War as well.

Homer certainly towers above the rest, but was he also the most important source of inspiration for depictions of the Trojan War? Only a small part can be traced back to the *Iliad* or the *Odyssey*. And this applies not only to illustrations:

Paris taking Helen to his ship? This painting on a krater from Thebes from ca. 730 BC is frequently seen as an early depiction from 'The Story of Troy', although nowhere is it made clear that this is in fact the Trojan Prince Paris and his Greek lover.

in Antiquity Aristotle noticed that the tragedians rarely took their material directly from Homer's poems, because the treatment – in particular in the *Iliad* – focused on only a small part of the Trojan heroic saga; other heroic poems now lost, such as the *Little Iliad*, the *Ilioupersis* and the *Kypria*, treated more episodes and, according to the philosopher, lent themselves much better as inspiration for tragedies (*Poetics* 1459a-b). The situation is no different in the representative arts: inspiration from lost works, including tragedies, is manifold, and it is by no means always clear that literature forms the basis for an illustration.

TROY: OTHER STORIES

The war was not the only thing Troy was famous for. The Trojans' beauty had also come to the attention of the gods. Zeus fell in love with the Trojan prince Ganymede, taking the shape of an eagle to abduct him. This is a popular theme in the first quarter of the 5th century BC: the ruler of the gods takes human form to pursue the youth who is depicted with a hoop and is sometimes also holding a cockerel, a common gift from a mature man to an adored youth. Rembrandt painted a memorable version of this story – an eagle seizing a crying and urinating toddler. Eos, the goddess of the dawn, is frequently depicted pursuing the young huntsman Tithonus. Memnon, the king of the Ethiopians, who also played a role in the Trojan War, issued from this love. Aphrodite adored Anchises, the father of her son Aeneas. In Attic vase painting nothing in these illustrations points to the exotic origins of these beautiful youths: they look as if they could be strolling over the Agora every day.

ON THE WAY TO THE TROJAN WAR

The first Trojan theme after the blinding of Polyphemus to gain popularity in Greek vase painting is the wedding of Peleus and Thetis. In the extant versions of the story the sea goddess Thetis marries the persistent prince Peleus. All the gods are invited to the wedding apart from Eris, the goddess of strife. She takes revenge by tossing a golden apple, with 'for the fairest' inscribed on it, into the midst of the wedding throng and so causes endless suffering. From the second quarter of the 6th century BC vase painters depicted the large and varied procession of prominent guests on large mixing vats for water and wine (*kraters* and *dinoi*). The painter Sophilos is the first to inscribe all the names alongside the figures, something that takes on extravagant form on the famous François vase (ca. 570 BC). The painter, Kleitias, even furnished horses and pieces of furniture with names.

Both the wedding and the conflict over Eris' apple are dealt with in the *Kypria*, a lost post-Homeric epic. The contest between the goddesses Athena, Hera and Aphrodite, submitting themselves to the judgment of the Trojan prince-shepherd Paris, is another popular theme in the arts. In these scenes

The so-called François Vase, showing the marriage of the Greek hero Peleus to the nymph Thetis. Peleus and Thetis were the parents of Achilles, the most important hero in the Iliad. Positioned in front of an altar, Peleus (right) welcomes the invited guests to the wedding ceremony. Below him Zeus, the king of the gods, is shown with thunderbolt on the chariot in the middle.

A lekythos (oil jug) from the end of the 6th century BC. Two warriors are attempting to attack each other with swords drawn, but are kept apart by their comrades. This could be the fight between Odysseus and Ajax over the weapons of Achilles, but there is no other evidence for this.

Paris undergoes a metamorphosis. While one might expect a young and attractive prince, he is depicted during the Archaic Period (600-480 BC) with a beard and wearing a stately cloak. By the beginning of the 5th century BC Paris is being shown as a beardless young man. A century later we see him dressed in colourfully adorned Phrygian dress, including his standard accessory, the Phrygian cap. This is an important characteristic of Greek art: the aim is to reflect the character or role of the figure in the story as clearly as possible; the idea of a photographic, momentary image was unknown to them. In the older illustrations Paris' status as prince is the most important, later it is his youthful attractions; the rich clothing of the late 5th century depictions point to the location of Phrygia and also to Paris' predilection for beautiful things.

IN FRONT OF TROY'S WALLS

Helen's abduction would lead ultimately to a Greek siege of Troy lasting 10 years. As stated above (see chapter 4) we find no depictions of massed armies, huge fleets or tented encampments in the art world of the ancients: the illustrations are instead strongly focused on individual heroes and their deeds, often in clearly recognisable scenes. But sometimes we may be

An Athenian lekythos from ca. 490 BC: Achilles armed to the teeth lies in ambush at a well (see also the drawing on page 80).

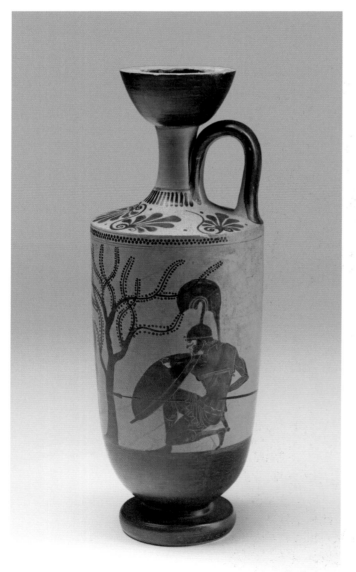

too eager to interpret an image as a myth. Combat scenes are often shown, particularly in the Archaic Period. For example a scene on a lekythos (oil jar) shows two warriors trying to attack each other but being kept apart by their comrades. This could be the argument between Odysseus and Ajax over Achilles' weapons, but the warriors are depicted impersonally, meaning that the scene cannot be linked to any known episode.

The *Iliad* was probably set down in writing in Athens around 530 BC. Illustrations of Trojan themes increase around this time, but very often derived from other sources than Homer's epics.. The vase painter Exekias conceived an illustration of the two greatest Greek heroes, Ajax and Achilles, around 540 BC. They are apparently playing a game that looks like backgammon. That Achilles is the more important can be discerned by the fact that he is a little bigger and also scores higher with the die (the inscription reads 4, while Ajax throws only a 3). This playful image clearly does not refer to an episode in the *Iliad* or the other epics: here the competition between the two heroes is fought out in friendly fashion on the gaming board.

In the same way the episode where Achilles kills the Trojan prince Troilos on the altar of Apollo, frequently depicted on Greek vases, does not derive from the Iliad. An oracle had predicted that Troy would not fall if Troilos reached the age of 20. When the Trojan prince accompanied his sister Polyxena to the well, Achilles was lying in ambush for them. Both fled and Achilles butchered the young prince on the altar of Apollo, where he had sought refuge – in vain. On a lekythos painted around 490 BC by the so-called Athena Painter, however, Troilos is not to be seen, but only his sister, who will later be sacrificed on the grave of Achilles. This is a good example of the way in which Greek artists convey a story. Instead of in a snapshot, the figures are shown in a way that illustrates their role in the story as aptly as possible: Achilles is lying in ambush, Polyxena take fright and flees. Certainly Troilos is shown on older vases depicted as a youth on horseback, sometimes riding quietly alongside his sister, sometimes at a gallop pursued by Achilles. The bird depicted on the well in is a raven, the bird sacred to Apollo, a reference to the fate of Troilos on his altar.

It is interesting that certain personalities and episodes that play a crucial role in the Iliad, are rarely depicted or not at all. For example we scarcely ever find Achilles' bosom friend Patroclus, apart from on the world famous Sosias cup on which Achilles is shown binding his comrade's wounds. Later, after Achilles has withdrawn in wrath from the conflict, Patroclus borrows his armour and joins the battle with the Trojans, to be slain in the end by Hector, the greatest of the Trojan heroes. But few traces even of this dramatic episode are to be found in the arts.

Hector does not long survive Patroclus' death. Achilles kills him and drags him behind his chariot a number of times round

Troy. The gods are enraged at this desecration of a corpse and he is instructed through his mother Thetis to cease his act of vengeance. At the end of the 6th century BC this cruel theme is popular: on occasion Patroclus' burial mound is depicted, with or without his shade, on others the Trojan gate from where Priam and Hecuba, Hector's parents, watch as their son's body is dishonoured. These vases were made in Athens, but have been found predominantly in in Etruria, just as many others with mythological representations. We may ask whether they were made with a view to Etruscan tastes.

Hector's corpse is ransomed by his father Priam in exchange for a large number of precious items. Schliemann believed he had found this treasure during his excavations at Troy (see chapter 2) – a nice piece of modern mythology. The ransom of Hector's body is a fairly popular theme. There are examples in both black-figure and red-figure pottery of the grey-haired king come to beg Achilles, reclining on a couch, for the body of his beloved son. Hector's corpse lies under the couch, in contradiction to the literary tradition. Priam is accompanied by his servants carrying the gifts.

Once Achilles re-joins the fight following the death of Patroclus, Trojan heroes rapidly fall in battle. One of them is Memnon, like Achilles the son of a goddess – Eos – but himself a mortal. He is king of the Ethiopians, and can be recognised on this vase from the dark appearance of his companions. The conflict between the two heroes is thus also a confrontation between the two goddesses, with Eos losing the argument. A touching illustration is Eos bearing the body of her son off the battlefield. Brave Queen Penthesileia of the Amazons also falls victim to the unchained hero. But Achilles falls in love with the Amazon as she is on the point of death. This tragic-romantic aspect of the story has made it a popular theme at various times, although it has been depicted in various ways. The most famous version is undoubtedly that of Achilles looking deep into the eyes of the dying Penthesileia, and we also see him supporting the body of the dying queen or bearing her off the battlefield over his shoulder.

But Achilles also dies. Although virtually invincible after his mother Thetis had dipped him in the Styx, his heel remained vulnerable where she had held on while submerging him. Paris, guided by Apollo, a god strongly sympathetic to the Trojan cause, loosed an arrow that hit the hero in the ankle. A fierce battle erupted over his body, before Ajax rescued it from the battlefield. The death of Achilles by an arrow from Paris is depicted just once, while the rescue of his body is a much loved theme that occurs on the François vase (see above) and remains popular, particularly in the Archaic Period.

A conflict between the Greek heroes Ajax and Odysseus ensues over Achilles' armour, which was made by Hephaestus, god of the forge. Odysseus manages to secure the armour to

Achilles and Ajax are engrossed in a game of backgammon. This amphora, made in 530 BC by Exekias, one of the best known Attic potters, was found in a grave in Etruria (Italy).

pass it on later to Neoptolemos, Achilles' son. Ajax resents the loss and plots vengeance. Struck mad he takes a flock of sheep for Greeks and hacks at them. He feels so much shame at what he has done that he sees suicide as his only option. His tragic death is sometimes depicted in excruciating detail in the Archaic Period, but the most beautiful example is that of Exekias, showing the hero planting his sword in the ground in preparation for falling on it.

THE END OF THE CITY, AND SUBSEQUENTLY

We know of the Wooden Horse holding the hidden Greek warriors primarily from Virgil's *Aeneid*. An unusual early relief *pithos* (storage container) from Mykonos, made around the middle of the 7the century BC, shows a horse on wheels with peepholes through which the hidden Greek heroes can be seen. The myth was part of the lost epic *Ilioupersis* about the Fall of Troy (Ilion). However it was never to be a popular theme in Greek art. Laocoön, the priest who saw through the trick and warned the Trojans against bringing the horse into the city, is seldom encountered. Poseidon sent two huge snakes to strangle him and his two sons. The Trojans saw this as punishment for rejecting the gift and hauled the ruse within the walls with even greater zest. We search in vain for a depiction of this dramatic

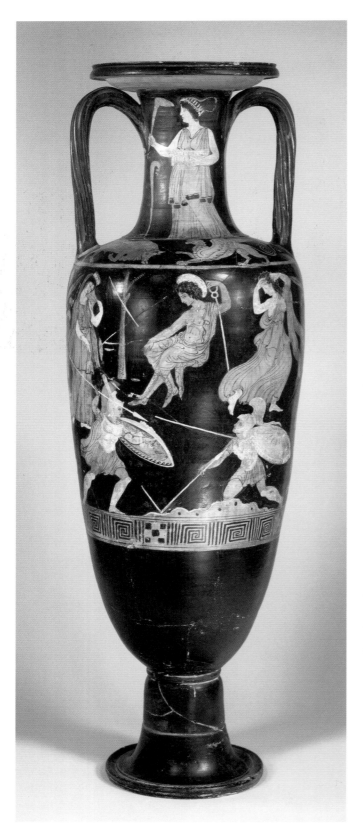

episode during the Archaic and Classical periods, but in the Hellenistic Period it is the subject of one of the most famous statues of antiquity, Laocoön and His Sons. The dramatic content, composition and powerful expressiveness of this statue, found in Rome in 1506, made a deep impact on Michelangelo and Rubens, among others. The superlative quality initially led to the assumption that the group was an original from the height of the Hellenistic Period (ca. 150 BC), but as an Italian variety of stone (travertine) turned out to have been used, it must have been carved after 50 BC. Besides this marvellous statue, depictions are rare, also in Roman art.

Depictions of the Fall of Troy are more popular in Greek art. Scores of atrocities are combined in these scenes. The two most striking are Ajax the Lesser raping Cassandra, who seeks refuge at the cult statue and altar of Athena, and the aged king Priam bludgeoned to death along with his own grandson, Astyanax, by the hand of Achilles' son Neoptolemos. The independence of the artists and the licence the Greeks took in retelling their myths emerges anew: according to the literary sources Astyanax is hurled from Troy's ramparts. Insofar as they are not murdered, the Trojans are taken as the spoils of war by the Greeks. Polyxena is sacrificed on the grave of Achilles, cruelly depicted on a Tyrrhenian amphora from around 550 BC and on a late Archaic sarcophagus from around 500 BC found near Troy in 1994.

Only a few escape the slaughter. The most famous of these is Aeneas, who is depicted fleeing the city with his father Anchises on his back. This prince from the area around Troy was a son of Aphrodite and was to become the forefather of the Romans after a long period of wandering. Caesar, who claimed divine ancestry through Aeneas, showed the hero on a coin.

CONCLUSION

Greek art of course does not take us to Troy itself. By far the most vases were painted in Athens. A large part of these ended up in Etruria, far from the walls of Troy. Recollections of Troy lived on in poems, stories and images. But the elements of these images derived from the daily lives of the Athenian producers and of the Athenian and foreign buyers. Priam is killed on a Greek, rather than a Trojan, altar. The Greeks, as well as the Trojans, wear armour that Athenian men knew from the battlefields of the Persian and Peloponnesian wars. The women in

In the war for Troy the Trojans received assistance from King Memnon of Ethiopia, son of the goddess Eos (Dawn). He was slain by Achilles, as depicted on this large amphora. The vase was made in Southern Italy around 320-310 BC. As it was once in the possession of the Dutch Stadhouder Willem IV (William IV Prince of Orange), it is known as the Stadhoudersvaas (Stadhouder's Vase).

their chitons and himatia (draped cloaks) appear like the Kore sculptures of young women, dozens of which were consecrated on the Athenian Acropolis. When Polyxena goes to fetch water she does it using an Athenian hydria (water vessel) at a well that could have been built by the Athenian tyrant Peisistratus. The focus of the painters and sculptors was on the human form, and they lacked historical data concerning the Trojan world Consequently, the representative arts reveal nothing of the way Athenians in the 6th and 5th centuries BC imagined "Priam's beautiful palace, adorned with polished colonnades" or "the wide camp of the Achaians". Yet the heroes lived on in the imagination of antiquity.

An exceptional early relief *pithos* (storage container) from Mykonos, made around the middle of the 7th century BC and showing the Trojan Horse. The horse is on wheels, and the heads of the concealed Greek heroes may be seen through the hatches.

THE TROY GAME: THE TROJAN HERITAGE IN THE JULIO-CLAUDIAN HOUSE

DIEDERIK BURGERSDIJK

THE TROY GAME

None of the rulers from the Julio-Claudian house, the first imperial dynasty to rule Rome (27 BC-68 AD), could withstand the temptation to participate either as actor or spectator in the highly dangerous Game of Troy: after Julius Caesar, the founder of the dynasty, had instructed this game to be put on in imitation of his predecessor, the dictator Sulla, it appears to have gained popularity and prestige among Rome's aristocratic youth. The imperial biographer Suetonius, writing at the beginning of the 2nd century AD, records this activity in no less than six of his biographies, beginning with his life of Caesar: 'two troops of older and younger boys played the Troy Game' (Suetonius, *Caesar* 39.3). The aim was for different teams to line up in two rows and compete with each other by racing through the Circus Maximus with horses, changing these during the race. The Emperor Augustus regarded the game as suited to young men of noble ancestry. In the biography of his adopted son and successor Tiberius we read that as a young man Tiberius, scion of the prominent Claudian family, participated in the Troy Game as leader of the older group of youths during the city games (Suetonius, *Tiberius* 6.4). At one point there was an accident: a certain Nonius Asprenas was paralysed, and later the grandson of the famous orator Asinius Pollio broke a leg (Suetonius, *Augustus* 43.2). This led to a temporary halt, as the game appeared again during the reign of the third emperor, Caligula, as *Troiae decursio*, 'the Trojan parade march' (Suetonius, *Caligula* 18.3), and again under Claudius, with whom it found favour (Suetonius, *Claudius* 21.3). Nero was very keen on the game from a young age (Suetonius, *Nero* 7.6), evidently to the delight of the spectators, who loudly signalled their approval, as we read in Tacitus, a contemporary of Suetonius (*Annals* 11.11).

Frequent reports of the Troy Game in histories of the emperors of the Julio-Claudian house during gladiatorial contests, of chariot races and other kinds of popular entertainment indicate their popularity. It is of particular note that the game appears to have been reserved for youths from the families of the elite. The origins may also be described as distinguished: Ascanius, the son of the forefather of the Roman nation, Aeneas, is said to have taught it to the Trojans during their flight from Troy to their new fatherland. In the fifth book of the *Aeneid*, Virgil, court poet to Augustus, relates how funeral games were held in honour of Aeneas' father Anchises at the site where he lay

Bronze coin from Smyrna, ca. 100 BC, showing a seated Homer holding a scroll. The head on the other side is that of the god Apollo wearing a laurel wreath.

buried, part of these games being given over to the Troy Game. Aeneas urges his son to join the competition, and a large group of young Trojans gleaming in magnificent armour show their skills before their watching parents on a playing field cleared for the occasion. There are three groups, each consisting of two wings of six, led in turn by Polites, the grandson of Troy's King Priam, Atys, a favourite of Ascanius, and Ascanius himself. Each of the troops has a leader, the one of Ascanius' troop has the name Epytides. The manoeuvres carried out by the troops, comparable with the undulating sea or the labyrinth on Crete, must have been beautiful to watch, if Virgil's extended description (*Aeneid* 5.545-603) is to be believed.

A MESSAGE TO THE ROMANS

The Troy Game forms part of a message to the Roman people propagated in all kinds of ways: the Trojan Aeneas – son of the goddess of love, Venus, and her mortal lover Anchises, fated to survive flight from Troy's destruction by the Greeks – is the forefather of the Julian clan and in a wider sense of all Romans. Note that two of the three leaders, alongside the grandson of King Priam of Troy, are Ascanius and Atys. Ascanius is renamed Julus in the *Aeneid*, making him the putative ancestor of the Julii (the family of Julius Caesar), a name directly derived from Ilion, or Troy. And Atys is the ancestor of the Atii, the family of which Augustus' mother is a member. Tracing their family name back to one of the crewmembers of Aeneas' ship was a popular pastime among prominent Romans. For example Virgil, poet in the service of Augustus, presented a family tableau in the form of the Troy Game dating back 12 centuries for the eyes and ears of an imperial audience, when the Trojans were in search of a new homeland to set up their household gods. This would ultimately result, some 15 generations after their flight, in the founding of Rome by the legendary twins Romulus and Remus, the sons of Mars.

From one point of view – that of Augustus – the city of Rome, arising out of the city of Troy, has two divine ancestors: the goddess of love, Venus – mother of Aeneas – and the god of war, Mars – progenitor of Romulus and Remus by Rhea Silvia, the female descendant of Ascanius, Aeneas and Anchises. It was for this reason that Julius Caesar had the temple of Venus Genetrix, the divine mother of his family, built on his own Forum Caesaris adjacent to the Forum Romanum. After Caesar had in his will adopted Octavian, the grandson of his sister Julia, on his death in 44 BC and after his name was transferred to his great-nephew, Roman history took a decisive turn: Octavian laid claim, apart from Caesar's name and possessions, to his power. This led to a power struggle with others from Caesar's circle that was ultimately decided in Octavian's favour. Invested with the honorary title Augustus in 27 BC, Octavian had his own Forum Augusti laid out directly across from that of his adoptive father, with the temple of Mars Ultor, Mars the Avenger, the god that had punished Caesar's murderers at the battle of Philippi in 42 BC, as the central sanctuary. In this way the two divine ancestors of the Julii were united architectonically, visible for all Romans. The right calf of the famous statue Augustus of Prima Porta reveals the same in sculptural terms: Venus' little son Cupid stands alongside this most famous scion of a victorious house.

Following the death of Caesar's murderers another pretender to the throne offered even more stubborn opposition to Octavian. Mark Antony was, as Caesar's supporter, the natural successor to his position in Rome, and this initially led Octavian to conclude an alliance with him, strengthening the bond by giving him his sister Octavia in marriage. The relationship deteriorated when Mark Antony established his base in Egypt. At the side of Queen Cleopatra, who had herself been installed by Caesar, he began to behave increasingly as an independent leader along Hellenistic lines: autocratic, exotic, decadent. Mark Antony also envisaged expanding his power eastwards into Asia in imitation of Alexander the Great. Octavian's countermeasures led to a civil war that ended with the sea battle at Actium on the north-western coast of Greece in 31 BC, and provided the impulse for the most important Augustan theme: following victory over the degenerate east, an era of peace, prosperity and stability was initiated, summarised by the term *Pax Romana*, political order for all Romans. A temple to Apollo, for assistance in the battle, on Rome's Palatine Hill, where Romulus once had his hut and where Augustus lived, was a permanent token of thanks for this divine intervention. Where Mark Antony had called on the alien god Dionysus, and had promoted Hercules as his ancestor, the Apollo of Augustus had restored order. A new era was dawning.

The Graeco-Roman theatre built on the ruins of ancient Troy. From the time of the first Roman emperors in particular (27 BC), Troy was a significant tourist draw. The mythical ancestor of the Romans, Aeneas, was said to have fled Troy in flames for Italy.

TROJANS IN LATIUM

Virgil's *Aeneid* gives an important place to Aeneas' sojourn in North Africa, specifically in Carthage, an episode that takes place in the chronology of the narrative following the stop in Sicily and before the funeral games there. After being shipwrecked, Aeneas meets his mother Venus disguised as a huntress, who shows him the way to the new city being built by Queen Dido, who has fled from Phoenicia. This episode, not long after the beginning of the first book, is a supreme example of storytelling: while Aeneas' recollection of the collapse of the city of his youth, related to Dido in the second book, is still fresh in his memory, he watches the diligent construction of a new city from a hilltop. Following his entrance into the city,

reception in the palace and the recounting of his vicissitudes, Aeneas is briefly bewitched by the charms of the Carthaginian queen, but in the end Jupiter restrains him through his messenger Mercury, who points out his appointed destiny and divine duty. *Pietas*, 'devotion to duty', wins out over all too human *amor*, 'love'. In a prophecy made by Jupiter (Virgil, *Aeneid* 1.257-96) it had been predicted that a man would arise who would rule over the nations: 'From this glorious line a Trojan Caesar will be born, who will bound the empire with Ocean, his fame with the stars, a Julius, his name descended from the great Iulus.' (Virgil, *Aeneid* 1.286-8). Aeneas is to be the human agent of this line. The narrative fits with Octavian's attitude towards Cleopatra: where Mark Antony, in imitation of Octavian's adoptive father Caesar, succumbs to human weakness and luxuriates in the love of the alien Queen Cleopatra, Octavian dismisses the decadence of the east that his empire is to be spared.

Given the perceived link between luxury and decay, is it noteworthy that an eastern prince from a once extremely prosperous Troy is designated as ancestor of the Roman people? The fact that Augustus did this is connected to the established tradition of a Trojan presence in the Latium region that gained acceptance from the 4th century. A large number of artefacts testify to the popularity of stories about Troy in both Etruria and among Latin speaking peoples. For example, the shrine to Venus in the coastal city of Lavinium (6th century BC) established by Aeneas according to the myth, various artefacts like a famous vase from the Etruscan city of Vulci with a painting of Aeneas fleeing Troy as it burns, with his wife, father and son (5th century BC) and votive images of Aeneas and his father from the Etrurian city of Veii. A solution was furnished for unwished for links with an eastern origin: the founder of Troy, Dardanus, was said to be originally from Latium, and to have moved to the west coast of Asia to found Troy (see for example Virgil, *Aeneid* 3.167-8: 'here [i.e. Italy] Dardanus was born, / … from whom our people first came'). Aeneas' travels to Latium have thus become a kind of *nostos,* 'return', like that of Agamemnon to Mycenae or Odysseus to Ithaca described in the Greek tragedies and epics. According to the myth, when Aeneas lands in Latium and enters into a coalition with Latin and Etrurian warriors to battle with the hostile Rutuli under the leadership of Turnus, he re-established Trojan power in Latium and creates order anew from chaos. Aeneas himself founds Lavinium, named for his wife, the daughter of the local King Latinus, and his son Julus

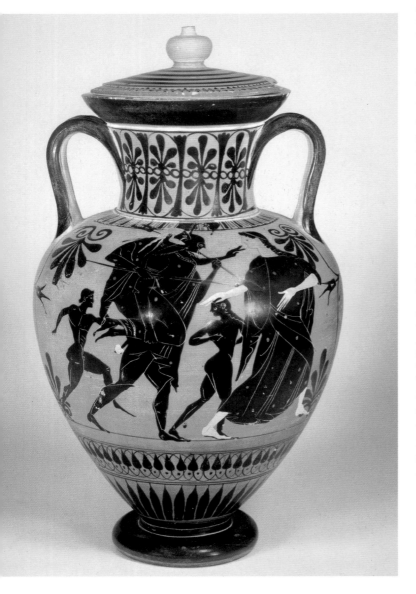

The Trojan hero Aeneas fled Troy as the city fell, with his father Anchises on his back. Aeneas' wife Kreousa walks in front of him. Greek vase from 510-500 BC

A silver denarius from North Africa struck during the rule of Julius Caesar, 47-46 BC. On one side there is a bust of Venus, goddess of love and the mother of Aeneas, and on the other Aeneas is shown fleeing Troy with his father Anchises on his left arm. The inscription reads: CAESAR. Caesar wanted to show through this depiction of Aeneas that he was of divine origin, thus justifying his position as dictator.

founds Alba Longa, where Rhea Silvia's father Numitor ultimately rules as king. His grandsons Romulus and Remus go on to found Rome, which is thus the continuation of Latin order by other means.

ORDER THROUGH WAR

Political order is obtained through military conquest. This is the message that Augustus disseminates in his historiographical testament, the *Res Gestae* (*RG*), 'Deeds Accomplished', inscribed on bronze plaques displayed on his mausoleum after his death: *parta victoriis pax*, 'order achieved through conquest' (Suetonius, Augustus 101 RG 13). The military campaign that he undertook in 16-13 BC in Gaul and Spain is significant for promoting the development of an extensive programme of art and literature. The lyric poet of Augustus' court, Horace, penned a eulogy in which he celebrates the longed-for return of the ruler as the start of a new golden era in Latium (Horace, *Ode* 4.5). Although Horace does not say so explicitly, he uses many motifs that conjure up the return of a paradisiacal existence: the presence of peace, law and work and the absence of

fear. He had previously written a eulogy on a similar theme, a campaign in Spain in 24 BC, in which the poet calls for public and private expressions of thanks (Horace, Ode 3.14). In this way Augustus' return is celebrated as a *nostos* that reflects with great ceremony the arrival of Aeneas in Latium, which after all recalls the lustre of a golden era resulting from the conquest of hostile powers.

Augustus decided to forego a triumph, instead requesting the erection of the so-called *Ara Pacis*, the 'Altar of Peace'. On it the new era is illustrated by extensive sculpted images of superabundant plant motifs and panels rich with symbolism: on both sides of the entrance and on the siding panels are friezes with senators, members of the imperial family and priests in grateful procession; at the rear the goddess Roma and Mother Earth (*Tellus* or *Italia*); in front the god Mars, the twins Romulus and Remus, and Aeneas sacrificing. The latter is just around the corner from where Augustus is proceeding with his family and the priests. In this way Virgil's heroic poem about Aeneas' quest for a new fatherland and Horace's eulogies on the grateful and happy welcoming of Augustus' return are given visual expression on an altar celebrating the return of the golden era. The last words of Horace's fourth book of Odes ('we sing the praises of Troy, Anchises and the offspring of all-nourishing Venus', *Ode* 4.15.31-2) reveal a striking similarity with Virgil's introduction to the *Aeneid*: ' I sing of arms and the man, he who, exiled by fate, first came from the coast of Troy to Italy, and to Lavinian shores' (*Aeneid* 1.1-2). The poets from the circle around Augustus – under the supervision of Maecenas, his patron of the arts – which included Horace and Virgil, sang along to the greater honour and glory of their patrons.

TROY AND THE TROJANS

The received idea of Troy in the early imperial period, as promoted by Augustan ideology, focuses more on the figure of Aeneas and his *Umwelt* of men, countries and gods, than on the city of Troy. The apogee of the idea of Troy as city is without doubt the second book of Virgil's *Aeneid*, even though the city as such does not play an important role, while providing the backdrop against which the flight of Aeneas is played out. The book's theme is after all Aeneas's flight from Troy as it falls, not Troy itself, much as is the case with Homer's *Iliad*. In it, Achilles' anger in the midst of the war's events, not the war itself, constitutes the theme, while the fall – which is not described as such in the book – is merely foreshadowed. While in the first six books of the *Aeneid* the word *Troia* occurs significantly more often than forms of *Troianus* (as adjective or substantive) and *Troes*, the opposite – unsurprisingly – is the case in the six final books, in which the war in Latium is described. In general the city of Troy, although doomed by fate, is shown as powerful and prosperous, as emerges from the description of the shipwreck, where the ships' cargoes bob on the waves: 'men's weapons, planking, Trojan treasure in the waves' (*Aeneid* 1.119). It is the Trojans led by Aeneas, fled from their city, who found a new power in Latium, whereby attention is fixed not so much on the perished city, as on those whose fate it is to found a new city: 'we head for Latium , where the fates hold peaceful lives for us: there Troy's kingdom can rise again' (*Aeneid* 1.205-6). Ultimately a new ruler will arise from the Trojan people, whose fame will be limited only by the stars.

The question is to what extent the stories about the Roman and more particularly the Trojan origin of the Julians was constructed by Augustus and his circle themselves. As we have seen, the association of Romans with Trojans was far from new. If we may rely on Suetonius, the claim to divine origins existed as early as 69 BC, when Caesar made an oration at the funeral of his aunt Julia: 'the Julii are descended from Venus, the family of which ours is descended' (Suetonius, *Julius Caesar* 6.1). Caesar emphasises his assertion by issuing coins with sides showing Venus and Aeneas, the reintroduction of the *lusus Troiae* and the consecration of the temple of Venus on Caesar's forum. Others too, for example the dictator Sulla, claimed to be descended from Venus, and the famous family of the Memmii flirted with its Trojan origins by stamping the image of Venus as patron of the Trojans on coins – compare the famous introduction by the philosopher poet Lucretius: *Aeneadum genetrix*, 'Foremother of the Aeneads', dedicated to Gaius Memmius. By contrast a novel approach was the Julians' emphasis on Aeneas as forefather, and the important role accorded his son Julus, previously Ascanius, as progenitor of the clan. It is generally accepted that the many illustrations in sculpture, coins and paintings of the 'triple A' structure of Anchises-Aeneas-Ascanius, fleeing Troy in

flames, are all derived from a sculpture group that must have stood on the forum of Augustus. Divine origins must certainly have played a role in this manner, but Aeneas was represented in his role of mortal hero as a 'model Roman'.

TROY THE CITY

It should be clear that not so much Troy as the Trojans were iconic in Augustan ideology. Nevertheless Troy at the time of Augustus was a living and inhabited city that was renowned for its honourable history. From the 2nd century BC onwards, the point at which Rome began making military incursions into Asia, Troy became a destination for the purposes of paying homage to the shrine of Pallas Athena or to visit the grave of Achilles, the Greek warrior who lay buried near Troy. This was in imitation of the Macedonian conqueror Alexander the Great, who claimed to be of Greek and Trojan descent. The fact that Troy occupied a strategic position with respect to the sea and to the hinterland contributed to this special attention. Following destruction by Fimbria in 85 BC – retribution for its assistance to Mithridates, an enemy of Rome – Troy could bank on a politically favourable position when Sulla awarded political independence to the city, which was part of the Troadic federation. Loyalty to Rome is reflected in a multitude of dedications to Roman figures, including Lucius Iulius Caesar, a member of the Julian family. It was possibly at this time that 'Iulus' began to be seen as an alternative to Ascanius as ancestor to the Julii.

During the same period, the last century of the republic, Troy was not yet advanced as the predecessor of Rome in literary works. The picture that Catullus provides in *Carmen*, in which he weeps over the Trojan grave of his brother, is by no means an attractive one:

> 'Troy (horror!), shared tomb of Asia and Europe,
> Troy, cruel funeral pyre of all men and virtues, which
> has even brought a miserable death to my brother!
> (…)
> A foreign land holds him deep under ground
> now, so far away, not among familiar tombs, and
> not placed
> beside the ashes of relatives, but buried unhappily
> in Troy, loathsome Troy!'
> (Catullus, *Carmen* 68.89-100)

Three quarters of a century later a location like this would have been able to evoke only honour and sympathy. Troy occurs frequently in the writing of Cicero, but only in connection with the war; on only one occasion is there a reference to Trojans as kinsmen, when it is reported that Aeneas had founded the Sicilian city of Segesta (Cicero, *In Verrem* 2.4.72). Sallust reports that

Rome was founded by Trojans, but without going into details:

> *' The city of Rome, according to my understanding, was
> at the outset founded and inhabited by Trojans, who were
> wandering about in exile under the leadership of Aeneas
> and had no fixed abode.'*
> (Sallust, *Bellum Catilinae* 6)

All of this reveals that Roman Troy did not yet have the prestige
it would later enjoy.

There is a great deal of speculation on the precise attitude
of Caesar and Augustus with respect to the city of Troy. According to the geographer Strabo, Caesar made concessions to
Troy, such as exempting it from taxation (*Geographika* 13.1.39).
Whether he ever visited it is difficult to determine. The sole
author to place Caesar in Troy is the poet Lucan, who has him
visit the city overgrown with grass and weeds in the *Pharsalia*,
his uncompleted epic about the civil war between Caesar and
Pompey (*Pharsalia* 9.950-999). The epic is named after the
Greek city of Pharsalus, where Caesar fought the decisive battle against his political opponent Pompey in 48 BC. Lucan may
have drawn his material from the last episodes written by the
Augustan historian Livy, but it is entirely possible that Caesar's
visit to Troy is poetic licence. In any event, Caesar's interest
is a response to the rumours, as reported by Suetonius (*Julius
Caesar* 79.3), that he intended to move with the state treasury
to Alexandria or Troy and leave Rome to the care of his friends.
It is certainly probable that Augustus visited Troy, presenting
himself as patron and supporter. His name is shown on the
architrave of the temple of Athena.

THE NERONIAN RENAISSANCE

It was during the Neronian renaissance that remembering Troy
as a city was given full attention. Nero, as emperor a patron of
the arts, carried on the family tradition of Trojan descent un-
checked. In 50 AD Nero's predecessor, the Emperor Claudius,
had taken up the Trojan cause:

> *'He allowed the people of Ilium perpetual exemption from
> tribute, on the ground that they were the founders of the
> Roman race, reading an ancient letter of the senate and
> people of Rome written in Greek to king Seleucus, in
> which they promised him their friendship and alliance
> only on condition that he should keep their kinsfolk of
> Ilium free from every burden.'*
> (Suetonius, *Claudius* 25.3)

The circumstances under which the proposal was made to Seleucus at the time – presumably in reaction to a request from
him to Rome – cannot now be discovered, nor precisely which

Seleucus is intended. What is important here is that the blood
ties to the Trojans are used to implement a political measure
along with an appeal to a distant past, as though there had
never been any doubt that the Romans were descended from
the Trojans. In addition it is not insignificant that Claudius had
the temple of Venus of Eryx, or Venus Erycina, a city founded
by Aeneas, restored:

> *'and had the temple of Venus Erycina in Sicily, which had
> fallen to ruin through age, restored at the expense of the
> treasury of the Roman people.'*
> (Suetonius, *Claudius* 25.4)

The worship of this cult associated with Aeneas had been introduced in Rome in 217 BC. At the age of 16, in 53 AD, Nero had
called for exemption from tax for the inhabitants of the region
around Troy in imitation of his adoptive father Claudius, an
emperor given to historicizing:

> *'Anxious to distinguish himself by noble pursuits, and the
> reputation of an orator, he advocated the cause of the peo-
> ple of Ilium, and having eloquently recounted how Rome
> was the offspring of Troy, and Aeneas the founder of the
> Julian line, with other old traditions akin to myths, he
> gained for his clients exemption from all public burdens.'*
> (Tacitus, *Annals* 12.58)

On being made emperor Nero gave further expression to
his powers of rhetoric through writing a poem entitled *Troica*, parts of which he recited in public (Suetonius *Nero* 10.2),
also reported by the poet Juvenal (*Satire* 8.221) and a century
later confirmed by the Greek historian Cassius Dio (*Roman
History* 62.29.1). This was so well received that he was accorded a
thanksgiving – something reserved for generals returning in triumph – and an inscription of the recited passage was displayed
in gold letters on the temple to Jupiter on the Capitoline. Only
a few brief and disputed fragments of the *Troica* are extant,
one of which has been transmitted by the already mentioned
Lucan. In Suetonius' biography of Lucan the poet, angry at
Nero's departure during one of his performances, while reliev-
ing himself in a public lavatory and to the amazement of those
present, shouts out half a verse from Nero: *sub terris tonuisse
putes*, 'you would have thought that it thundered beneath the
earth' – one of a few scanty remains of what must once have
been a great work.

Nero's performances, extended to include tours to southern
Italy in order to train his voice according to Tacitus (*Annals*
15.33), had a sequel in 64 when Rome caught fire and the emperor gave voice to his composition *Halosis Iliou*, 'The Fall of
Troy' from the Tower of Maecenas, dressed in his stage cos-

194

tume and accompanied by a lyre. *Flammae pulchritudine*, 'in the beauty of the flames' Nero declaimed himself (Suetonius, *Nero* 38.2). The report is confirmed by Cassius Dio (*Roman History* 62.18.1), who has him singing from the roof of the palace, adding that eyewitnesses called the poem 'The Fall of Rome', but only partly by Tacitus (*Annals* 15.39), who dismisses the performance of *excidium Troiae*, 'the demise of Troy', as speculation, given that Nero was in residence at his country house in Antium at the time of the fire. The aftermath of the fire presented Nero with the opportunity to realise his dream of a *domus aurea*, 'golden house': he had a large palace complex built around the valley between the Oppius and Palatine hills that was intended literally to revive the golden era and that was enlivened with brilliant frescoes recalling Troy in all its glory.

THE IDEA OF TROY IN THE EARLY IMPERIAL PERIOD

Setting aside how the idea of Troy in the early imperial period was received, it is noticeable that republican Roman traditions surrounding Trojan descent were strongly linked to a single clan by Julius Caesar and his adoptive son Octavian Augustus: that of the Julii. Just as the Trojans, mingled with the indigenous Latins and to a lesser extent the Etruscans, were ancestors of the Roman people, Aeneas was the ancestor of the Julian clan. His mother was Venus, while Mars was the father of Romulus, founder of Rome. The latter, previously the uncontested leader in the foundation myths, was pushed into second place by the rise of the Julian clan: there was now an earlier ancestor to hand. A certain evolution in the reception of the Troy theme may be discerned: where Julius Caesar created a personal family cult on the basis of Trojan origins, as common among prominent families, Augustus continued this cult in an extended literary and artistic cultural programme with the abundant means he had at his disposal. The last emperor from the clan, Nero, continued the line all too faithfully by taking it in hand himself through the composition of a *Troica* and the accompanying destruction of Rome, seen as Troy risen from the ashes.

Romanaque Pergama surgent, 'and the Roman Troy will rise again', as predicted by Lucan (*Pharsalia* 9.999).

Virgil has Aeneas setting duty above love in his departing speech to the disappointed Dido:

> *'If the fates had allowed me to live my life under my own*
> *auspices, and attend to my own concerns as I wished,*
> *I should first have cared for the city of Troy and the sweet*
> *relics*
> *of my family, Priam's high roofs would remain, and*
> *I'd have*
> *recreated Pergama, with my own hands, for the defeated.'*
> (Virgil, *Aeneid* 4.340-4)

In his biography of Virgil, Suetonius notes the wish of the great poet that his epic should be burnt on his death, but this plan was frustrated by his heirs to posterity's good fortune, upon which a certain Sulpicius of Carthage penned an epigram with the closing lines: 'unhappy Troy almost fell twice, / and Pergamon was almost burnt again on a pyre'. The citadel of Troy rose again in the Julio-Claudian house, starting with the *lusus Troiae*, a game as popular with the spectators as it was played in earnest – but all too perilous, as in Neronian times.

Augustus, the first emperor of the Julio-Claudian dynasty. He and his adoptive father Julius Caesar traced their origins to the Trojan hero Aeneas and his mother, the goddess Venus. Aeneas' son Ascanius Julus was seen as the first 'Trojan' prince on Italian soil. At the behest of Augustus the myth of the Trojan flight to Italy was immortalised in Virgil's *Aeneid*. Plaster copy after a marble original from the 1st century AD.

TROY IN BYZANTIUM

WILLEM AERTS

The conflict between the Greeks and the Trojans over Troy has been set down in verse by the greatest poet of Antiquity, Homer, in his epic the *Iliad*. The epic tells of just one period of a few weeks centred on Achilles. This great hero feels himself insulted by his commander-in-chief Agamemnon and refuses to continue the battle, but then takes revenge for the death of his friend Patroclus on Troy's greatest warrior Hector, who had slain Patroclus.

The story of Troy's destruction was told centuries later in the second book of the *Aeneid*, an epic by the Roman poet Virgil. The hero of the title, Aeneas, escapes from the ruined city with his father, small son and a group of trusted friends, manages to reach Italy, seizes land along the Tiber and becomes the mythical founder of the Roman Empire. The empire is afflicted by civil wars in the 4th century AD. Constantine the Great, who emerges as winner of this conflict, decides to abandon Rome as capital and to found a new capital at a safer and more central spot in the empire. What could be more obvious than to return to the place where it all began – Troy? Alas the spot where that famed Troy once lay was not to be found, and 'in desperation' the choice fell on Byzantium, a small city on the Bosporus that would develop into the metropolis Constantinople.

THE CITY AND THE WAR IN BYZANTINE LITERATURE

The Byzantines knew nothing of the site of this famous city that had been immortalised in the epic. Nevertheless, resulting from Homer's creation, there is quite a bit to say about Troy in relation to Byzantine society, even if it centres on literature rather than topography. In Antiquity and during the early Byzantine period, great epics in Homeric jargon were composed, such as the *Argonautica* by Apollonios of Rhodes (3rd century BC) and the *Dionysiaca* by Nonnus of Panopolis (5th century AD). For the Byzantines the *Iliad* and the Odyssey were the greatest poetic creations conceivable, and were studied, commented upon and read in schools down the generations. The Byzantine historian Anna Komnene (1083-after 1147), daughter of (Alexius I Comnenus), emperor from 1081 to 1118, relates in the introduction to her work, the *Alexiad*, that she has studied Homer's poems thoroughly – an achievement on its own given that Homeric idiom is far removed from the Byzantine of the 11th/12th century. The renown of the Homeric epics has ensured that commentaries on the Trojan War exist in all shapes and sizes in Byzantine literature.

An epic directly related to the Trojan War and written in Homeric style is attributed to Quintus Smyrnaeus, who in the 4th century AD set down the events following Hector's death – which marks the end of the *Iliad* – in 8,772 verses spread over 14 books. In the 12th book the seer Calchas announces that Troy will be taken not by violence but by cunning. Odysseus proposes building a wooden horse with warriors hidden inside, while the burning of the camp and setting sail with the ships suggest the departure of the Greeks. The ruse works, and when in the 14th book the Trojans have drunk themselves into a coma, Odysseus and his men emerge to sow death and destruction. In book 13 Calchas warns the Greeks to spare Aeneas, the son of Aphrodite, as the gods have decided that he will found a 'holy city' on the Tiber.

John Malalas, a chronicler from the time of the Emperor Justinian (527-565) devotes an entire book (chapter), the fifth, of his *Chronographia* to 'the period of Troy'. He starts his story as follows:

'At the time of (king) David there ruled over Ilion, that is to say the land of the Phrygians, Priam, son of Laomedon. And during his rule both Ilion and Dardanon, Troy and all of Phrygia were destroyed by the Achaeans (Greeks), among them, by report, Agamemnon, Achilles, Menelaus and all the others with the ruddy Neoptolemus, who went to war against Ilion because of the abduction of Helen by Paris, also called Alexander. He had fallen madly in love with her. No wonder: she was perfect: well-bred, bountiful bosom, white as snow, beautiful eyebrows, beautiful nose, beautiful face, curly light blonde hair, big eyes, charming, mellifluous voice, in short a fantastic woman to see, 26 years old. The first of the catastrophes that led to the demise of Troy and the land of the Phrygians and its royal house occurred for the following reasons.'
(John Malalas, *Chronographia* Chapter 5)

Constantinople was the capital of the Eastern Roman (Byzantine) Empire from 330 AD to its conquest by the Ottoman Turks in 1453. Map of Constantinople from the 15th century.

There follows an exposition on Paris, the Judgement of Paris, his choosing of Aphrodite over the other goddesses Hera and Athena in the beauty contest, the abduction of Helen from Sparta while her husband Menelaus is away, Helen's reception in Troy, equipping the expedition against Troy by Agamemnon and Menelaus, the catalogue of warriors on both the Trojan and the Greek sides, and so on up to the taking of Troy and developments thereafter, with the murder of Agamemnon by his wife Clytemnestra and Odysseus' long voyage home.

One way and another it is evident that Malalas wanted to hold up both the pre-history and the aftermath of the Trojan War to his audience. But not only that: to him the Trojan War was not so much the subject of an heroic epic as an historical event which the criteria of historiography applied to, as is shown by setting the period by reference to the Biblical King David. The passport-like description of Helen is also interesting. There are three differing types of personal description in Byzantine literature: a romantic type derived from Achilles Tatius, a passport-like description as used primarily by Malalas, and a combination of the two in the *Iliad* by Hermoniakos (see below) and in novels. Malalas made use of passport-like description in other parts of the *Chronographia*, for example in the presentation of the heroes fighting in the Trojan War and of Roman emperors.

TROY AS PSEUDO-HISTORY

Malalas is not the first to see the Trojan War as historical fact. It is clear that he took his views and material to a significant extent from two anonymous authors that have become known by the names of Dares Phrygius and Diktys Cretensis. Dares is said to have written the history from a Trojan standpoint, Diktys is reported to have kept *Ephemeriden*, 'diaries' of events that took place around Troy. A few Greek fragments have survived, but the stories they tell are known from reworked translations into Latin from the 5th and 4th centuries AD respectively.

It is probable that the Byzantine man of letters Johannes Tzetzes (1110-na 1180) still had access to the Greek texts just as Malalas had, although Malalas probably understood Latin. He also worked extensively on Homer's epics and dealt at length with events before, during and after the Trojan War in his poems *Antehomerica*, *Homerica* and *Posthomerica* written in hexameter. But he also provides a commentary on the *Iliad*, as well as an allegorical interpretation of the world of the gods and the events. In this there is also a certain degree of rationalisation, whereby the gods are seen as natural phenomena (Zeus is the air, Aphrodite is pleasant weather) or mental qualities (Zeus is common sense, Ares is anger).

The Trojan War is also comprehensively dealt with in the *Chronicle* by Constantine Manasses (c. 1130-1187), in 6,733 typically Byzantine "political verse" (verse of 15 syllables). This is

also a work of history, thus historicising the Trojan War (verses 1107-1476). Manasses also locates the war during the time of King David and states expressly that he will place the facts as they actually occurred in the forefront, all admiration for Homer's political licence aside. In turn, Manasses toys with all kinds of mythical traditions that have been dealt with elsewhere. When Hecuba, King Priam's wife, is pregnant with Paris she has a dream in which she sees a flaming torch that shoots from her lap and reduces Troy to ashes. The soothsayers urge that the child should be offered up to wild animals or fire at birth. The child is abandoned, found by shepherds and brought up by them – compare the tale of the Persian King Cyrus and the story of Oedipus. Paris returns to Troy, and it is believed that the web of fate has been evaded, but its strands prove ineluctable. He commits murder and is forced to flee, turning up in Sparta where he is welcomed with open arms by Menelaus and Helen. Her beauty seduces him and he abducts her, is shipwrecked in Egypt, is seized and banished by the Egyptian ruler Proteus, who keeps Helen with the intention of returning her to Menelaus. The reunification takes place 10 years later after the Greeks, seeking vengeance on Paris had attacked Troy and ultimately taken and razed it with the aid of the ruse of the Wooden Horse. Here Manasses follows Herodotus (*Histories* Book 2, Chapter 112 ff). Manasses also goes to work with gay abandon on the deeds of Achilles and Odysseus in front of Troy. There is much agreement with Malalas, for example in how Helen and the heroes are portrayed.

A *BYZANTINE ILIAD*

Manasses and/or similar sources provide the material for the so-called *Byzantine Iliad*. This is a poem of 1,166 political verses, in an extremely modern Byzantine vernacular. Three loosely connected parts tell the story with a strong moral undertone. The main part simultaneously exudes the atmosphere of the Byzantine love novels. The romance encapsulates the love affair between Paris and Helen. As with Manasses, a repeated dream predicts Troy's demise, with this time Priam seeing the burning torch emerging from Hecuba's lap. The child has to die, but is entrusted to the waves in a watertight box (compare Moses), found by shepherds on the shore at the city of Tarsus and brought up by them. He commits a crime, is forced to flee and ends up in Sparta at Menelaus' court. There the love between Paris and Helen erupts. Paris even gives Helen lessons in music. The ardour cannot wait: Helen falls pregnant. Flight is the sole option, but where? Back to Troy after all, where the prediction has been forgotten and where Helena is happily accepted into Trojan society on account of her beauty. The poet then refers to Homer and goes over to Achilles, his love for the Trojan Briseis (his war spoils), and his refusal to continue fighting if he has to return her to her parents (as a result of an outbreak of plague in the Greek camp, as described in the *Iliad*). He rejoins the battle only after Patroclus has been slain, kills Hector, is seduced by an offer to marry the Trojan Polyxena to conclude peace (a ruse thought up by Paris) and is himself killed by the brothers Paris and Deiphobus in the temple where the marriage was to have been concluded. Brief mention is then made of the construction of the Wooden Horse, the Fall of Troy and the slaughter of Priam and his family on the grave of Achilles.

The *Byzantine Iliad* differs also in the fact that there are no descriptions of Troy, although the poem does provide a decryption of Priam's palace, namely in the passage where Priam summons prominent Trojans to discuss the dream:

> 'The furnishings of the palace, how am I to describe them?
> The entire floor a mosaic made of Sardinian marble,
> With chairs, ostentatiously inlaid with sapphires,
> And side doors all of gold with silver decorations.
> The beautiful great throne of Priam the king
> Stood higher than the others, inlaid with onyx.
> Five birds, above the throne, could be seen flying about,
> Precisely where King Priam was seated on his throne,
> And you could say with certainty that they were alive!
> Streams of water spouted from the beaks of the birds
> The jets flowing into silvered embossed basins.
> And around the palace stood beautifully carved statues,
> One playing an instrument, another the lyre
> And yet another playing plaintively on a reed pipe,
> One gave voice to song, so that it seemed a human voice.
> In the middle there was the king seated on a high throne
> And around him the rulers showing their respect.'
> (*Byzantine Iliad*, verse 50 ff)

No further argument is needed to state that Byzantine court ceremony and the magnificence of its palace has been transposed to Troy. The source for this magnificence is the interior of the great palace of the Emperor Theophilos (829-842), with its lifelike images of birds and other animals, derived from the opulence of the Arab court of Harun al-Rashid and intended to be its equal. Romantic descriptions of palaces, forts and bathhouses also occurred in the Byzantine popular novels of the 14th and 15th centuries.

TROY AS ROMANCE

Romantic descriptions also found their way into the *Achilleid*, a novel that has scarcely anything to do with the Trojan War or Troy, even though it takes its name from the admired hero of the *Iliad*. The *Achilleid* is a the romance novel par excellence. The central character is the son of a royal couple that had been childless for 12 years. The boy is exceptionally handsome, grows up strong and healthy, is trained in the arts of war, and sallies forth with his cousin Patroclus (who warns him against the arrows of Eros!) against a hostile king. By chance he catches sight of his outstandingly beautiful daughter, more beautiful than Aphrodite herself. The invincible hero is of course won over by Eros – love. He writes letters to the girl who wants nothing to do with Eros. But victory is to the persistent, and when Achilles prays to Eros, the girl is also struck by his arrows. A rendezvous follows in a beautiful park and a marriage is ultimately concluded. But even stronger than Eros is Thanatos – death: the girl dies after six years of marriage. Achilles is in deep mourning when he hears of the Trojan War. In Troy Paris (!) is king. The Greeks with Achilles among them ravage the Trojans, and Paris offers his sister (the name Polyxena is not mentioned) in marriage to Achilles. Achilles is murdered by Paris and Deiphobus during the exchange of vows. After six years of war the Greeks take Troy. The end also provides a moral: beauty, love, courage, luck, wealth, whatever – all end with the grave. The Trojan War is merely a brief appendage. The birth, upbringing, military campaign, correspondence, marriage, sickness and death of the girl, and the grief of Achilles take up 1,758 verses, while the battle at Troy, including the moral ending, are dealt with in 162.

The Trojan War is definitely the main theme of another vernacular poem: the work attributed to Constantine Hermoniakos, who composed 8,799 octosyllabic verses in 24 'songs' commissioned by the despot of Epirus, John II Komnenos (Comnenus) Angelos-Ducas (1323-1355), and his wife Anna Palaeologina. As the title shows, it is conceived as a 'translation' of Homer's *Iliad*. The author's intention is to convert Homer's difficult language into contemporary language in order to render Homer's work more accessible, but in fact the works of Tzetzes and Manasses were the paradigms. The fact that Hermoniakos added a life of Homer is unusual. But for the rest the pattern to be seen in Malalas is followed in principle: the pre-history, the Judgement of Paris, the abduction of Helen, the war and the conquest of Troy. To this Hermoniakos adds the vengeance taken by Hecuba on her youngest son Polydoros, who had killed his sister Polyxena, a motif taken from the 5th century BC Greek tragedian Euripides. The personal description as with Malalas and Tzetzes are characteristic. His description of the beautiful Helen occupies at least 120 verses, based on Malalas, but with a combination of the passport-like and the romantic types of description. Not just the fair skin, radiant glance, flush on the fair cheeks, neck of crystal and beautiful breasts like apples are described, but even her toenails. No one who looked on her could escape the spell of her beauty. And thus Paris fell for her allure!

The works above in which the Trojan War is a theme for discussion are completely overshadowed by the *Polemos tis Troados*, a huge work of 14,401 verses in late Byzantine / early modern Greek, probably from the 14th century, the author of which is unknown. This is not an originally Greek version but an edited

Hagia Sophia (Ayasofya), built in the 6th century on the orders of the Roman Emperor Justinian. The architects, Isidore of Miletus en Anthemius of Tralles, were ordered to build the largest church in Christendom. To this day it is one of Istanbul's architectural landmarks. Hagia Sophia was the centre of the Byzantine Empire until 1453, when the church was turned into a mosque following the fall of Constantinople, with minarets being added. The building was secularised in 1934 under Turkish President Kemal Mustafa Atatürk. It has been a museum since and one of the most frequently visited tourist attractions of the city. Watercolour by William Turner (1775-1851).

translation of the *Roman de Troie* by the 12th century French poet Benoît de Sainte-Maure. It is extremely broad in scope and presents a surprising version of events – for classicists at any rate – when for example it has Troy being destroyed by the Greeks not once but twice. The first occasion was the result of offensive treatment by Trojan King Laomedon of the Greeks Iasous (Jason) and Herkoulios (sic, Heracles) who rest at Troy while on their way to Colchis to retrieve the Golden Fleece. Following the success of their expedition with the aid of the witch Medea, the Greeks with Heracles among them and also the old King Nestor take vengeance on the Trojans, seize the city, plunder it and leave with the spoils. Priam, son of Laomedon, rebuilds the city. A retaliatory expedition is planned against Greece, and Paris abducts Helen during a religious festival, bringing her to Troy. A delegation led by Odysseus to secure Helen's return fails as a result of his 'boorish' behaviour. The war is described from many aspects, with Hector being more sympathetically portrayed and as a better warrior than Achilles. Hector is seriously wounded after being struck by a projectile from an unknown source and dies. His funeral is attended by the Greeks as well, where Achilles sees and falls in love with Polyxena. He avoids battle, disadvantaging the Greeks. Polyxena's mother backs the marriage, although Priam is furious. Achilles takes up the fight again. Paris now lures Achilles into a trap with the false promise of marriage and kills him. Finally the Wooden Horse emerges with the Fall of Troy and the aftermath, including the murder of Agamemnon by Clytemnestra (predicted by Cassandra), Menelaus arriving on Crete with Helen, and Odysseus reaching Ithaca after long wandering, before being killed by the son that he fathered by Circe...!

Benoît expanded his work to huge proportions, but the core rests on the version as presented in the Latin translation of the work attributed to Dares Phrygius. This probably lent credence to the work in Byzantine eyes, as is shown by the fact that it has been transmitted in at least five complete and two incomplete manuscripts.

Another work of a completely different nature should not go unmentioned. This is in the form of commentaries that Archbishop Eustathius of Thessalonica (1115-1197), the great Byzantine scholar, made on the *Iliad* and the Odyssey. These commentaries form a huge work, comprising virtually everything that was extant at the time on the Homeric epics. Eustathius gives space not only to the many mythological traditions, but also to comparisons with his own era, defines Homeric words using 'modern' (Byzantine) terminology, provides etymologies, and details geographic directions, often using as source the Greek historian Strabo, sometimes taking an ironic tone. Referring to the *Iliad* (3, 158) when the Trojan notables remark: 'Small blame that Trojans and well-greaved Achaeans should for such a woman long time suffer woes; wondrously like is she

to the immortal goddesses to look upon,' he says tersely that the Muses provided Homer with the simile. He could not know this from his own experience, as little as the converse, that the goddesses were similar to Helen. No, Euripides, the tragedian with his 'the most beautiful woman lit up by the gold-rayed sun' (*Hecuba* 636) was more realistic. Eustathius also refers to the view that Helen was merely a figment of the imagination in Troy and the war a shadow conflict, and he cites Herodotus with some approval:

'Surely the Trojans were not so "crazy" that they would have taken the risk of not returning Helen, with or without the agreement of Paris?'

CONCLUSION

For the Byzantines, Troy existed purely as a literature. The location of the action had literally perished. The language of Homer had certainly become inaccessible – radically changed pronunciation and more importantly the shift from 'sung' verse to stressed verse rendered correct recitation of Homeric metre, the hexameter, impossible. Nevertheless they continued to cherish, copy, study and comment upon the epics as 'landmarks' of their literary past. In addition the trend evolved of bringing the epic tales up to date, whether by embedding them in history or reworking them in the contemporary vernacular. In this regard the romantic historicisation (Diktys and Dares) and the Frankish contribution through Benoît de Sainte-Maure are significant. 'La Troie est morte, vive la Troie!'

THE SECOND ROUND: THE BATTLE FOR TROY IN THE RENAISSANCE

DAVID RIJSER

Ottoman Sultan Mehmed II may in 1453 not have had the cultural legitimacy in Western eyes that would have been able to buttress his claim to the Eastern Roman Empire, but he certainly had something that his Byzantine opponents urgently lacked: money. It was this money that made it possible for him to buy a huge Hungarian cannon that the Byzantine emperors were unable to afford. This cannon was to play a key role in the fall of Constantinople that year. In the end it was cash that finally brought down the Roman Empire. But Mehmed was not satisfied. He had perceived the significance of cultural capital and had a keen awareness of the importance of continuity with the classical past. In his case that meant Troy. Both historical precedent and the site of ancient Troy were there for Mehmed's taking.

AVENGER OF TROY

Mehmed was a cosmopolitan with a great interest in cultural matters. He commissioned the Venetian master Gentile Bellini to paint his portrait, which now hangs in London's National Gallery, collected classical manuscripts, and had Italian humanists read to him the works of Diogenes Laertius, Herodotus, Livy, Curtius Rufus and from papal history – according to his Venetian doctor Jacomo Langusto. He also maintained a Byzantine historian who had defected and who politely immortalised Mehmed's heroic deeds in the ornate Attic of the ancient Greeks. This Michael Critobulus, who changed his name to make it resemble a character from one of Plato's dialogues, relates a fascinating anecdote in the *Historiae*, a hagiography dedicated to Mehmed. During one of the many military campaigns conducted by Mehmed to pacify the surrounding

Sultan Mehmed II smelling a rose, ca. 1480, attributed to the Ottoman court painter Şiblizade Ahmed or his master Sinan Bey. The painter has been inspired by the portrait of the sultan by Gentile Bellini (see page 106), although the small scale and seated position are also in the oriental tradition of dynastic portraits. The roses could perhaps refer to his intellectual and spiritual refinement and his interest in gardens, or the three roses could point to Mehmed's royal power in Asia, Greece and Trebizond, and the archer's ring on his thumb to his military achievements and his skill as a huntsman.

territory following his conquest of Constantinople, he passed by Troy:

'And after he had arrived at Troy, he admired the ruins and the traces of the old city, the surroundings, the position and other details of the area that were located at a particularly favourable intersection of sea and land. Moreover he inspected the graves of the heroes on site, in particular those of Achilles, Ajax and others, saying they were fortunate not only in their immortality and their deeds but also in having the poet Homer as panegyrist. Shaking his head slightly he remarked: "God has appointed me following the passage of so many years as the avenger of this city and its inhabitants. I have defeated their enemies indeed. I have razed their cities and made use of their possessions as 'booty of the Mysians'. Because it was Greeks, Macedonians, Thessalians and Peloponnesians that once pillaged Troy. I have now finally punished their descendants after so long a time for their arrogance towards us Asians at the time, and so often since."*
(Critobulus, *Historiae* 4.4 ff)

Mehmed had obviously paid attention to the readings from Herodotus, who had after all in his *Histories* (1.1-4) placed the Trojan War in the context of a series of campaigns of mutual revenge between East and West. Alexander the Great, whose conquests in the East had been placed in the same context by the 2nd century historian Arrian, had also visited Troy, paid ritual homage to the grave of Achilles and remarked: "Thou youth favoured by fate whose lot it is to have found Homer as herald of your courage!" (*Anabasis* 1.12.1). Critobulus' account of Mehmed's contemplation is directly linked to these words. Mehmed's visit to Troy also should be seen in the context of his identification with Alexander, whose reincarnation he wanted to be seen as. Alexander slept with the *Iliad* under his pillow, and Mehmed acquired a valuable edition of Homer that can still be admired in the library of the Topkapı Palace.

Mehmed's publicity campaign thus envisaged identifying the Turks with the Trojans: in this way he could obtain the desired historical legitimacy while at the same time delivering a sensitive blow beneath the belt to Western Christian identity. The latter after all had been shaped by Troy to as large an extent:

through the myth of the most important of the survivors of Troy, Aeneas, who after his peregrinations was to become the legendary founder of Rome.

MEHMED II AND TROY

Like other famous rulers, such as Xerxes I, Alexander the Great and Caesar, Ottoman Sultan Mehmed II the Conqueror (1432-1481) also paid homage to the Trojans. Sultan Mehmed II was highly interested in the heroes of classical antiquity. Byzantine and Latin advisers surrounded him, and his personal library in the Topkapı Palace included Greek copies of the *Iliad*. He commissioned, in all probability, also copies of medieval Arabic manuscripts dealing with the story of the Trojan horse.

The Troad and the Dardanelles – controlled by the Trojans in ancient times – became a place of major importance during the reign of Mehmed II. After the conquest of Constantinople in 1453, he ordered the construction of strong fortresses for the defence of the Dardanelles. Evidently Mehmed II attached great importance to the strategic waterway, but Troy must have fired his imagination as well. Medieval sentiment in Europe favoured the Trojans, famed as the glorious warriors. European countries traced their founders to the Trojans to provide themselves with honourable ancestors. Mehmed II joined in this European tradition: he claimed Troy and identified himself with the legendary warriors of Troy.

According to Michael Critobulus from the island of Imbros, a chronicler in Ottoman service, Mehmed II visited the site of Troy in 1462. He praised Homer during his stay and declared that the citizens of Troy had, finally, been avenged. Referring to the conquest of Constantinople, Mehmed II celebrated the victory of 'us' Asians over the descendants of the 'Greeks, Macedonians, Thessalians and Peloponnesians'. According to the chronicler, the sultan said that these nations had 'ravaged this place in the past, and their descendants have now through my efforts paid the right penalty, after a long period of years, for their injustice to us Asians at that time and so often in subsequent times'.

Sultan Mehmed II's declaration of vengeance for the injustice to 'us' Asians, in fact, corresponds with the classical idea of the contrast between East and West, the orient and the occident, Asia and Europe. Actually, Homer was an important source for this notion. In the history of Greek ideology, the war for Troy played a significant role in the military conflicts with the East. From a political point of view, it was crucial for the Trojan War to be interpreted as a battle of East against West, Europe against Asia. The very epic model was recalled by many nations in war.

Günay Uslu

AENEAS AS PRECURSOR OF CHRISTIANITY

Virgil took up the tale of Aeneas in his *Aeneid* in order to give shape to his myth of the founding of Rome, in which the tragic fate of Troy and its inhabitants is presented as a so-called "founding sacrifice" necessary for the creation of a greater good, namely Rome. In particular in the second book that deals with the Fall of Troy, Virgil subjects his paradigm, the Homeric epic, to significant revision. Whereas Homer treats the warring sides objectively by and large, without definitively turning either of the two into the scapegoat for all the suffering, Virgil has this objective reading make way for a radically subjective presentation: Aeneas, victim of Greek violence and stratagem, himself relates the story of the city's fall to Dido. He does not hold back from making clear repeatedly how blameless the Trojans and how ruthless, treacherous and godless the Greeks were.

Although in Virgil's epic this subjective version is subsequently overshadowed by a more objective account, in which the Trojans turn out to be as morally ambiguous as their

THE RENAISSANCE OF TROY

Greek edition of the *Iliad* by Homer from the library of Mehmed II. Sultan Mehmed II was inspired by Homer's work and regarded his conquest of Constantinople in 1453 as ultimate revenge for the sack of Troy.

Mehmed II (1432-1481), sultan from 1444 to 1446 and from 1451 to 1481, was the founder of the Ottoman Empire, securing for himself the honorific *Fâtih* (Turkish for conqueror). In 1453 he seized Constantinople, modern Istanbul, finally putting an end to the Byzantine Empire. In Turkey sultan Mehmed II is seen as a national hero. Portrait by Gentile Bellini in 1480.

History of Mehmed the Conqueror, by Michael Critobulus (c. 1410-c. 1470), dedicated to Mehmed II. Critobulus described the rise of the Ottoman Empire between 1465 and 1467 and its conquest under Sultan Mehmed II of the Byzantine Empire. The work contains a report on the sultan's visit to Troy in 1462. According to Critobulus, Mehmed II declared at the time that he had, through his conquest of Constantinople, finally avenged the destruction of Troy by the Greeks, and the injustice done to 'us Asians'.

erstwhile opponents, the poetic persuasion and rhetorical brilliance by means of which in Book II the Trojans are presented as 'good' and the Greeks as 'bad' have had as result that this very bias came to dominate the way the *Aeneid* and its conceptual contents were perceived. Church Father Augustine already presented the Roman Empire as the typological precursor and worldly counterpart to the Kingdom of Christ. The patriarch of the Romans, *pius Aeneas*, could subsquently be seen as a precursor of Christianity, and his 'innocent' Trojan character was well suited to this, however much this character was based on a misrepresentation of what Virgil had intended. The *locus classicus* here is Dante's *Inferno* (2.10 ff). The idea of a Trojan origin thus went to make up part of Europe's identity: not merely the abstract idea of 'Rome' as the Christian Promised Land of the Middle Ages in Dante, but also for example in the highly entertaining confabulations of Geoffrey of Monmouth of the

first half of the 12th century in his *Historia Regum Brittaniae* (1.2-18). This has the British descending from Ascanius' grandson Brutus, to whom Geoffrey dedicates a fascinating and highly original novel at the beginning of his work. Mediaeval allegory could even have Aeneas standing for the *Sainte Église*, the Holy Mother Church. Anyone able to take Troy away from Christianity, as Mehmed intended, was thus striking a mortal blow.

A ROMAN TROY

Initially Mehmed did not in any way appear to have been bent on polarisation. There is even evidence that he sought rapprochement with Europe through the Trojan-Turkish link. In the West itself, the identification of Trojan with Turk seems at any rate to have been unobjectionable in the 15th century. The Trojans had after all long ruled over the region now controlled by the Turks. Moreover Virgil referred mostly to the Trojans as *Teucri* (after their ancestor Teucer), and what could be clearer than to associate the name with the *Turchi* or *Turcae*? The dubious reputation the Greeks had gained in the West after Virgil not infrequently lent support to the view that they had finally got what they deserved with the fall of Constantinople. Mehmed himself appears to have wished to to exploit ideas of this kind. Montaigne, probably based on the Chronicles of Enguerrand de Monstrelet, cites an apocryphal letter from Mehmed to Pope Pius II (in reality it should have been Nicholas V), in which he stated:

'I am amazed that the Italians are allied against me, given the fact that we have common origins in the Trojans and they have as much interest as I in avenging the blood of Hector on the Greeks, whose blood they nevertheless prefer over mine.'
(Montaigne, *Essais* 2.36)

However it is clear even without the letter that the identification *Turcae = Teucri* was not particularly welcome in the Vatican. Pius II stated his explicit opposition in his *Europa* of 1458:

'I note that many authors, not only poets but even historians, have fallen under the spell of referring to the Turks as Teucri*, perhaps as a result of the fact that the Turks are now in possession of Troy, which was once inhabited by the* Teucri*.'*
(Enea Silvio Piccolomini (= Pius II), *Opera Omnia*, p. 394)

This is the background that needs to be taken into account with perhaps the most famous appearance of Troy from the Renaissance: the decor of the papal apartments of Julius II (1503-1513) and his successor Leo X (1513-1521) in the Apostolic Palace in the Vatican by Raphael and his workshop in the first two decades of the 16th century. Troy plays an extremely important role in the decorations, even if this is not noticeable at first sight and has not always been fully acknowledged by critics. The scene on the left of the fresco of the *Fire in the Borgo* in the Sala del Incendio, the hall that concludes the enfilade and the last to be completed by Raphael and his workshop, is the one that stands out most of all. The group is perhaps related to an ancient prototype that has been lost but is known from a 16th century engraving by Giovanni Jacopo Caragli: a sculpture group of Aeneas with his father Anchises on his back and Ascanius holding his hand. But even if so, this concerns more than the borrowing of a motif from Antiquity *tout court*. The hall, dedicated to the works of the popes Leo III (795-816) and Leo IV (847-55), contains portraits of Leo X, the pope that commissioned them, who is presented in this way as a typological complement to his earlier namesakes. The *Fire in the Borgo* illustrates how Leo IV miraculously extinguishes a large fire threatening St Peter's by making the sign of the cross. Raphael's

A man fleeing Rome in flames with his father on his back. This detail from *Fire in the Borgo*, a fresco by Raphael in the Apostolic Palace in the Vatican, is a reference to Aeneas' flight from Troy.

Laocoön is a Trojan priest from a later version not by Homer who issued a warning about the Wooden Horse that the Greeks had left in front of the walls of Troy. He is said to have been strangled along with his sons by snakes sent from the sea by Poseidon. This statue, the famous Laocoön Group from the end of the 1st century BC, shown here in copy, was found in 1506 and bought by Pope Julius II for his art collection that would later become the Vatican Museums.

Alexander the Great visits the grave of Achilles, 1649, Aert Jansz Marienhof (ca. 1626-na 1651). Alexander the Great visited Troy on the eve of his campaign through Asia. He made sacrifice to the goddess Athena and paid a visit to the grave of Achilles, whom he idolised. He regarded himself as 'avenger of the Greeks' and the story is told that he kept a copy made by Aristotle of Homer's *Iliad*.

pictorial citation from the *Aeneid* (Virgil describes the scene in 2.721-729) suggests a comparison between Leo IV's miraculous quenching (and his campaigns against the Saracens), and Leo X's intention of bringing peace to Christendom by embarking on a crusade against the Turks – as he had been motivated to do after almost being taken prisoner by Muslim pirates in 1516. The fire that consumed Troy – this is the suggestion – rages once more, has even reached the gates, but the legitimate successor of Aeneas (who is also presented as the typological precursor of Leo), the Pope, will once again bring the penates (household gods) to safety.

The symbolism of this pictorial language was not new. Leo's predecessor Julius II in his central state chamber, the *Stanza della Segnatura*, had referred pointedly to Homer and Virgil, the two poets immediately next to Apollo, the god of the Muses, on Mount Parnassus, and had also included the scene in

which Alexander the Great visits the grave of Achilles near Troy in *grisaille*. The window framed by the fresco of Mount Parnassus moreover looked towards the *Cortile delle Statue*, the courtyard where Julius had commissioned a cycle of Trojan antique statues to be erected. These statues all referred unambiguously to the *Aeneid* – including the *Laocoön*, the *Apollo Belvedère* and the *Venus Felix*, alongside a statue that his advisers regarded as an Aeneas with Ascanius – statues that were described by his court poets as Julius' *marmoreos Lares* (household gods of marble). Here too the intertextual network of visual references pointed at the Trojan heritage that the Pope laid claim to, with Virgil's *Aeneid* as its Holy Writ. It is clear that, just as Pius II before them, Julius and Leo used these means to contest the Turkish appropriation of the *Teucri* and claimed emphatically that the papacy was the legitimate heir of the Trojan tradition.

This 'reconquest' of Troy from the Turks by the Pope in Rome has had a long aftermath. The 'Roman Troy' tradition forms the basis for example of one of the few 'classical' works from the Low Countries in the shape of Vondel's *Gijsbrecht van Aemstel* (1637). The author repeatedly drives home the point in his dedication to Hugo de Groot and in his 'Prologue' that Troy is symbolically linked to Amsterdam, Gijsbrecht to Aeneas, Gozewijn to Priam, Vosmaer de Spie to Sinon, de 'Schuit 't Zeepaardje' to the Trojan Horse and so on, and by implication, unsurprisingly, Vondel to Virgil. This schoolmasterly emphasis should perhaps be attributed less to Vondel's somewhat deficient poetic and dramatic skills – something the play bears ample witness to – than to the intention to push Rome into the background precisely in order to make room for Troy in the foreground. The play's premiere was in fact postponed as a result of Protestant objection to 'the portrayal of superstitions of popery like the mass and other ceremonies'. Vondel, who

Achilles slays Hector. This sketch in oil painted by Pieter Paul Rubens for a wall hanging is part of the series *The Life of Achilles* (1630-1632). Hector is forced onto his knees as the Greek hero in his magnificent armour thrusts a speer through the neck of his opponent. Athena floats above the two combatants, and to the right one of Troy's gates may be seen.

converted to Catholicism shortly after producing *Gijsbrecht*, nevertheless used the parallels to suggest only too clearly that just as Troy had risen again from the ashes as Rome, Amsterdam had now risen from humble and troubled beginnings to become a metropolis, and thus had Rome as its model.

THE DEATH OF THE OLD TROY

But the fair appearance of a virtuous Troy did not fool everyone. It is interesting that precisely Troy as scene of the action inspired Shakespeare, who never wrote for the squeamish, to write his most cynical play, *Troilus and Cressida* (1603). Instead of transporting Trojan-Roman concepts to Haarlem and Laren, like Vondel, Shakespeare uses the play to project 'modern' contradictions between chivalry and pragmatism, courtly love and raw sex, onto the conflict between the Greeks and the Trojans. He does this in a now highly postmodern-seeming potpourri using medieval (in particular Chaucer's *Troilus and Criseyde*) and ancient sources (primarily Chapman's translation of the *Iliad*), replete with glaring anachronism (Hector cites Aristotle) that must have been intended as a deliberate provocation of scholars and classicists. The end result is an exceptionally bitter satire on all forms of pretention, whether in politics, war or love. The structural principle that informs this deconstruction, is opposition: between Greeks and Trojans, battlefield and bedroom, rhetoric and *debunking*. Shakespeare ruthlessly juxtaposes scenes in Troy with those in the Greek camp- the most poignant at the start of the second act which turns on the debate in Troy over whether Helen should be kept or handed back. This debate, which includes an extremely subtle analysis of the concept of 'value', in absolute or relative terms, is framed by the appearance of the scurrilous Thersites, Agamemnon's boils, Odysseus' cynicism, Patroclus' effeminacy and the arrogant indolence of Achilles. The Trojans are courtly, intellectual and honest. They hesitate and philosophise as though within the impenetrable walls of a mediaeval abbey. But reality awaits outside in the form of the Greeks. Nevertheless Shakespeare does not allow himself to idealise the Trojans. Hector is brought down by vanity, Cressida forgets her vows to Troilus as soon as she ends up in the Greek camp and falls for the advances of Diomedes. Shakespeare appears to have seen through the traditional ideological *casting* of the Trojans as naïve, honest and courtly, and of the Greeks as cunning and ruthless, and simultaneously through the pretentions of politicians who tried to present themselves in a good light on the basis of contradictions of this kind. In the brave new world that Shakespeare conjures up for us no virtue exists. The old Troy, romantic fatherland, was dead.

HOMER AND TROY: FROM EUROPEAN TO DISPUTABLE *LIEUX DE MÉMOIRE*

PIM DEN BOER

Homer and Troy are the ancient Greeks' first *lieux de mémoire* – concrete or abstract places to which identity-defining memories attach and on which e.g. national recollections are anchored. Although Homer's personal details could never be established with any certainty, for centuries there have been no doubts about his existence as a person. For the historians of Classical Antiquity, like Herodotus (ca. 485-425/420 BC) and Thucydides (ca. 460-400 BC), it was evident that Homer had existed, even if they did not know when he lived. They did believe that he could not have witnessed the Trojan War in person.

Homer's great significance was that he was the first poet to describe the many gods of the Greeks with their various traits and characteristics. Much of the knowledge we have of the gods derives from Homer, according to Herodotus. Homer was honoured but was not accorded divine status. His words were not divine words which could not be subject to doubt. His verses were not a holy revelation of the sole almighty God, but the first hymns on the many Greek gods with all their human failings.

From the beginnings of the Greek educational system in Athens in the 5th century BC up to the capture of Constantinople by the Ottomans in the 15th century – for 2,000 years – Homer retained a permanent place in this system. The same education in Greek was provided to the elite of the Roman Empire, where Latin usually was the *lingua franca*. The Greek gods merged with the Roman ones. The founding of the city of Rome itself was traced back to the destruction of Troy. Virgil wrote a Latin epic about the Trojan prince Aeneas who had made his escape from Troy as it burned and finally settled in Italy. Powerful Roman families traced their family trees back to Trojan heroes.

After the rise of Christianity, Homer's texts were spared despite the harsh repression of heathen polytheism. Following the collapse of the Roman Empire in the West, Homer's writings continued to be studied in the centres of Greek knowledge in the East. A contemporary compared the seizing of Constantinople by Sultan Mehmed II in 1453 with that of Troy and saw Ottoman expansion as punishment for the destruction of Troy (see 6.1).

In the West in the centuries before that, Homer had been no more than the name of a great poet without his own voice. Only in the 14th century did the *Iliad* and the *Odyssey* return to Western Europe. Under the influence of burgeoning human-ism, the successful hunt for ancient Greek manuscripts began in Latin Christendom.

HOMER AND TROY AS EUROPEAN *LIEUX DE MÉMOIRE*

By the second half of the 16th century Homer was being referred to as the first among the most exceptional figures in history. In his *Essais* Montaigne wrote that no one was better known than Homer. Who does not know of Troy, Helen, Hector and Achilles? We even name our children using the names found in Homer. According to Montaigne, not only families, but also most of the world's nations tried to find evidence in Homer for their Trojan origins. Naturally he could not omit mentioning that even Mehmed II had written to the pope to the effect that they had the same fraternal Trojan origins and that he, Mehmed, had aimed to avenge the blood of Hector. Montaigne regarded this as a *noble farce*, but nevertheless as clear proof of Homer's renown throughout the world.

In fact, for centuries it was the Roman poet Virgil who was the most highly esteemed, not Homer. This was not merely a question of applying the rules of *poetica*, but also of moral principles. Homer's world had been too young to have learnt the principles of true honesty, in the arrogant assessment of the era of Enlightenment.

For as long as courtly society dominated the patterns of behaviour in the highest European circles, there was revulsion at the vulgar behaviour depicted by Homer. The heroes roasting whole lambs, the princesses washing the dishes and their own clothes – all this was considered ridiculous. There could not have been a greater difference than with Virgil, in whose epic we recognise the civilised world of a nation with taste, high art, sculptors, painters and architects. With the rise of pre-Romanticism, this predominant view was increasingly disputed. The simplicity of manners in Homer became an argument used against courtly culture.

THE SITE OF TROY

In the second half of the 18th century Homer's geographical context was discovered and archaeological interest awakened. In 1767, an important step was taken by the British amateur Robert Wood. To him Homer was not only the most original of all poets, but also a meticulous observer of nature. Wood

The Burning of Troy, 1631, Simon de Vlieger. After the Greeks had successfully implemented their plan with the Wooden Horse, they plundered Troy and set it alight. In the left foreground Aeneas is seen fleeing the city with his small son Ascanius carrying his father Anchises on his back, along with two soldiers. This story from the Trojan War is not in Homer but is told in Virgil's *Aeneid.*

Oppugnant Troes Græcorum castra frequentes,
Illas projecti tentant convellere saxis. 12.
Sarpedon magno comitatus Hectore portas
Deijcit, adij ipsos fervent tunc prælia naves.

Synoptic depictions of well known *lieux de mémoire* came into vogue in the early modern period. The fantasy depiction shown here by Crispijn van de Passe is taken from *Speculum heroicum principis omnium temporum poëtarum*, the 24 books of Homer published in 1613 by J Hilaire Larivière. The plate shows a battle scene in front of the gates of Troy. The 'modern' armour is worthy of note, as is the similarity of Troy to contemporaneous European cities.

drew authority from the fact that he was one of the first to base his judgements on a visit to the places described in the *Iliad* and the *Odyssey* during a *Grand Tour* through Greece and Asia Minor. Wood was an early forerunner of Heinrich Schliemann, who in turn a century later was to take seriously Homer's tale with respect to location and thus create the basis for Homeric archaeology.

HOMER IN EDUCATION

Homer made his entry into the European classroom in the 19th century. On the introduction of ancient Greek into the curriculum of the Latin schools of Europe, studying Homer became obligatory. Germany and Britain led the way; other European countries followed. According to the standard view, the Germans were the first to rediscover Classical Greece. Following the Napoleonic occupation of German territory, the Roman past was identified with the French Empire and for that reason vigorously rejected. Ancient Greece was now regarded as the embodiment of the ideals of freedom, beauty and true knowledge.

Undoubtedly, many Germans were fond of Greece – the level and intensity of academic study of the Greek classics at German schools and universities had no equal – but they were certainly not alone in their ardent philhellenism. All well-educated Europeans shared it. That the Germans were not all that exceptional in this regard is shown by the example of Britain, where the famous schoolmaster Thomas Arnold played a key role in introducing Greek authors into the classroom. Arnold aimed to take education to a higher level in a moral sense and believed that reading the classical Greek authors was the best route. At the same time he introduced contemporary history and gymnastics into the educational programme. High moral standards, knowledge of affairs, skill in speaking and a healthy body were the educational ideals thought to be found in their highest form in Classical Greece.

But it was Plato rather than Homer who was installed in prime position by Arnold and other teachers, and he provided the best-loved exam material. Nevertheless, Homer also became increasingly important in classical education in and outside the classroom, in Britain, in German-speaking regions and in other European countries. For a later generation of pedagogues – the generation of Thomas' son Matthew for example – reading Homer in the formative years even became crucial. They laid greater emphasis on mythology and aesthetics than the previous generation, being less interested in politics and strongly influenced by German idealism. For Matthew Arnold *cum suis* Greek poetry and tragedy, rather than Greek philosophy, constituted the most precious classical heritage. To them Greek literature was a primer for life itself and true beauty. For this reason Homer deserved pride of place.

Across the whole of Europe an idealised image of Hellas as a fundamental pedagogical place of recollection arose. The introduction of Greek authors into classical education was seen as essential for the creation of an elite to provide leadership for the country. In the analysis of the elitist education system the role of the classical languages is often limited to the exclusion of other social strata. That may be correct in the broad social sense, but the question remains why it was Greek that was introduced. Within the elitist educational system deliberate choices were made with a view to the desired identification of the pupils. The 19th-century German *Bildungsbürger* and British Utilitarians were fascinated by Plato. In the heyday of European colonial expansion around 1900 it was not only ardent classicists, but also British and German imperialists who promoted the necessity of reading Homer. Social Darwinists in particular cherished Homer as a pedagogical frame of reference.

Of course there were politico-cultural differences depending on the country concerned. In France in the 19th century Homer was not by any means as venerated as he was in Germany and Britain. Greek was introduced into the French grammar schools, but Latin continued to predominate. Homer did not achieve the outstanding position in the French tradition that he enjoyed at English boarding schools and German gymnasia. In the period 1880-1900, when the French Third Republic had established itself, teachers gave preference to Greek texts from the period of the Greek *poleis* (city states). Not Troy, but Athens was the favourite *lieu de mémoire*. In France philosophy and tragedy took pride of place, the earliest poetry contenting itself with a more modest rank. Homer continued to be part of the past of an aristocratic society. French Republican teaching retained a preference for Athenian democrats and Roman Republicans. True democrats were anti-Homer, was the motto.

HOMER AS LIBERAL *LIEU DE MÉMOIRE*

Translating Homer was seen as an extremely useful activity from the middle of the 19th century in particular, given that he represented a European *lieu de mémoire* of a liberal world view. It was mostly implicitly that Homer's texts as foundational texts for the classical tradition started to function alongside the Bible. Homer was thus promoted to a position as one of the cornerstones of contemporary liberal European culture.

In England, where the liberal tradition developed furthest, the great appeal and huge interest in Homer had a clear political and moral dimension. Homer became the first historical point of reference for 19th-century European liberalism. It was in this context that the influential liberal British statesman William Gladstone developed a fascination for Homer. In the midst of his onerous political duties he published many articles and books on the Greek bard. Alongside his Christian convictions, Homer for Gladstone meant nothing less than the historic introduction to modern humanity. This is also the background to his famous statement to the effect that two things remained for him to do: 'One is to carry Home Rule [for Ireland] and the other is to prove the intimate connection between the Hebrew

and Olympian revelations.' In fact Gladstone aimed to reconcile the Old Testament and Homer.

How to comprehend the fundamental significance of Homer for 19th-century British liberals in general and Gladstone in particular? What turned reading Homer from a language exercise to a moral lesson? Gladstone had expounded clearly for a broad public on why Homer offered perfect lessons in life for a liberal, while remaining an ideal source of inspiration for identification with Homeric heroes. Homer, according to Gladstone, is replete with moral choice and devotion to duty. The *Iliad* incorporates great national consciousness and embodies the Greek idea of a state. Achilles excels in martial prowess and is at the same time the paradigm of the liberal and courteous gentleman. The *Odyssey* is focused on family life and the restoration of his rights to Odysseus. Odysseus possesses the highest qualities of the statesman; not only does he excel in racing, boxing and wrestling, but he is also prepared to set his hand to the plough and work the earth as a farmer.

Reading Homer is inspiring not only for men but for women as well. With respect to the position of women, comparison with female figures in the Old Testament comes out in Homer's favour, in Gladstone's view. Homer describes female characters such as Penelope, the 'queenly matron', and Nausicaa with her 'maiden freshness and her great intellect of an Elizabeth'. Even the beautiful Helen shows deep humility and turns out to be capable of a self-condemnation that closely approaches Christian repentance. In Homer Gladstone finds a great sense of virtue. Divorce is unknown and incest is abhorred. Moreover, Homer points to the moral fellowship of man and woman.

Given the accustomed European feelings of superiority, the Trojan for Gladstone represents the alien, Asian element. He contrasts the strict monogamy of the Greeks with Priam's

Priam (Priamos Basileus) on a bronze plaquette by Alessandro Cesati (ca. 1550). On the reverse a walled city is shown, a 16th century interpretation of Troy, with a number of ships in the foreground that resemble Venetian gondolas.

A so-called jeton (a coin used for bookkeeping calculations on a counting table) from Middelburg in the Netherlands from 1608. On the front is a crowned coat of arms from Zeeland Province and seven escutcheons of cities linked together with a ribbon. On the reverse of the silver jeton the Wooden Horse is being dragged into Troy.

Juppiter e somno surgens, Troes᷎ fugatos
Cernens, iratus sæva Iunonis ob artes, 15 *Imperat iniussis Neptuno abscedat ab armis:*
Hector et assumit priscas ab Appolline vires.

The Greek gods Jupiter, Hera and Poseidon are to be seen on this engraving by Crispijn van de Passe floating above the confusion of the battle around Troy. From *Speculum heroicum principis omnium temporum poëtarum*, published in 1613 by J Hilaire Larivière.

polygamy. Gladstone believes that Homer is already drawing a distinction between European Greeks and Asian Trojans. He even perceives a European trait here: 'a finer sense, a higher intelligence, a firmer and more masculine tissue of character (...) have since, through long ages of history been in no small measure European and Asiatic respectively.'

Political life in Homer is also surprisingly familiar for a 19th-century liberal. The form of government is not the divine or despotic dominion of the Oriental empires. Public affairs are discussed in an assembly and decisions usually taken on the basis of rational powers of persuasion. For Gladstone, Homer reveals the origins of the modern English monarchy, tempered by parliament's influence. In the area of religious observance, Homer also provides the earliest example of a liberal state: without theocracy, without an omnipotent church, without an infallible Pope. In Homer, the individual speaks to the gods directly and not through a caste of priests.

In England and Germany in particular, but also in other countries, Homer in the second half of the 19th century began to be seen as the earliest and unsurpassed *lieu de mémoire* of the European liberal classical tradition. Reading the epics in ancient Greek came to be seen as superbly suited to forming the bourgeois middle classes and the future social elite. In this regard Homer was interpreted as the earliest poetic expression of middle-class humanism and liberalism. Homer's verses

also did service in proclaiming a modern European civilising mission and expansion overseas.

HOMER FOR EDUCATING AND CREATING IMPERIALISTS

Liberal European idealisation of Homer was interrupted by the excavations at Troy in Ottoman-Turkish territory by Heinrich Schliemann and subsequent archaeological research from the end of the 19th century onwards. A great deal of attention was paid to these excavations by the press. The Homeric world was suddenly revealed to a wide public through photographs and drawings in popular magazines. Troy turned out to lie within the Ottoman Empire, outside Europe, and to be rather different from the dreamy ideas of virtuous middle-class Hellenism. Homer's image needed serious retouching: he had in fact been the court poet of an old and violent society. The epics were not composed for peaceful Hellenic burghers but for warlike Mycenaean nobles. The Homeric verses had resounded through the magnificent palaces of the ruling aristocracy. The texts may have reflected primitive times, but certainly not ancient popular wisdom nor the earliest expressions of humanism and liberalism. Homer sang of an aristocratic elite, not of a bourgeois middle class.

This change of outlook did not mean that Homer was regarded as less suitable reading; quite the contrary. There was simultaneously a sea change in the cultural climate in *fin-de-siècle* Europe. Liberalism was increasingly confronted by popular vitalist, racist and elitist ideologies. Did the future elite, especially that of the British Empire, not need to be drilled through arduous schooling for the global imperial mission? In the heyday of European expansion the duty to excel had to be impressed on education as never before. An aristocratic-imperialist, Mycenaean Homer was even better suited to this end than a bourgeois liberal, Hellenic Homer. The desire to stand out through merit, not only in intellectual achievement, but also in sport and games, was more important than ever. This was true in particular of the British boarding schools, but also of the elite educational institutions in other countries during the highest phase of European expansion and imperialism.

This elitist vision of education reinforced Homer's position in the classical curriculum. National differences aside, European society and education became intensely competitive from the end of the 19th century. Social Darwinism, with its touchstone of *survival of the fittest* and theories on the essential role of the elites gained ground and the moral code of the *Iliad* was subsumed under the motto: *always excel*. After the discovery by cultural philosophers of Homer as the expression of Greek *Volksgeist*, after Homer was made middle-class, the aristocratisation of Homer by imperialists schooled in the classics took over. They appropriated the heroes of the *Iliad* in a particular way. Schoolboys were able to identify with warriors engaged in hazardous enterprises overseas. Homer offered a whole series of heroes as paradigms for schoolboys in the age of colonial expansion.

All Homeric ideals appeared to end in the squalid European war of 1914–1918. Nevertheless, following the war Homer remained required reading in the classical education systems of both the old and the new nation-states of Europe during the 1920s and 1930s. But with the crumbling of liberal predominance in the political regimes of Europe, the Greek bard also lost his unique political position as a liberal *lieu de mémoire*. The old Homer did not have the least significance for either the right or the left of the political spectrum, and he failed to evoke even a trace of recollection. This was down to the fact not so much that 'democrats dislike Homer', as that the classical tradition as such was no longer able to fill its previous dominant inspirational role in modern education.

HOMER AND TROY AS DISPUTABLE *LIEUX DE MÉMOIRE*

The popularity of the *Iliad* coincided with the creation of modern educational systems in Europe. In previous centuries Homer had been studied in Greek by only a handful of devotees. In the 19th and the first half of the 20th century Homer was required reading for innumerous boys and later girls at schools throughout Europe.

Homeric society is today no longer seen as a far-off mirror of the contemporary world. As the distance in history grows and identification in every respect is absent, it becomes difficult to defend Homer as required reading. But Homer's tales remain fantastic popular entertainment. For example the 2004 film *Troy* directed by Wolfgang Petersen, with Brad Pitt as Achilles, was a great success. From oral poetry at the dawn of history, through written text, illustrated, reprinted innumerable times, treated in film and the new media, Homer is now reaching a larger audience than ever before – even without the support of the classical school system.

We now know for certain that Troy was where the ships lay waiting for favourable southern winds to sail through the Dardanelles, which at the time were the only link with the settlements around the Black Sea. Europe's customary claim of ownership is up for debate. The question may legitimately be asked whose *lieu de mémoire* Troy really is. According to recent archaeological research, Troy was an Anatolian fortress falling within the Hittite sphere of influence. This is something to get used to. Trojan origins would then mean Asian origins. Advancing knowledge is dismantling trusted certainties and the identifications of centuries are becoming disputable.

SHAKESPEARE'S *TROILUS AND CRESSIDA*

RUDOLPH GLITZ

To Shakespeare's contemporaries, the legend of Troy felt much closer and more familiar than it does to us. The educated among them first learnt about it in the classrooms of their local grammar schools, where they encountered it through Homer's *Iliad* itself, Roman re-workings of that classic, and numerous exercises and summaries in the humanist textbooks of the day. Yet even outside the schools and universities, many of the stories surrounding the fall of Troy formed part of common knowledge. They were widely disseminated by the first translations of Homer into English fresh from the recently imported printing press, by imaginative adaptations and additions to the legend as can be found for instance in the tales of Boccaccio and the poetry of Chaucer, simply by word of mouth, and last but not least by theatrical dramatizations. What made Troy and the Trojans in particular a matter of public interest in England was their historical connection with the British people: according to medieval and early modern history books, the Roman founder and name-giver of Britain, Brutus of Troy, descended directly from the Trojan hero Aeneas.

It was against this background of widespread popularity, close familiarity, and even presumed kinship with the Trojans that Shakespeare wrote *Troilus and Cressida* (1602) – a play critics count among his darkest, most difficult, but also most prophetically modern works. It largely revolves around the doomed love between one of the sons of King Priam and the daughter of the Trojan priest Calchas. Shakespeare's version of their story can be summarized as follows: the beautiful Cressida loves and is courted by Troilus, who has already proven himself as a warrior and distinguishes himself politically by successfully dissuading his brother Hector from returning Helen to the Greeks. The couple is united by Cressida's uncle Pandarus, but just after their first night together, Cressida is handed over to the Greeks to re-join her father, who has defected, in an exchange of hostages to which Troilus agrees out of patriotism. Once among the Greeks – to the lasting distress and anger of the proverbially 'true' Troilus – the proverbially 'false' Cressida gives in to the suit of her assigned protector Diomedes.

Although loosely based on characters mentioned by Homer, the story of Troilus and Cressida does not appear in the *Iliad*. It was added to the Troy-related folklore by a medieval French poet and popularized in England by Chaucer's celebrated *Troilus and Criseyde* (ca. 1385). However, the setting, battle

Portrait of William Shakespeare (1564-1616), attributed to John Taylor, ca. 1610. Shakespeare's plays comprise 38 tragedies, histories and comedies centring on universal and eternal themes that continue to be drawn on today for theatrical interpretations, operas, musicals and films.

scenes, speeches, and public events in Shakespeare's play are clearly informed by Homer's classic, albeit not always straightforwardly and sometimes through the mediation of other texts. Switching back and forth between Troy and the Greek camp before finally taking us to the battlefield before the city walls, Shakespeare's play shows us such memorable Homeric scenes as the Greeks' war council and the fight between Hector and

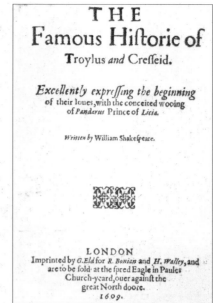

Ajax. It also reflects, at least to a certain extent, the British sympathy with the Trojans. On the one hand, it presents Hector, Troilus, Aeneas, and Paris as pompous and silly but still occasionally glamorous idealists who abide by the chivalric code of honour. On the other hand, it has Thersites, the jester of the Greeks, denounce his own master Ajax as an 'idiot', 'camel', and 'peacock', his general Agamemnon as someone who 'loves quails' (i.e. prostitutes) and 'has not so much brains as earwax', Menelaus as 'both ass and ox' because of the horns of cuckoldry that Paris has put on him, Diomedes as a 'false-hearted rogue', Nestor as a 'stale old mouse-eaten dry cheese', Ulysses as a 'dog-fox', and Patroclus as Achilles' 'masculine whore'.

As Shakespeare's irreverence towards both Trojans and Greeks makes clear, his play is a far cry from Homer's frequent celebrations of their grandeur and heroic exploits. The foul-mouthed Thersites is himself denounced by Ulysses as 'a slave whose gall coins slanders as a mint', yet Shakespeare's play as a whole actually seems to share the jester's cynical perspective on events. Perhaps the most striking example of this is the confrontation between Hector and Achilles near the end of the play. Even the maker of the anti-war movie *Das Boot*, Wolfgang Petersen, felt obliged, in his 2004 production of *Troy*, to present their encounter as a thrilling duel between two paragons of stalwart masculinity. Not so William Shakespeare! In his account of the struggle he has the two warriors meet in the midst of a thoroughly chaotic and undignified to-and-fro on the battle field, where Hector first has the upper hand and foolishly grants Achilles a break from fighting, then chases and kills a random

The Dutch actors Coen Flink and Ellen Vogel in Shakespeare's *Troilus and Cressida*, performed during the Holland Festival in 1959.

Frontispiece of the first edition of *Troilus and Cressida*, 1609.

Greek merely for the pretty armour he is wearing, and finally, while preparing to change into his newly acquired trophy, gets brutally butchered in a surprise attack by Achilles' Myrmidons. The petty and dishonourable reality of war as Shakespeare presents it here was clearly meant to clash with his audience's expectations. It exposes as unreliable not only poetic accounts of war such as Homer's but also, quite generally, what Shakespeare elsewhere calls 'the bubble reputation'.

To the play's thoroughly disillusioning view of warfare, heroism, and fame – a view, by the way, which made it especially popular in the years after World War I – Shakespeare adds an almost equally sobering demolition of the myths of chivalric love. While Troilus and Cressida's relationship is clearly based on mutual attraction and passionately declared by both of them, it is also shown to be governed by male interests and vanities. From the beginning, Troilus speaks of Cressida in commercial terms that, for all their implicit praise, mark her out as little more than a prized possession: 'Her bed is India; there she lies, a pearl, [...] Ourself the merchant'. In his subsequent speech in favour of keeping Helen, the young prince tellingly compares

Troilus and Cressida presented by theatre company Cheek by Jowl in London, 2008.

the taking of a wife to the buying of clothes, which 'honour' and the rules of ownership, rather than love, keep one from returning: 'We turn not back the silks upon the merchant / When we have soiled them'. In such a crudely misogynist context it is hardly surprising that Cressida sees even her own love for Troilus as a threat to her personal autonomy:

> *I have a kind of self resides with you*
> *But an unkind self that itself will leave*
> *To be another's fool.*

Cressida later reproaches herself for her stereotypically female inconstancy, but when the same Troilus whose eloquence and machismo manage to keep Helen in Troy accepts with little protest her handing over to the Greeks and keeps doubting her faithfulness at the moment of their parting, the spectator is given good reason to sympathise with her betrayal – even without considering her vulnerable position among the preying lechers in the Greek camp, where the blunt but honest Diomedes does not seem the worst choice of partner.

With both love and war stripped of their heroic aura and exposed as different expressions of male competitiveness and greed, the ending of *Troilus and Cressida* on the battlefield leaves us with the aftertaste of a world in which nothing is worth 'aught but as 'tis valued', a past world whose reality fails to live up to its future reputation – even though strictly speaking Troilus ends up true, Cressida false, Achilles triumphant, and Hector fallen in battle. In its bleakness, this world resembles that which Ulysses warns his fellow Greeks against in Act I, but which equally threatens the more glamorous-seeming Trojans, and hence perhaps also the British of Shakespeare's own day. Once a community loses its respect for 'degree', Ulysses warns, once it loses its respect, in other words, for the values and distinctions that structure it and are guaranteed by more than merely the fluctuations of the market,

> *Then everything includes itself in power,*
> *Power into will, will into appetite;*
> *And appetite, an universal wolf,*
> *So doubly seconded with will and power,*
> *Must make perforce an universal prey*
> *And last eat up himself.*

TROY IN THE OPERA

HEIN VAN EEKERT

Ominous low chords in the strings. A soprano sings almost monotonously: 'Dark, hideous night, deathly without end, the terrible night of Ilion.' The beautiful Helen is speaking, describing the demise of the great city of Troy from the banks of the Peneios in the opera *Mefistofele* (1868) by Arrigo Boito. As the music starts to rise and a female choir urges the queen to compose herself, Helen speaks of clouds of ashes, the looming shadow of the Greeks and the licking flames. Then the orchestra suddenly falls silent. 'Immediately there is only total silence where once Troy stood.' This one of the few musical retellings of the city's demise, come down to us via Goethe's *Faust* reworked by Boito, who was his own librettist.

THE WAR FOR TROY AS SEEN BY TIPPETT

In terms of opera, cantata and song, the story of the war for Troy is in the first instance a history of the period before and the period afterwards. Composers are less interested in Homer's lengthy recounts of who struck which enemy in what part of the chest with a spear or a stone. When the battle or the downfall is turned to music it is primarily, as with Sir Michael Tippett's masterful *King Priam* (1961), given from the viewpoint of those witnessing it from a distance. Tippett takes us above all to the chambers of various Trojans to hear their reactions to what is going on outside the city walls – Andromache's despair, Helen's inapproachability or Hecuba's doggedness alternate with Paris or Hector arriving to report what is happening in battle. In the other camp, Achilles is sitting in his tent, singing about his fatherland to the accompaniment of the guitar – Homer after all describes him as playing the lute. He sends Patroclus into battle and receives Priam to negotiate over Hector's body.

While Tippett does base his work on events in the *Iliad*, his opera is not a musical version of the epic. This is true in the first instance because so much more happens in *King Priam*. We see the birth of Paris, the Judgement of Paris, in which the singers playing Hecuba, Andromache and Helen double up as Athena, Hera and Aphrodite, and the death of Achilles and Priam. The composer is more interested in what in Homer's epic seems to serv as an intermezzo: the sadness, frustration and fear in those involved in the war. Martial music in the brass section and shouts from the choir in the background provide reports from the battlefield in musical form. Tippett's Achilles is like the character drawn by the Greek poet – a man full of rage – but as soon as this hero joins the battle, we hear him only from a distance, through his enraged battle cry that is heard by Priam and his sons on the walls of Troy. The cry found its way into the three *Songs for Achilles* for tenor and guitar, in which Tippett combines Achilles' song accompanied by the guitar in the tent, as we hear it sung in the opera, with two others. Achilles' battle cry sounds in the second song, once Patroclus has gone on to the field of battle, while in the third he speaks to his mother Thetis about his comrade's death.

Tippett's opera is one of the most moving musical evocations of the Troy story: ageing Priam becomes a sorrowful, occasionally emotional and even aggressive King Lear, and the three major female figures are beautifully contrasted. The music emphasises the significance of the libretto, does not skirt round the violence of the story, but also radiates incredible intimacy in a number of scenes. After Achilles has promised Priam the body of his son Hector, they meditate together on death: Achilles will die at the hands of Priam's son and Priam will be killed by Achilles' son Neoptolemus.

THE FALL OF THE CITY AS SEEN BY BERLIOZ

Hector Berlioz, like Tippett and Boito his own librettist, also shows us the fall of the city: and once again not the final battle itself but mainly the run-up to it, as seen through the eyes of Cassandra. In the first two acts of *Les Troyens* (1858) she is the focus of attention. As the woman who foresees and understands everything, but who is not believed by those around her, she knows as much as the audience but is equally powerless to do anything about it. She bears witness to the report on the death of the priest Laocoön and his sons, and she looks on with horror at the entrance of the Wooden Horse. She is powerless against Sinon, who was cut by the composer from the final version of his work. Berlioz has his opera begin at the scene depicted by the following verses from Virgil:

> *So all the Trojan land was free of its long sorrow.*
> *The gates were opened: it was a joy to go and see*
> *the Greek camp,*
> *the deserted site and the abandoned shore.*
> *Here the Dolopians stayed, here cruel Achilles...*
> (Virgil, *Aeneid* 2.26-29, translated by A.S. Kline)

When the Trojans at the start of Berlioz' masterpiece walk about freely outside the walls for the first time again, driven on in restless ecstasy by the orchestra's rapidly resounding quavers, they find lances, spears, helmets and a huge shield on the plain. The Greeks appear to have fled in panic. 'Quel potrons que ces grecs!' (What cowards, these Greeks!) Berlioz has them sing, but then a Trojan soldier says: 'Do you know whose tent stood here? That of Achilles!' The mere name of this Greek hero causes the people to flinch. 'Remain here! Achilles is dead,' says the soldier. 'Look, here is his grave.' Only then everyone recalls once more that Paris has slain the superhero.

Berlioz turns a few verses from Virgil's *Aeneid* into a beautiful dramatic scene: before the Trojans rush off to the Wooden Horse standing on the banks of the Scamander, to make way for a deeply dismayed Cassandra, this scene reminds the audience of the fear that the Trojans have lived through. Achilles stands symbol for this fear: even after his death, the mere idea of his former presence fills everyone with dread.

The fact that Berlioz is an admirer of Virgil – or rather became one after hating the complicated verses as a teenager –

has led to there being a direct line between classical poet and composer: in *Les Troyens* Berlioz translates Virgil's lines to the opera stage. He is able to do this, by his own account, only with the help of a great playwright: Shakespeare. Berlioz, who is both composer and librettist of Les Troyens, learns something of stagecraft from Shakespeare. Moreover Shakespeare, and not Virgil, is the source for the words Dido and Aeneas sing to each other at night on the coast of Carthage: a dialogue taken from *The Merchant of Venice* serves as model for a great love duet, to ensure that the two actually have something to say to each other at this joyful moment, before the appearance of Mercury with the simple word, 'Italy!' puts an end to their bliss.

CAVALLI AND OTHERS ON QUEEN DIDO

The role of Aeneas in Berlioz' opera is a difficult one, and tenors will say that four voices are in fact needed to interpret it properly. Nevertheless he does not come into his own in *Les Troyens* to the extent of the *leading ladies* of this opera, Cassandra and Dido. In *La Didone* (1641) by Francesco Cavalli (1602-1671), which makes use of roughly the same narrative material as Les Troyens, somewhat more attention is given to his lot. We see him in conversation with his father Anchises, his mother Venus and, following her death, with the shade of his wife Creusa. Woven through all of this is the ill-starred love between Cassandra and the warrior Coroebus, and there is an opportunity for a moving lament by Hecuba. Sinon, here a booming bass part – and not as in Berlioz a guileful tenor – lumbers across the stage in unsubtle and boorish triumph. In the background we hear voices calling to arms.

In *La Didone* Cavalli and librettist Gian Francesco Busenello stick closely to the *Aeneid*, although they allow Dido to live, following a moving lament, in order to marry her former archenemy, the African King Iarbas, who moves through the second part of the opera as a besotted dreamer. Nevertheless we get much more of Virgil from this work that from *Dido and Aeneas* by Henry Purcell, which enjoys the greatest popularity as a result of its beautiful melodies and its moving, if somewhat one-sided, image of Dido. There is not much in the way of *Aeneid* elements to be found in this short opera, in which witches – possibly stand-ins for nasty anti-English Catholics – decide on the fate of Carthage's queen.

For the rest, Dido comes out strongly in the opera repertoire. Pietro Metastasio (1698-1782), who had translated the *Iliad* into Italian verse by the age of 12, had a hit with his first libretto,

The Wooden Horse of Troy on the stage of the opera *Les Troyens (The Trojans)* by Hector Berlioz, during a production by the Royal Opera House in London, 2012.

Didone abbandonata (Dido Abandoned) in 1724. Metastasio's libretto does not follow Virgil slavishly but includes a generous role for Iarbas, who wanders through Dido's palace in disguise and under the pseudonym Arbace. Dido's sister is renamed Selene. The libretto was initially set to music by Domenico Scarro, but it proved popular and was re-used frequently. Scarro's interpreters of the roles of Dido and Aeneas themselves appeared in a further two versions of Metastasio's *Didone* – by the composers Tommaso Albinoni and Nicola Porpora respectively. Around 50 composers, including Niccolò Jomelli and Baldesarre Galuppi, were ultimately to compose Dido operas using Metastasio's libretto, occasionally having it adapted it to their own needs. Thus, the encounter between the Trojan hero Aeneas and Dido, Queen of Carthage, became one of the most popular themes in the repertoire, probably surpassed only by that between the Saracen sorceress Armida and the crusader Rinaldo in *Gerusalemme liberata* by Tarquato Tasso, and perhaps by Jason and Medea.

On the long list of Metastasio composers we find the German composer Johann Adolf Hasse, who came up with a version in 1742 that he reworked a year later. Earlier in his career he had focused, along with librettist Luigi Maria Stampiglia, on an earlier part of the *Aeneid*: Aeneas' visit to the island of Chaonia, where he meets the Trojan Helenus who has meanwhile married Andromache, the widow of his fallen brother Hector (*Aenea in Caonia* from 1727). Giuseppe Sarti, who also has two versions of *Didone* to his name, followed Aeneas to Italy in *Enea nel Lazio* (1799), which was written for Saint Petersburg.

There is a long list of cantatas with a role for Dido, some with, but more often without, Aeneas. She is an evocative figure. In the early Renaissance, her welcoming of death in 'Dulces exuviae, dum fata deusque sinebat' (*Aeneid* 4.651-660) was set to music by various composers, including Josquin Desprez and Roland de Lassus. Her suffering continued to resound into the 19th century in operas, lieder and other music, usually centring on her suicide.

THEMES ON THE TROJAN WAR

A summary of the operas and musical pieces on the Troy theme thus becomes a poor version of the second book of Homer's *Iliad*: names, number of versions and specific characteristics, running the danger that its author, by contrast with the Greek genius, can never aim for completeness, because libretti – in particular in the 17th and 18th centuries – are often re-used and it is by and large impossible to provide a complete and correct summary without ending up with something that has all the attractions of long groceries list.

The extensive way in which Francesco Cavalli dealt with the narrative material serves as example: his first opera is *Le Nozze di Teti e di Peleo* (1639) about the wedding of Thetis and

Peleus, with Discordia who tosses the notorious golden apple, as the sole contralto among the leading roles. With *Il Rapimento d'Helen* (The abduction of Helen, also known simply as *Elena*) from 1659, *La Deidamia* (a lost work from 1644 about the successful attempt to have an unwilling Achilles participate in the Trojan War) and *La Didone*, Cavalli runs through the most important events around the war, without turning to music anything related to Homer's *Iliad*.

The *Iliad* leaves most composers cold. They prefer to concentrate on subsequent events, as related by Virgil in his *Aeneid* and in Homer's Odyssey, or in the various wanderings, homeward voyages and homecomings of other Greek and Trojan heroes, or also on the departure for Troy.

Le Nozze di Teti e di Peleo by Rossini, *The Judgement of Paris* by John Eccles, *Paride ed Elena* by Gluck and *La belle Hélène* by Jacques Offenbach are the best known works dealing with the causes of the war. The operas telling of departure or homecoming are much more numerous. Various versions of *Ifigenia* and *Iphigénie* being sacrificed by her father in the city of Aulis bear witness to this, as well as Campra's *Idomenée* and Mozart's *Idomeneo*, or *Die ägyptische Helena* by Richard Strauss; Odysseus musical dramas like Monteverdi's *Il ritorno d'Ulisse in patria*, *Ulisse*, the *tragédie lyrique* by Jean Féry Rebel (in which the enchantress Circe follows Odysseus to Ithaca), Gluck's *Telemaco*, Gabriel Fauré's *Penelope* (in which her beloved son Telemachus is quite notably absent) and Luigi Dallapicola's *Ulisse*; a large number of operas dedicated to Andromache, some of which were inspired by the *Andromaque* by Jean Racine, like the opera of the same name by André Grétry of Rossini's magnificent *Ermione*.

ACHILLES

This is bad news for Achilles, whose *finest hour* strikes just at the moment of the battle for Troy and who thus gets a raw deal as operatic hero. Little of the serious, but awe-inspiring hero in Tippett's *King Priam* or the terrifying, even if no longer living, warrior in *Les Troyens* by Berlioz, whose name alone sows panic, is found in the majority of operas about Achilles. For example, listen to the countertenor Philippe Jaroussky on his cd *Caldara in Vienna* sing a lovely aria as concluding piece. All ear-teasing *pizzicati* from the violins and a melting song line, repeated in whispered tones by a choir: 'If you are able to chain a heart and inflame a soul, what can you not do, tyrannous love?' This is the hero too: a still-young Achilles who sounds as though he could not hurt a fly through the libretto of Pietro Metastasio and music of composer Antonio Caldara, With his high-pitched, and, to our 21st century ear, feminine sounding voice, he sings a song during a meal presented to Odysseus. Odysseus comes to fetch him but is forced to realise that the girl standing singing in front of him is in fact Achilles in women's dress.

Popular among composers of the 17th and 18th centuries is the post-Homeric story – chronicled in the *Achilleid* by Statius – of Achilles' youth spent on the island of Scyros, where his mother Thetis has hidden him, aware that participating in the Trojan War would spell his death. King Lycomedes has him running around dressed as a girl; although the dress does not prevent Princess Deidamia from falling head over heels in love with the young hero. Things become complicated once Odysseus turns up on the island, with a prediction of his own as motivation: without Achilles the Greeks will never be able to take Troy.

The story has at first view a comic slant: a young man in a dress is always good for a laugh, but the story gets even better when the Greek envoys start paying court to the ladies on Scyros, including Achilles dressed up as Pyrrha. It is an outstanding story for a large-scale ceremonial occasion, such as the very first production of an opera outside court: in 1640 the Teatro Novissimo in Venice opened its doors with a production of *La finta pazza* (The Feigned Madwoman) by Francesco Sacrati. In it *Deidamia* pretends to be mad, in order to keep her beloved Achilles on Scyros by this means. The audience is played to when a eunuch asks whether there is a doctor in the house. At the same time the gods appearing in the story point the spectators to the fact that there is a direct link between the Fall of Troy and the rise of Venice. The role of Achilles is sung by a castrato: while 17th and 18th century audiences associated this voice type with the young lover, it is also useful for a convincing disguise as a girl.

The story works well as libretto, and versions of Deidamia by other composers follow in the years after *La finta pazza*. In 1736 Pietro Metastasio – who wrote *Didone abbandonata* – writes an *Achille in Sciro* in 18 days, a libretto that is passed from hand to hand. Composers largely unknown to the wider public, like Caldara, Chiarini, Corselli and Sarro, set the words to music with a high-voiced Achilles as the hero. For his *Deidamia* Handel makes use of a libretto by Paolo Antonio Rolli that focuses primarily on the feelings of the girl and her interaction with Ulisse/Odysseus. Achilles, sung at the premiere by a 20-year-old woman, storms through the opera with youthful exuberance. When he finally exchanges his dress for armour, he sings that he will raze Troy to the ground in an aria full of pubertal arrogance, emphasised with magnificently boastful musical heroics: 'That kingdom's fate depends purely on my hatred. By my deeds the pilgrim will say, Troy once stood here.' Deidamia is the one that holds our sympathy, thanks partly to the colourful and sensitive musical portrait that Handel draws of her. She accuses Odysseus of destroying her future in the delicate aria 'M'hai resa infelice' – 'You have made me unhappy. How can you be proud of that?' Her sorrow sounds so sensitive and adult that it is clear Handel perceives that girls are always a bit

more advanced than boys at an emotional level. Here we hear a foreshadowing of the 10 years older sorrow-wracked Deidamia from the epic *The Fall of Troy* by Quintus Smyrnaeus. In a moving central section the girl explodes at the hero, with more than a little insight into his future, that he should be cast into eternal night by a severe storm when within sight of his safe harbour. Odysseus, sung originally by a castrato, is not unfeeling towards *Deidamia*'s situation, which after all resembles that of his wife Penelope. He, and not Achilles, turns out to be her true counterpart, with whom she sings the opera's only duet, although she is in reality pledged to Achilles. Handel's *Deidamia* is an opera full of youthful effervescence, overshadowed constantly by a veil of doom and grief.

Achilles soon find another love in Iphigenia. In *Iphigénie en Aulide* (1774) by Gluck (with a libretto by François Gand-Leblanc du Roullet based on Euripides via Racine) he is not merely the bait that is to lure Iphigenia to Aulis to be sacrificed; but he also gains her as his wife through divine intervention, as the operatic conventions of the time demanded a happy ending.

On the field of battle at Troy there is at first just one genuine operatic heroine: the slave Briseis. She is far from home, her love for Achilles is thwarted by the commander of the Greeks, Agamemnon, and she thus suddenly has to cope with two lovers, only one of whom she desires. What is more: once returned by Agamemnon to Achilles, she provides for a (temporary) happy end because Achilles then returns to join the battle against the Trojans once more. Her fate lies at the centre of *La Briseïda* (1768) by Antonio Rodríguez de Hita (1724-1787): a *zarzuela* (Spanish opera with spoken dialogue) in Italian style in which Achilles and Briseis are both played by sopranos and Agamemnon and Patroclus also have high-pitched voices. The story is told again in *Achille* (1801) by Ferdinando Paer, drawing the hero into the Italian bel canto style. As supple tenor he takes on the baritone of Agamemnon, sending his comrade Patroclus into battle after a duet in which they call on the help of the gods in a musically exciting way. As Patroclus is a part for a bass voice, he cuts almost an elder brother or fatherly figure alongside Achilles. Giuseppe Nicolini and a young Gaetano Donizetti also transform the narrative material into bel canto in *L'ira d'Achille* dating to 1815 and 1817 respectively.

SCENES FROM THE *ILIAD*

Scenes taken from the *Iliad* that are not directly linked to the conflict are usually too brief for a full opera. Schiller tries to make something of the scene between Hector, Andromache and their little son Astyanax on the walls of Troy, but he overplays his hand by shifting them to the point just before the fight between Achilles and Hector. In addition he leaves out Astyanax in his 'Hector's Abschied' as a result of which the scene loses its tenderness. In 1815 Schubert turns it into a duet as though part

Deidamia

G.F.Händel

Concerto Köln

15 mrt – 1 apr 2012 www.dno.nl

De**NEDER LANDSE OPERA**

het muziektheater
the amsterdam
music theatre

of an Italian operatic scene: a beautiful opportunity for male and female singing parts to show their dramatic musical talents. Antonio Contis writes a solo scene for Cassandra in which the fight between Hector and Achilles is reported. Johann Christoph Friedrich Bach set the words to music around 1769, while Benedetto Marcello did the same 40 years previously.

The youthful Nicola Manfroce (1791-1813) in his *Ecuba* from 1812 links the hero Achilles to yet another woman: Priam's daughter Polyxena. Jean-Baptiste Lully, who designated himself the inventor of French opera, had attempted this much earlier, but died before completing his work. *Ecuba* had its premiere in Naples: Manuel Garcia, father of the singing prodigies Maria Malibran and Pauline Viardot, sang the tenor part of Achilles, which he had also sung a couple of months earlier in Gluck's *Iphigénie*. As Neapolitan audiences were crazy about tenors, Priam was also given a high male voice. The story turns on Hecuba: she is unable to forget Hector's death and sees in a peacemaking marriage between her daughter and the Greek hero a chance to kill the latter. In the nature of things this makes for enormous internal conflict in Polyxena, who is truly in love with the Greek. This kind of situation provides plentiful scope for arias and fiery ensembles, with the death of Achilles and the subsequent razing of Troy as climax.

This should have rounded off Achilles' musical biography if Othmar Schoeck had not come up with an exceptionally taut opera in 1927 in which Achilles takes on the Amazons. *Penthesileia* is based on a play by Heinrich von Kleist (1771-1811) in which the heroine of the title is to blame for Achilles' death, by contrast with the version in the first book of Quintus Smyrnaeus *The Fall of Troy*, after which she also dies from inconsolable grief. The scenes between Achilles, a low baritone part, and the Amazon burn with mutual eroticism and the music gives full rein to depicting the raw tumult of battle.

Is it coincidental that this war story is taken up again by composers in the war-ridden 20th century? *Troades* by Aribert Reimann, which begins with the prologue between Athena and Poseidon declaimed over crushing hard organ tones, depicts the fate of Hecuba, Cassandra and Andromache in the words of Franz Werfel's translation of Euripides. Cassandra gives voice to her madness as a modern Lucia di Lammermoor and *Andromache's farewell* to her little son Astyanax inspires Reimann to extremely dramatic music. The same scene, this time translated into English, forms the basis of Samuel Barber's Andromache's Farewell.

AN INCOMPLETE LIST

And there we have it. What was intended not to be a dry summary of the works has become precisely that, whereby the author regrets that he has been unable to find space in this list for Walton's *Troilus and Cressida*, Kreutzer's *Astyanax*, Kraus' *Aeneas i Carthago* and Trojahn's *Orest* (in which Menelaus and Helen have significant roles) and has been unable to do anything about Schubert's other Troy lied 'Memnon', or Jarrell's melodrama *Cassandre*.

As the war continues to rage – the son of Achilles is slain in operas by Rossini and Grétry by the son of Agamemnon, so that Hector's widow is released and is able to marry her brother-in-law – so the list of Troy-based operas will continue to grow over the years ahead: not so much because new works are being written apace, but rather as older works are dusted off. It is time now to vanish singing into the night of the kingdom of fables along with Helen from Boito's *Mefistofele*.

Poster for the opera *Deidamia* by George Frideric Handel (1685-1759), performed by De Nederlandse Opera (The Dutch Opera) in 2012.

7 SCHLIEMANN AND THE REDISCOVERY OF TROY

HEINRICH SCHLIEMANN, SCIENTIST AND ROMANTIC?

GERT JAN VAN WIJNGAARDEN

Heinrich Schliemann is probably the most famous archaeologist of all time. The numerous biographies and television documentaries about him, along with the more than 600,000 hits when his name is googled, demonstrate this. But Schliemann's fame emerges more particularly from the way the mention of his name evokes reaction from a wide public: admiration on occasion, but also ridicule and a certain degree of contempt.

Admiration predominated in the years immediately after his death in 1890. Colleagues lauded Schliemann on the grounds of his services to archaeology and the significance of his discoveries. E Ludwig's 1931 biography may best be described as hagiographic. But after the Second World War increasing attention was paid to the contradictions in Schliemann's life and to the ways in which his archaeological results were achieved. A 1995 biography by DA Traill (1995) goes so far as to call him a pathological liar and a fraud. In recent years a more nuanced picture of Heinrich Schliemann has emerged, for example in the catalogue of the 2002 German exhibition *Troia. Traum und Wirklichkeit (Troy. Dream and Reality)*, in which he is portrayed as a romantic who generated his own myth.

It is evident that the man who, in his own words, chased the dream of his youth and went on to discover ancient Troy is an evocative figure. But who in fact was this man? And why does he continue to cause controversy?

PERSONAL LIFE

A great deal is known about Heinrich Schliemann as he kept a diary and was a copious letter writer. And he kept a careful record of what he wrote. This information trove has led to a number of biographies. These supplement the autobiographical forewords that he himself wrote to various archaeological publications. An autobiography edited by his wife Sophia was published following his death.

Drawing from Heinrich Schliemann's book *Troja* (1884) showing Schliemann sketching seated on a wall in Troy. Schliemann is often accused of having destroyed a great deal as a result of his extensive excavations. But his publications were good and richly furnished with illustrations of artefacts and architecture.

Johann Ludwig Heinrich Julius Schliemann was born on 6 January 1822 in Neubukow, a small German town near the Baltic. He was the son of a Lutheran pastor, who was transferred two years after Heinrich's birth to the village of Ankershagen, where there is now a museum in the house of the the Schliemann family. The family was poor and suffered setbacks. Heinrich's mother died when he was 10, and his father had to give up his career after being accused of fraud. Schliemann had to abandon his ambition of a university education, finding work instead with a shipping company.

After recovering from an illness, Schliemann decided in 1841 to try his luck elsewhere and he boarded a ship bound for Venezuela. The vessel was shipwrecked, and he ended up in Amsterdam. He soon showed a talent for learning languages, and by the end of his life he had mastered English, French, Dutch, Italian, Spanish, Portuguese, Swedish, Polish, Greek, Latin, Russian, Arabic and Turkish, along with his native German. He knew most of these languages well enough to be able to publish and correspond in them.

Schliemann's knowledge of Russian led to his being sent to St Petersburg as an agent in 1846. A few years later he left for the United States where he amassed a fortune during the Californian Gold Rush. In 1850 he became a US citizen, but returned to Russia where he engaged in various kinds of trading. He was particularly successful in the sale of saltpetre, sulphur and lead – components needed for munitions – to the Russian government during the Crimean War 1854-1856. After 1858 Schliemann was rich enough to retire and to pursue his dreams.

The love of Schliemann's youth had been Minna Meincke, whom he had hoped to marry after his time in the United States, but she did not wait for him and married someone else. Schliemann continued to correspond with her for the rest of his life, and he never again fell truly in love. In Russia he married Katherina Lyschin, who bore him three children: Sergei, Natalia and Nadeshda. Katherina was accustomed to a luxury lifestyle and could not understand why her husband chose to lead the life of an intellectual and archaeologist. She left him, and Schliemann used his US citizenship to divorce her. He subsequently commissioned a friend to find him a young and subservient Greek wife, who was required to love Homer. In 1869 he married Sophia Engastromenos, who was 17 at the time and 30 years his junior. Sophia had everything that

Portrait of Heinrich Schliemann (1822-1890), painted in 1877 by Sidney Hodges.

the Dutch island of Texel. However, archival sources indicate that the ship ran aground on the island and that those aboard were able to disembark easily. Schliemann ended up in Amsterdam, finding work as a messenger with the Hoyak & Co trading company. He subsequently became bookkeeper with the trading company Schröder & Co., which was based at 71 Keizersgracht. He lived in Amsterdam for almost five years, from 1841 to 1846.

Schliemann lived in a house on the corner of Bloemgracht and Tweede Leliedwarsstraat, a 'miserable, unheated garret' in his own words. It was in this room that he began his tireless study of languages, beginning with English, French and Russian and using a method consisting of reading out loud every day. This did not endear him to his co-residents in the thin-walled house, and Schliemann was compelled to move during his Russian studies. On account of his knowledge of this language he was given the opportunity in 1846 to open a branch of Schröder & Co. in St Petersburg.

In Amsterdam Schliemann discovered his trading talent and his facility with languages. He continued to correspond with friends in the Netherlands all his life, in particular with the Prussian consul W Hepner. Schliemann returned just once to the Netherlands. In 1875, and by then famous, he visited Queen Sophia at Huis ten Bosch in The Hague. He presented her with six Greek terracotta figurines, two of which were fakes as it was subsequently discovered. A letter has been found in Schliemann's correspondence in which he asks his wife to buy a number of figurines for the queen at an antiquary in Athens. The famous archaeologist was evidently not able to excavate everything himself.

SCHLIEMANN AND TROY
According to his own version of events, Schliemann's fascination with Troy began in childhood when his father read the *Iliad* to him and gave him a copy of L. Jerrer's *Illustrated history of the world* (1829). However, it is more likely that he became interested in Homer during one of his trips in his middle years. He finally found the opportunity in 1868 to undertake the trip of his dreams, arriving on the plains of Troy after first visiting Ithaca, Mycenae, Athens and Istanbul.

Schliemann, like others, initially believed a mound near Pinarbaşi was the site of ancient Troy. However, a number of trial excavations there yielded nothing. Following a meeting with the British diplomat and commercial representative Frank Calvert he became convinced by Calvert's theory that Troy must have lain at the mound of Hisarlik. In 1870 he carried out an exploratory excavation there without the permission of the authorities or the owners of the land. The following year he started the systematic excavations that would, with interruptions, continue until shortly before his death in 1890.

Schliemann desired: she was pretty and she was interested in Antiquity. She accompanied him on his expeditions and stands immortalised in the photograph showing her wearing jewels from Priam's Treasure. The marriage produced two children: Andromache and Agamemnon. But Sophia was a weak personality and Schliemann was jealous of her youth. In the end they lived separately.

On his return from Germany to Athens, Schliemann stopped over in Naples in 1890. After a visit to Pompeii on Christmas Day he collapsed on the street, dying later in hospital. His friends carried his body to Athens where his grave may still be seen.

SCHLIEMANN AND THE NETHERLANDS
On 1 December 1841 Schliemann sailed from Hamburg as a cabin boy with the brig Dorothea bound for Venezuela. According to Schliemann's autobiography, a severe storm arose, and passengers and crew had to abandon ship, after which they floated for hours before being washed ashore on the beach of

Schliemann was initially disappointed by the finds, which scarcely seemed to correspond to the picture of the wealthy Troy of Homer. But on 31 May 1873, just after he had decided to halt the excavations, he discovered a group of golden, silver and other metal objects, that has become known as Priam's Treasure. Aside from the jewels that Schliemann allowed his wife Sophia to pose wearing, the treasure contained a gold cup with two ears that he compared with the *depas amphikypellon* mentioned in the *Iliad* (*Iliad* 1.584; 6.220).

For Schliemann this was proof that he had found the remains of Homeric Troy. Rapid publication of details of the excavations and the treasure in the book *Trojanische Altertümer* (Trojan Antiquities) (Leipzig 1874), made him world famous as the excavator of Troy – and gave rise to his first detractors.

DISCOVERER OF THE AEGEAN BRONZE AGE

The discovery of Troy spurred investigation into other locations mentioned in Homer's epics. Between excavation campaigns in Troy, Schliemann also conducted excavations at various sites in

Schliemann and his wife Sophie during excavations at Mycenae, shown on Schliemann's mausoleum in Athens. The mausoleum was designed by the Austrian architect Ernst Ziller using as model the Temple of Athena Nike on the Athens Acropolis. The frieze depicts scenes from the *Iliad* and from Schliemann's life. On the monument significant finds from Troy are depicted.

the Aegean region. Many of them are now known as centres of the Mycenaean culture (ca. 1600-1100 BC), which probably served as inspiration for the Homeric and other Greek myths. Schliemann was not always able to excavate where he wanted. For example he was unable on account of political tensions to excavate at Knossos on Crete, where the British archaeologist Sir Arthur Evans later discovered the Minoan palace. At Pylos Schliemann looked for the palace of Nestor, but it was found by the US archaeologist C Blegen only in 1939 and at a completely different site from where Schliemann had looked. The site of the palace of Odysseus on Ithaca remains undiscovered.

The excavations at Mycenae, the city of the Greek leader Agamemnon in the *Iliad,* and the publication of the findings in 1878 confirmed Schliemann's renown as an archaeologist of genius. He had shown that Greek culture had flourished during periods before Classical Antiquity, and that archaeology was a suitable method to research these early times. Schliemann's reception at the British Archaeological Association in London in 1877 and his membership of many scientific institutes all over the world turned him into a scientist with a status well beyond his education and training.

SCHLIEMANN'S EXCAVATIONS

1867	Ithaca – trial excavations
1868	Pinarbaşi – trial excavations
1870	Troy – (illegal) trial excavations
1871-1873	Troy
1874	Mycenae – (illegal) trial excavations
1875	Orchomenos – Treasury of Minyas
1876	Mycenae
1878	Ithaca
1878-1879	Troy
1880-1881	Orchomenos
1882-1883	Troy
1884	Marathon, Tiryns; Nauplia
1888	Cythera, Sphacteria
1890	Troy – International Troy Conference

THE CONTROVERSIES

Schliemann's archaeological work was surrounded by controversy from the start. One of his sharpest critics in the initial years was the amateur archaeologist Ernst Bötticher, who insisted that Schliemann's finds at Hisarlik could not possibly have anything to do with ancient Troy. There are still many, including scholars like Frank Kolb, who openly doubt that the site of ancient Troy is at Hisarlik. The background to this discussion is of course the question whether archaeology is in any sense able to reveal ancient myths.

Less theoretical is the issue of who really discovered Troy. Although Schliemann acknowledged that he was spurred on by Frank Calvert's idea that Troy must have lain at Hisarlik, he unambiguously put himself forward as the finder. More significantly, he openly obstructed Calvert in his attempts to do his own research. Nevertheless, it is absolutely clear that the idea came from Calvert. At the same time, it was Schliemann's capital and energy that were needed to substantiate the idea and to make the discovery known to the world in spectacular fashion.

Controversy surrounds Priam's Treasure, which was, according to Schliemann, excavated by himself and Sophia while their contracted workers were having lunch. It is evident that this is not true, as Sophia was in any event not in Troy on the appointed day. Schliemann smuggled the treasure out of the country in an act that caused him a great deal of difficulty with the Ottoman authorities (see 7.2). Following a court case, he was obliged to pay the Ottoman Empire a large sum of money. The treasure itself has also become the subject of doubt. Were the artefacts really all found together? Some even believe that Schliemann had the treasure made or simply bought it, or parts of it. Although it will never be possible to disprove the latter, subsequent finds of gold in Troy have shown that several items in the treasure have good archaeological parallels.

The most significant controversy is in fact the issue whether this 'most famous archaeologist' really was a good archaeologist or not. He had had scarcely any archaeological training, but was ultimately awarded an honorary doctorate at the University of Rostock. His archaeological interpretations were, to put it mildly, somewhat one-sided: all the material evidence was interpreted in the light of the *Iliad* and the *Odyssey.* Many, if not most of, Schliemann's conclusions turned out later to be incorrect. The most remarkable revision certainly is that Priam's Treasure did not originate from the time of the Trojan War, as Schliemann believed, but must be dated at least 1,000 years earlier. Although he paid attention to archaeological stratigraphy, Schliemann failed for a long time to realise that he was digging right through Troy's most important layers. But in 1890, the year of his death, he acknowledged that he had been wrong.

In contrast to his shortcomings as an archaeologist it is noteworthy that Schliemann described his archaeological finds and their location extremely precisely. His publications are full of detailed sketches, many of them of unappealing pottery items or of small objects like spindle whorls. His books on Troy provide a good overview of the material culture. And modern archaeologists could take Schliemann as an example with regard to the speed and comprehensiveness with which he published.

Heinrich Schliemann was clearly a controversial man. He was by no means always honest. From his initial campaigns in 1870 on he smuggled finds out of the country, and there are demonstrable errors in his publications, diaries and letters. At the same time his energy and decisiveness changed the archaeology of the Greek world for good. Schliemann has himself become part of the Trojan myth.

SCHLIEMANN AND THE OTTOMAN TURKS

GÜNAY USLU

The excavations of Heinrich Schliemann (1822-1890) at Hisarlık in the second half of the 19th century are definitely among the most imposing archaeological activities that took place in the Ottoman territories. With Homer as a significant source of inspiration in 19th century Europe, Schliemann's first campaign of excavations in search of the historicity of the *Iliad* between 1870-1874 was impressive and received global acclaim. It resulted in his discovery of what he believed to be Homeric Troy, and the finding of what has been termed Priam's Treasure, which he illegally removed from the Empire.

There has been a great deal of valuable historical research into Schliemann's archaeological activities in the Troad. Most research, however, relies largely on Western sources. Hardly any attention has been paid to the archaeological concerns and interests of the Ottomans themselves. In fact, what was the Ottoman attitude towards Heinrich Schliemann's first campaign of excavations and the illegal transportation of Priam's Treasure? Ottoman official correspondence sheds more light on the role of the Ottoman Empire regarding the archaeological research on their territory in the 19th century and their involvement and interest in the Trojan heritage.

SCHLIEMANN'S EXPERIMENTAL EXCAVATIONS AND OTTOMAN REACTIONS

Schliemann's enthusiasm to start excavations on the hill of Hisarlık was born during his first visit to the Troad in 1868, in which he conducted experimental excavations and met Frank Calvert (1828-1908), who believed that Hisarlık was the site of Troy. After this meeting, Schliemann asked Calvert, as an influential inhabitant of the Dardanelles, to arrange a permit for him to excavate at Hisarlık. However, Calvert's attempts were not successful. From 9to 19April 1870, Schliemann actually conducted excavations on the north-western corner of the hill without a formal permit and without approval from the two Turkish owners.

In his aim to control the site, Schliemann asked Calvert, in several letters, to buy the land from the Turkish owners for him as soon and as cheaply as possible. However, the two owners refused to sell the field at any price. Schliemann was not able to continue his excavations. In fact, his unauthorized excavations caused irritation on the Ottoman side. He was faced with formidable obstacles. Besides, Schliemann had boasted of

Letter from Ottoman Education Minister Safvet Pasha (1814-1883) to Grand Vizier Mehmed Emin Âli Pasha (1815-1871) on Schliemann's request for permission to excavate at Hisarlık (20 June 1871). Schliemann's trial excavations without the permission of the Ottoman authorities and his attempts to buy the site from the local owners had not escaped the minister's attention. Safvet Pasha makes clear in the letter that he has instructed the governor of the Dardanelles to buy the land in Hisarlık for the Imperial Museum. He emphasises the great significance of Troy's city walls.

Mehmed Emin Âli Pasha was one of the most prominent reforming politicians of the late Ottoman Empire. Apart from being a politician, he was also a linguist and scientist of note. He represented the Ottoman sultan at the Conference of Paris in 1856 that brought the Crimean War to an end.

the arbitrary way he had proceeded and having acted without authorization. As a result of this, he was obliged to tender his regrets to the Minister of Public Instruction, Safvet Paşa, on 31 August 1870. Nevertheless, there was little chance of obtaining a permit to excavate since the government was opposed to it. As a matter of fact, the Ottoman Turks themselves were also

SCHLIEMANN'S EXCAVATION PERMIT

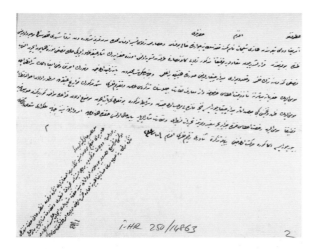

Letter from Grand Vizier Mehmed Emin Âli Pasha to the palace secretary of Sultan Abdülaziz (1830-1876) about Schliemann's request to excavate at Hisarlık (29 June 1871). In the letter the grand vizier emphasises the significance of the quest for Troy. He sees major advantages for science and for the understanding of human development in the excavations and possible discovery of the city walls and artefacts. He subsequently lays down conditions for the excavation, which are later ratified by the palace secretary through royal decree (text below left on the photograph). The conditions stipulated that Schliemann had to finance his excavations himself, including the cost of the Ottoman supervisor. The decree also laid down equal division of the antiquities discovered between the Imperial Museum and Schliemann. This was the normal course taken whenever foreigners received permission to excavate up until the Ottoman Antiquities Act took effect in 1874 and 1884. In conclusion the decree also promulgated conditions regarding the conservation of the city walls and opening them to the public.

collecting ancient works of art for their recently established Imperial Museum in the capital.

Indeed, by the time Schliemann conducted his test excavations at Hisarlık in 1870, Ottoman interest in antiquities was already increasing and official archaeology notably expanding. In the 19th century, due to the reformations of the *Tanzimat* (1839-1876), known as the 'Ottoman Enlightenment', a new intellectual group had been established, consisting mainly of bureaucrats, with a significant interest in European culture

and literature, and a vast appreciation of Graeco-Roman artefacts. As a result of these developments, the emerging new institutions during the *Tanzimat*, such as ministries of trade and commerce, health, education and public works, also included a museum. Although Hagia Irene, a former Eastern Orthodox church located in the outer courtyard of Topkapı Palace in Istanbul, had served as a depot for the sultan's collection of military equipment and as a place where valuables were kept since 1723, the formal collection of antique objects began approximately in 1846. This collection was initially entitled The Depository of Antiquities, but in 1869 the name was changed to the Imperial Museum (Müze-i Hümayun).

Together with this transformation, efforts to collect antiquities increased and formal acquisition of ancient works of arts intensified. In 1869 and 1870, Safvet Paşa, the Minister of Public Instruction and a prominent representative of the *Tanzimat*, instructed governors of different provinces, to collect antiquities and to transfer these to the museum in Istanbul. The latter decree in particular received acclaim: the Imperial collection increased with artefacts sent by the governors of several provinces, such as Salonica, Crete and Aydın. The Ottoman newspaper *Terakki* covered these shipments, which indicates a public interest in the formal efforts to collect antiquities.

Heinrich Schliemann's experimental excavations at Hisarlık took place in this climate, in which the appreciation of classical heritage by the Muslim cultural elite of the 19th century Ottoman Empire had already become apparent. As we have seen, Schliemann's efforts to buy the field at Hisarlık were not successful. His requests to obtain immediate permission to conduct excavations at Hisarlık were not productive either. All the more interesting is the fact that during this period, in which Schliemann was trying to obtain an official permit, the Ottoman government acquired the land from the two Turkish owners on behalf of the Imperial Museum. The government realized the transaction to ensure that the Imperial Museum would be a beneficiary of the excavations at Hisarlık. Schliemann was enraged at the Ottoman transaction. Schliemann's letter to Calvert on 12 March 1871 is illustrative at this point: '...but the field must be my property and as long as this is not the case I will never think of commencing the excavations, for if I dig on Government ground I would be exposed to everlasting vexations and trouble...'.

The Ottoman official correspondence concerning Schliemann's request for permission to excavate at Hisarlık is also clear on this point. In his letter to the Grand Vizier, Mehmed Emin Âli Paşa, on 20 June 1871, Safvet Paşa states that preliminary research uncovered Schliemann's attempts to buy the land at Hisarlık. In consequence, the governor of the Dardanelles was instructed to buy the field for the Imperial Museum. The Ottoman government did not appreciate the possibility that

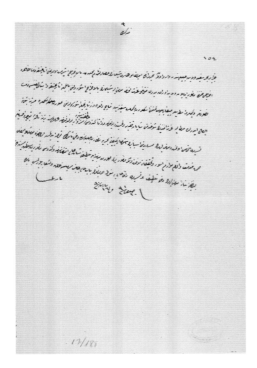

Report dated 29 March 1874 from the Education Ministry to the Sublime Porte (the administration of the Ottoman Empire) on the investigation into the illegal export by Schliemann of gold artefacts from Troy. This investigation was conducted at the behest of the Education Ministry and focused on the modus operandi of Schliemann who is reported to have 'stolen the antiquities'. The investigation's outcome had negative consequences for several Ottoman bureaucrats, who were accused of negligence and lack of interest.

Schliemann owned the field at Hisarlık. And yet, Schliemann, in a letter to Calvert, expresses his frustration at the fact that Safvet Paşa mentioned to the American ambassador Wayne MacVeagh that 'he could not let' Schliemann 'have the land'.

At any rate, it is obvious that the Ottoman government had not disregarded the test excavations at Hisarlık. In fact, the incorporation of the land demonstrates a great interest in the search for Troy. In the same correspondence the Grand Vizier calls Troy 'the eminent city of Troy from ancient times' and emphasizes that the discovery of objects during the excavations would improve knowledge. Furthermore, in the case of the discovery of the city walls, both Safvet Paşa and Mehmed Emin Âli Paşa insist that their preservation as a whole and their public display are of utmost significance.

SCHLIEMANN'S LEGAL EXCAVATIONS

Thanks to the mediation of John P. Brown, diplomatic agent of the United States in Istanbul, Schliemann received the permit that allowed him to realize his dream of uncovering Homeric Troy. According to the Imperial decree of 29 June 1871, Schliemann's excavations were at his own expense, including the costs of an Ottoman overseer. Furthermore, the decree required an equitable division of the discovered antiquities, half for the Imperial Museum and the other half for Schliemann. Actually, this was until the enactment of the Ottoman Antiquities Law in 1874 and 1884, common practice when granting foreigners permission to excavate. Finally, the Imperial decree included the requirements concerning the preservation and public display of the city walls, mentioned above.

Having arrived at the Dardanelles on 27 September and despite his permit, Schliemann yet again encountered difficulties caused by Ottoman officials. This time the local governor, Ahmed Paşa, refused permission to dig, as according to him the official permit did not indicate the excavation area accurately enough. The governor required more detailed instructions from the Grand Vizier. Once again owing to diplomatic support and the change of ministry, Schliemann finally began his first season of excavations on the 11 October 1871. The campaign continued until 24 November 1871. The second full season ran from 1 April to 14 August 1872 and his final season covered the period between 2 February and 14 June 1873. It is quite clear that Schliemann smuggled the majority of the artefacts that he found between 1871 and 1873 out of the Empire, since the photographs taken of the antiquities between the seasons of 1872 and 1873 show he had a rich Trojan collection in Athens during this period. Smuggling out Priam's Treasure, however – a large cache of gold and copper bowls and vessels, spectacular jewellery and other valuables – was the apex.

OTTOMANS CLAIMING TROJAN ARTEFACTS

The publication of Schliemann's report on the discovery of Priam's Treasure in the *Augsburger Allgemeine Zeitung* on 5 August 1873, received acclaim all over the world and impressed scholars as well as the general public. On the Ottoman side, however, it created a feeling of loss. The government held an internal inquiry into the smuggling of the Treasure, questioning the method of the 'robbery', in particular 'by whom, from which quay, with whose vessel, how often and on which date'. The keeper of the archives of the province of the Dardanelles was recognized for his 'excellent' services on behalf of the investigation into the 'robbery of the antiquities'. The outcome of the investigation had negative consequences for several Ottoman administrators, who were accused of negligence and a careless attitude towards the illegal handing over.

The Ottoman government clearly had no intention of throwing in the towel. The Ottomans claimed their share of Priam's Treasure and took legal steps to acquire it. The correspondence of the Ministry of Public Instruction addressed to the Bab-ı

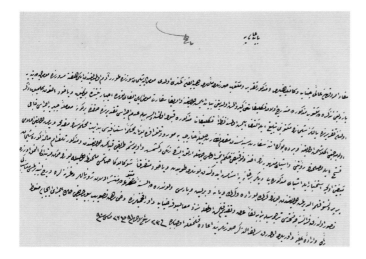

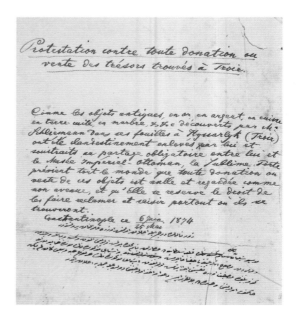

Ali, the Ottoman Sublime Porte, clearly highlights the key motives of the lawsuit. Since Schliemann was not willing to hand over the Ottoman share of the artefacts in Athens and the objects were put up for sale, the director of the Imperial Museum had to be sent to Athens to initiate legal action. In fact, the Ottomans were correct in their perception of Schliemann's intentions to sell his Trojan artefacts. Schliemann did try to sell the complete Trojan collection, including Priam's Treasure, to both the British Museum and the Louvre in September and October 1873 respectively.

The legal conflict between the Ottoman Empire and Schliemann in the courts of Athens started in April 1874 and ended in an agreement in April 1875. In response to the incompetence of the Greek court and the subsequent Ottoman appeal, the appeal court ordered the confiscation of the Trojan collection. However, since Schliemann had transferred the objects to a secret location, it was untraceable. The Ottoman government, furious about this development and concerned about 'a possible sale of the entire collection or in parts, by Schliemann', decided to publish a protest letter in prominent newspapers and periodicals within the Empire, as well as in Vienna, Berlin, Paris and London. This course of action in the form of a published protest, in French, against a donation or sale of the Trojan treasuries, demonstrates a determined Ottoman claim on Trojan artefacts.

The Empire finally gave up its Trojan claims and settled for an agreement that included financial compensation of 50,000 francs, which was used to fund the construction of the new building for the Archaeological Museum in Istanbul. Since the Ottoman government had to deal with a financial collapse in 1875, the motive for giving up the legal struggle was, in fact, the considerable expense involved.

Letter from the Education Ministry to the Sublime Porte of 9 June 1874, about the items that Schliemann had illegally taken to Athens. After the Athens court had declared that it was not competent in the case, and the Ottomans had launched an appeal, the judge ordered the confiscation of the Trojan artefacts. However, the collection could not be found, as Schliemann had transferred the items to a secret location. The letter reveals that the Ottoman authorities were concerned about 'the possible sale by Schliemann of the collection in its entirety or in part'. A decision was taken to publish a letter of protest in order to avoid this.

Draft of the letter of protest of 6 June 1874 that was published in prominent newspapers and magazines in the Ottoman Empire and in Vienna, Berlin, Paris and London. This public protest – in French – against the donation or sale of the treasures reveals how determined the Ottoman authorities were in their claim to the items that Schliemann had taken from Troy.

TROY: PROTECTED AREA

After Schliemann's illegal transportation of the Treasure, the Ottoman government declared the site of Troy a protected area, in which excavations were no longer permitted. When the Ottoman army started to construct military buildings at the hill of Dardanos in 1875, they had received a note from the Ministry of Public Instruction to stay away from Troy. Furthermore, if any antique objects were found during the construction at Dardanos, notification to the Ministry would be required, upon which the Ministry would send an official to investigate. In addition, the governor of the Dardanelles was instructed to be watchful regarding possible secret or public excavations at Hisarlık.

The remaining Trojan artefacts were added to the collection of the Imperial Museum by an order of the Ministry of Public Instruction in 1874. Moreover, this directive also demonstrates that there were plans for continuing excavations at Hisarlık, albeit on behalf of the Imperial Museum. The same order is even more explicit concerning the Ottoman attitude towards Schliemann. It is clear that Schliemann was no longer wanted, since the Council of the Ministry of Public Instruction had decided that 'from now on there is no need and no possibility for Schliemann to do excavations and research'. He was 'only allowed to obtain pictures of future findings at the Imperial Museum'.

However, Ottoman excavations at the Troad did not take place. Being faced with a major financial collapse, an anti-Ottoman revolt in Bosnia and Herzegovina, Montenegro and Serbia in 1875 and the following Bulgarian April uprising of 1876, it is hardly surprising that excavating for Troy was not the main concern of the Ottoman authorities. Schliemann, on the other hand, was determined to resume the excavations in the Troad. All things considered, the chances that Schliemann would receive a permit to recommence excavations at Hisarlık after his illegal deeds and the following clash with the Ottoman government seemed to be very small. Nevertheless, he achieved his goal with diplomatic pressure on the Ottoman government, and in 1876 received a permit to resume excavations for a period of two years.

The permission was granted, indeed, although in fits and starts. The Ottomans turned out to be extremely uncooperative this time. In fact, because of the opposition of the authorities the venture was foredoomed to failure: the permit was inoperable. For all that he tried, Schliemann did not succeed in excavating at Troy. In fact, he had to wait until 1878. In that year he received a permit for two years and was at last able to carry out his much-desired excavations at Hisarlık.

It is obvious that the loss of Trojan artefacts increased Ottoman appreciation of Troy. Indeed, a number of Ottoman sources regarding the excavations at Troy between 1870-1875 show a significant Ottoman interest and involvement. The Ottoman Turks were obviously much more interested in the classical heritage than the historiography of archaeology has previously acknowledged.

THE DISCOVERY AND SMUGGLING OF PRIAM'S TREASURE

RÜSTEM ASLAN – ALI SÖNMEZ

Heinrich Schliemann's excavations at Hisarlık can arguably be seen as a landmark in Anatolian and Homeric archaeology. The excavations shaped the future of archaeological research at Hisarlık and Schliemann's status in the academic world. "Priam's Treasure" in particular, has been the subject of debate ever since its discovery on the 31 May, 1873. In view of the numerous discussions in both academic and more popular media, it hardly seems necessary to dedicate yet another paper to this spectacular hoard.

Yet, there are two reasons to do so nonetheless. Firstly, all studies that have dealt with Schliemann and Priam's Treasure have, so far, taken Schliemann's own records – his diary and publications- as the starting point of the discussion; other sources have been largely ignored. One of the aims of this article is to rectify this omission. The second reason to write yet again about Priam's Treasure is that doubts about the veracity of Schliemann's record on the Treasure have, over the years, increased. Various studies, carried out especially after 1930s, proved that Schliemann had substantially manipulated his diaries and reports. In view of the doubts regarding the credibility of Schliemann's records, the value and credibility of Ottoman sources have become more important.

While it is clear that Schliemann frequently presented 'his own truth' about certain situations and events (possibly because of personal ambitions and to improve his reputation as an academic) this is not the case with numerous Ottoman records. Indeed, these – often rather dry and bureaucratic – accounts are of great help in reconstructing certain important events and in correcting some of Schliemann's assertions. The discovery of Priam's Treasure is an important case where Ottoman sources correct the picture presented by Schliemann.

Cartoon published by *Hayâl*, an Ottoman satirical magazine (12 September 1874):
Mrs Schliemann: 'You have promised these to the Ottomans, and these to the Greeks. And now you say you have promised these to the American ambassador. What's left for us?'
Schliemann: 'Everything!!!'

Schliemann's article "Priam's Treasure" which was published in the *Augsburger Allgemeine Zeitung* on 5 August 1873, initiated a number of legal and archaeological discussions, of which the following questions appear to be the most relevant:

1) The date of the discovery: when exactly was Priam's Treasure found?
2) The context of the finds: where was the Treasure found, and at what 'depth' (which stratigraphic layer) was it found?
3) Who assisted Schliemann during his discovery of Priam's Treasure and how was it subsequently smuggled from Ottoman lands?
4) Why does Schliemann's description of the archaeological artefacts in his diaries differ from his reports?
5) Is Priam's Treasure complete set of a great treasure, or a group of finds thrown together later?

Most likely it will be impossible to answer any of these questions with absolute certainty, and most of the observations and conclusions that are presented here are should be considered as preliminary results. Noting these caveats, we will now try to analyse Ottoman sources. This article is organized in a roughly chronological order, starting with documents dating to the time of the Treasure's discovery. The debate surrounding Priam's Treasure started with Schliemann's article *Priam's Treasure*, which was published on 5 August 1873 in the *Augsburger Allgemeine Zeitung* (though the article was dated 17 July). By making his discoveries at Troy known to the public, Schliemann immediately became world-renowned. However, his successes at Troy also aroused the interest of Ottoman officials and around the time of the publication in the *Augsburger Allgemeine Zeitung*, the Ottoman State launched an investigation into the matter and took the first legal steps. Schliemann's letter dated 19 June, 1873 to Anton Dethier, the director of the Istanbul Archaeological Museum, seems to indicate that some ten-

sions had already arisen, and makes the whole affair even more interesting. Schliemann writes as follows:

"Dear Director,
I am honoured to inform you that I discovered the Great Tower of Ilion, the double door of Skaia, the altar of Ilion Minerva, Priam's palace and treasure, the grand boundary wall of Neptune and Apollo, and a large number of Trojan houses. I believe that my mission here is over and leave the region forever... I have excavated more than two thirds of the hill after three years of hard work. I wrote a long article on this subject for the Augsburger Allgemeine Zeitung that I want to bring to your attention. I intend to write another article about the small treasure I have discovered lately. I had to put Priam's Treasure out of sight hastily to protect it from greedy workers; therefore I even do not know what it comprises, but I am sure of the following: bowls among others, a big depas amphikypellon (cup used to drink wine) made of pure gold, four or six silver hatchet-like objects which – I suppose – are the "talents" mentioned by Homer (metals used instead of money in the Iliad), furthermore a raft of pots and pans, a few dozens of spearheads etc. In my opinion, it is impossible to share the treasure with the Ottoman State since I found it by working for three years with 150 labourers and spending 200.000 francs."

This letter (remarkably offensive from an Ottoman point of view) reveals Schliemann's point of view about the issue clearly. While it is not clear when, exactly, the Ottoman State initiated an investigation in the wake of the letter, the available data suggests that the state reacted rather swiftly, at least immediately after the official publication of the news. Because the first official enquiry (which, according to a later document, was initiated as early as 20 September 1873) into the matter did not satisfy the Ottoman officials, a second enquiry, under de direction of İzzeddin Efendi, was launched in order to establish what had been found, and how and by whom these objects had been smuggled out of the country. Meanwhile, the case was brought to court in April 1874 in Athens. Schliemann, understanding the seriousness of the situation, tried to sell the findings to different museums. The incident is even caricatured in a magazine

(*Hayal*, 9th of September 1874) published in Istanbul. Legal procedures lasted a long time but the issue was finally amicably settled. In view of the swift reaction of the Ottoman authorities after the discovery of Priam's Treasure became known, including two official enquiries, it is clear that the Ottoman government was acutely aware of Troy and the value of its treasures. However, the serious political and economic crisis with which the Ottoman State was grappling forced the authorities to focus mainly on a financial settlement – resulting in a (from a cultural perspective) rather unsatisfying settlement with Schliemann.

Regardless of the outcome of the juridical procedure, the report of İzzeddin Efendi (dated July 24, 1874) offers various interesting details:

"From the Ministry of Education to the Prime Ministry

The artefacts dug out during the charge of Emin Efendi have been smuggled by Schliemann twice in the same year: once at the beginning of April, 1289 (1873) and once at the end of May, by placing the artefacts into a ship which belongs to a Greek shipper called Andrea, who came to Karanlık Port located in Kumkale to load timber. Schliemann put the gold jewellery in a box, and small part in his and his family's pockets, and brought it from Kumkale Port to the customs office in Kale-i Sultaniye on the boat of Abdullah Reis, and later smuggled the jewellery to Athens. For that reason, a criminal process was initiated against the director of Kumkale, Rüstem Ağa, customs officer Emrullah Efendi and the other customs officers in Çanakkale that had heard of the case; but no legal action was taken on Halil Efendi, the customs manager of Çanakkale and his subordinate officers. In fact, it is understood that they were interrogated not properly but superficially. Thereupon the case was assigned to the Assembly of Education in order to be investigated again and Emrullah Efendi, Abdullah Reis and İsmail (a member of the crew) insisted that the aforementioned box and the objects were taken to the Çanakkale customs office across the bazaar around 14-15 pm by the Schliemann family; they were kept in the port for nearly half an hour and allowed to pass without a search or any inspection. Whilst there is no doubt that the director of Çanakkale customs office and the officers should have known about the transfer, it is unacceptable for them to say the exact opposite in the inquiry. That's why it would be appropriate to interrogate the director and the officers objectively and act upon the result; likewise to penalize Emrullah Efendi and Rüstem Ağa, who neglected their duty during the transfer of the relics, in accordance with criminal code. In the meanwhile, it is decreed to

arrest Kostandi and Alexander from the Kalkanlı village and the jeweller Yanniki from Erenköy concerning an issue regarding four kilograms of gold[....]. The relics that fell into the workers' hands during excavations but were seized afterwards have been sent to the Imperial Museum in a box. It is decreed to refer the case to Court of Appeals if the matters described above are deemed appropriate.

Let us try to sum up the situation and comment upon it: Schliemann smuggled the treasure finds on two occasions; once in the middle of April and once at the end of May. In addition to this, while he was leaving Troy, Schliemann himself and his companions hid various antique objects in their clothing, thus smuggling parts of the Treasure for a third time. The first and the second smuggling incidents were carried out from Karanlık Port by a Greek ship. At the third occasion, finds were taken to Çanakkale from Kumkale Port by Schliemann and then smug-

Report by İzzeddin Efendi of 24 July 1874 on the items smuggled from Troy. He describes in detail Schliemann's methods and stratagems. According to the report Schliemann put 'the gold jewellery in a box and the smaller items into his own and his family's pockets' and 'smuggled' the artefacts to Athens on the boat of his collaborator 'Abdullah Reis'.

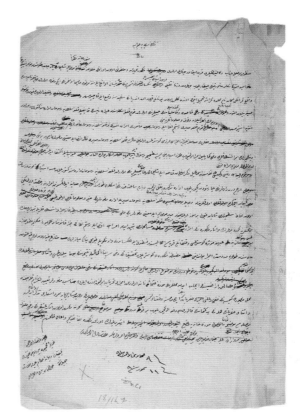

gled to Athens. We understand from the records that the officers in Çanakkale customs either took bribes or neglected their duties. The officers listed in İzzeddin Efendi's letter were punished as a result of these transgressions, while various objects were recovered from Schliemann's workers. (Those objects, now known as the "Worker's Treasure", are now exhibited in the Archaeological Museum at Istanbul). Towards the end of the report, İzzeddin Efendi indicates that the litigation concerning four kilograms of gold between Kostandi and Alexander from the Kalkanlı village and the jeweller Yanniki from Erenköy, ought to be resolved. Moreover, İzzeddin Efendi notes that all the excavations in the area were the Treasure was supposedly found had now completely ceased.

The first photograph of Priam's Treasure, released by Heinrich Schliemann in 1874. Shown among other items are the 'Jewels of Helen' along with gold and silver eating utensils. The treasure was surrounded by controversy from the start, because of inaccuracies in Schliemann's report on their discovery.

Trésor de Priam découvert à 8½ mètres de profondeur

DISCOVERING THE TREASURE

We enumerated the problems relating to Priam's Treasure at the beginning of this article. One of these problems was the day of its discovery. Various dates between 27 May and 17 June have been put forward so far. In İzzeddin Efendi's report, the end of May is mentioned as the period during which the Treasure was discovered, yet no specific date is stated. This information does, however, not contradict the date which is now by many specialists considered to be the most probable candidate: 31 May of 1873.

DATING 'PRIAM'S TREASURE'

Another problem concerns the chronology: to which period of Troy does the Treasure belong? Calvert and Dörpfeld had already pointed out that many of Schliemann's finds were at least 1,000 years older than he had supposed, and hence that these finds could not belong to Homer's Troy; and thus not to Troy's legendary King Priam. It is still being discussed whether Schliemann's statement about the location of findings was true or not. The latest archaeological analysis on the matter was performed by Manfred Korfmann. Korfmann asserted that "Treasure A" may belong to the first or second phase of Troy II or even Troy III, but definitely not Troy IV. In other words, Priam's Treasure dates to ca. 2500 BC.

While it can thus be reasonably argued that the Treasure most likely belongs to Troy II, much remains unclear about the way in which the Treasure was found, and by whom it was found. In contrast to what is written in Schliemann's excavation report, we know from previous studies of Schliemann's documents that his wife Sophia was not in Troy when the Treasure was found. This is also evident from the writings of William Copeland Borlase (1848-1899), an English Antiquarian and Liberal politician who visited Troy and published his impressions in *Frasers Magazine* in January 1878. Borlase talked with Yannikis from Erenköy, who had been Schliemann's most trusted employee, on how the Treasure was found. Yannikis stated that he was the only one with Schliemann when the Treasure was found. (According to Yannikis it included copper and some golden objects.) Although some academics still argue for the presence of a third person when the Treasure was found, this seems unlikely on the basis of Borlase's account.

We know that Yannikis from Erenköy was important to Schliemann, which adds to the credentials of Borlase's account. The name Yannikis frequently occurs in Schliemann's diaries. He made payments, scheduled and settled financial affairs on Schliemann's behalf and seems to have been a trusted lieutenant, who was on occasion sent to the Ottoman authorities to arrange the allocation of Trojan finds. It was Yannikis who organized the smuggling of Helios Metopes in 1872. Yet he may have done more for Schliemann than just that, for even after Yannikis' death in 1883 (he drowned in the Karamenderes River), Schliemann regularly sent money to his family.

It remains unclear what the conflict of Yannikis with two *Rums* (the local, Greek speaking population) concerning four kilograms of gold was about. Perhaps these two were workmen in Troy. Had Yannikis been buying the gold which they found in Troy or somewhere else, on behalf of Schliemann? Why did they fail to agree? Why did Schliemann stay in Troy for ten days after smuggling the Treasure to Athens on 6 June 1873? Many questions remain unanswered. From Schliemann's letter to Anton Dethier, we learn that he had to stay in Troy to finish some small jobs; but we do not know what this entailed. We do know that workers in Troy stole finds during the excavations, as Schliemann touched upon this in his diaries many times. The finds comprising the "Workers' Treasure" in the Archaeological Museum in Istanbul are an example of this practice. Interestingly, these finds were seized by the authorities in Yenişehir, a Rum village. There are tantalizing clues about what might have happened, but in the end we simply do not know anything for sure. We also do not know whether the four kilograms of gold listed in İzzeddin Efendi's report represented treasure that had not been mentioned in Schliemann's first report, or whether Schliemann included a number of additional finds in the report after buying these objects through Yannikis. When we analyse all the available evidence, including the important report of İzzeddin Efendi, however, we may reconstruct the events that occurred in 1873, as follows:

From 1872 onwards, small items had been discovered in layers of the Troy II excavations by Schliemann. At this time, Schliemann, in his desire to show the world that Hisarlık was the site of Homeric Troy, was digging on a massive scale; employing some 120 workers whom he could not possibly control. As a result, workers were hiding finds from him. Schliemann himself smuggled plenty of valuable objects, which he discovered until April 1873, via Karanlık Port. At this time Yannikis was making an effort to buy some items found by workers, most likely on behalf of Schliemann. Schliemann himself, with the help of Yannikis, found more valuable objects on 31 May 1873. As he was anxious about Amin Efendi's inspection, he sent these objects, stacked in six baskets, to Frank Calvert's farm near Troy. From there, they were smuggled to Greece via Karanlık Port, again under the supervision of Yannikis and Spiridon Demetrios. At that point, Yannikis probably bought back some gold from the workers for Schliemann. After a payment problem occurred, the incident was submitted to court. Schliemann then smuggled the last of the Treasure past the Çanakkale customs office to Athens by hiding the objects in his (and his companions') clothes. On 5 August, he presented his finds in the

Schliemann's wife Sophia draped in the golden jewellery from Priam's Treasure. At the end of the Second World War the treasure was shipped by the Soviets from Berlin to Moscow, where it was kept in secret for decades.

Augsburger Allgemeine Zeitung as a single coherent set of finds; as a great treasure – as Priam's Treasure. Soon after, the "Treasury Case" commenced in the Athens court, the first of a long series of conflicts over the ownership of Priam's Treasure.

8 HOMER AND TROY IN MODERN TURKEY

هيدروفوخ‌

منرجمى فرائثارى

صاحب وناشرلرى

هودنت وقصصار

PANNEMAKER SC

هومرك رسمى

معارف نظارت جلیله‌سنك رخصتله طبع اولنمشدر

استانبول

HOMER AND TROY IN 19TH CENTURY OTTOMAN TURKISH LITERATURE

GÜNAY USLU

Although repeatedly translated into European languages, the fact that these two famous, valuable and old works [the Iliad and the Odyssey] have still not been translated into the Ottoman language is a reason for grief. Therefore, I started at once to translate, print and publish, step by step, the aforementioned work from its original language.
(Na'im Fraşeri, Istanbul 1885/86 (1303))

As far as we know, there is no Ottoman-Turkish version of the poems of Homer until 1885. Na'im Fraşeri's abovementioned words in his preface to his translation of the first song of the *Iliad* (*Ilyada. Eser-i Homer*) confirm this view. Although Ottoman Turks knew Troy and Homer long before, they obviously did not feel an urgent need to translate Homeric poems into Ottoman Turkish until the 19th century. In fact, literary attention given to Homeric epics, such as translation attempts of the *Iliad* into Ottoman Turkish, biographical notes on the poet, informative articles on Homeric literature and the topographical characteristics of Homeric locations, occurred in an era that was characterized by an increasing penetration of Western works and ancient Greek and Roman authors into Ottoman literature.

Heinrich Schliemann's archaeological activities in Troy from the 1870s onwards, obviously stimulated Ottoman interest in Homeric literature. Yet, also the 19thcentury intellectual modernizations, the progress in public education, the rise of printing and publishing, and the innovations within the Ottoman literature created suitable conditions and the appropriate atmosphere in which Homer and mythology could enter Ottoman art, culture and literature.

Title page of Na'im Fraşeri's, *Ilyada. Eser-i Homer*, Istanbul 1885 or 1886. This is the first attempt to translate the *Iliad* into Ottoman Turkish. Na'im Fraşeri, born in Frashër now in modern Albania, was a civil servant with the Ottoman Ministry of Education. His prose translation of the First Book of the *Iliad* – in all a booklet of 43 pages – has a 15-page foreword in which he introduces the *Iliad*, Homer and Troy in some detail.

For all the interest and enthusiasm, however – even in the new literary era – translations of the epics into Ottoman Turkish were not numerous. In fact, not one complete Turkish version of Homeric literature had been produced in the Ottoman Empire. Obviously, the translators pioneered and undoubtedly experienced the complexities involved. To get a better understanding of the role of Homer in Ottoman literature and to position the rising interest of the Ottoman intellectual in Homeric epics in the 19thcentury, it might be useful to take a quick look at the early Ottoman interest in Homer and the literary developments within the late Ottoman Empire.

HOMER IN EARLY OTTOMAN LITERATURE

Ottoman Turks were no strangers to Troy, Homer and Homeric subjects and figures. In fact, as has already been mentioned in the special issue dealing with Sultan Mehmed II, the conqueror of Constantinople (1432-1481) was highly interested in Homer and Troy. It might be illuminating to mention that the epic stories of the heroic age of the Turkish tribe of the Oğuz, that make up *the Book of Dede Korkut*, include narratives which are analogous to the Homeric poems. These mythic narratives of the Turkic people had been orally transmitted for centuries before they were recorded, probably in the 15th century. The episode in which the Oğuz hero Basat kills the Cyclops-like figure Tepegöz shows a strong similarity to Odysseus' struggle with Polyphemus. Also the epic *Alpamysh* (*Alpamış*), which most probably existed during the period of the Turkic Kaghanate as early as the 6th to 8th century in Central Asia, includes Homeric aspects.

Early Ottoman works, such as the comprehensive 17thcentury history *Camiu'd – düvel* (The Compendium of Nations) in Arabic and its Ottoman-Turkish version *Sahaif-ül Ahbar* (The pages of the Chronicle), by the Ottoman astronomer, astrologer and historian Ahmed Dede Müneccimbasi (1631-1702), as well as the 18thcentury publication of *Cihannüma* by Mustafa ibn Abdullah, better known as the prominent Ottoman scholar Katib Çelebi (1609-1657), dealt with Troy and Homer as well. Moreover, in *Tarih-i Iskender bin Filipos* (History of Alexander the son of Philip), published in 1838, which is an Ottoman Turkish translation of Flavius Arrianus' *Anabasis Alexandrou*, Troy and Homeric characters were again included in the subject matter.

The Ottoman Turks knew the ancient Greek and Roman world also through the medieval Arabic studies of ancient Greek literature. Ancient philosophy was a major part of the Ottoman political and cultural world. Classical figures such as Plato, Aristotle, Hippocrates and Galen happened to be the basic classics of the Islamic and Ottoman culture. Within this context, classical figures, such as Alexander the Great, Plato, Aristotle and Socrates were considered to be important religious characters within Islam. Their historical position was disregarded and they were seen as legendary characters of an Islamic era. From this point of view, Plato, for instance, was considered to be a prophet by several Islamic scholars and some scholars were even accused of preferring Aristotle to the Koran in the 9th century.

Homer was known as the 'wandering poet' in the Muslim world. Although Greek poetry was not the main focus of the Arabic studies, Arabic translations of ancient works included fragments and quotes of Homer. His biographies, moreover, were incorporated in dictionaries and encyclopaedias. Still, Ottoman intellectuals were circumspect about Homer's pagan gods. Reservations towards mythology were closely connected to religion. Therefore, the long-term absence of particular attention to Greek literature – contrary to antique philosophy – was essentially a result of the incongruity of mythology with Islam. In this context, Na'im Fraşeri emphasizes that Muslims had their own Homer and Virgil, namely Firdevsi and Nizami from Iran: 'During the civilization of the Arabs, the Islamic community adopted some scientific writings from the Greeks, yet they did not favour Greek literature. This is why Islamic poets formed a separate caravan, in which the poets of Iran obtained a superior position'.

NEW OTTOMAN TURKISH LITERATURE: NEW PERSPECTIVES

The 19th century was a most turbulent period for the Ottomans. The period was characterized by emerging domestic movements to separate particular regions from the Empire resulting in enormous territorial losses. It was a time of weakness and disintegration par excellence. Leading figures of the Ottoman society tried to save the Empire by far-reaching modernization. During the *Tanzimat* (reforms) era (1839-1876) the government explicitly accepted European values, the basic principles of the French Revolution, and moreover, it made Westernization a state programme. We may say that with the *Tanzimat* edict in 1839, the Empire and its society left a circle of civilization in which it had lived for centuries and declared its entrance into another civilization, the Western European one, which it had been in conflict with for centuries. These reforms and changes in social, economic and political life triggered the search for change in Ottoman literature. Therefore, the literary

production from the 1850s onwards is called above all the *New Turkish Literature*. Inflamed and nourished by the *Tanzimat* reforms and the process of Westernization, the Ottoman literature of the period became interwoven with Western literature.

The translation activities were at the basis of the new literary movement. The growing reception of European culture into Ottoman literature was strongly related to the establishment of various translation institutions such as the *Terüme Odası* (Translation Chamber) (1832), the *Encümen-i Daniş* (1851) and the *Cemiyet-i İlmiye-i Osmaniye* (1860). On the other hand, intellectuals – whether connected to these institutions or not – also translated Western works on their own initiative. In fact, translating was a way to learn a foreign language or to practise that particular language. In their selections, Ottoman intellectuals primarily preferred the important literary figures of the French neoclassical period, like the dramatists and tragedians Racine, Molière, Corneille and the fabulist La Fontaine. A distinct preference for philosophical works was also noticeable.

Given the dominant position of the culture of Ancient Greece and Rome within neoclassical works, Ottoman preference for these works resulted in increasing influence of the ancients and mythology in the Ottoman literature and arts. Correspondingly, intellectuals at the basis of the new literary movement frequently referred to Greek antiquity in their essays and prefaces to their publications. The incorporation of significant neoclassical Western works in their literature, moreover, gave Ottoman Turks the opportunity to enrich their hitherto dominant Islamic view on classical authors. In fact it inspired them to compare their existing Islamic view with the newly acquired Western perception. By doing so, Ottomans were able to see ancient works in a different light and revaluate the ancients from their recently acquired Western point of view.

One of the most popular translations of the era was that of Fénelon's novel *Les Aventures de Télémaque*. In fact, the travels of Telemachus, the son of Odysseus, was reading material in Ottoman schools and was used in high schools to teach prose composition. The first translation of *Télémaque* into Ottoman Turkish (*Terceme-i Telemak*), made by the prominent statesman and Grand Vizier (in 1863) Yusuf Kamil Paşa (1808-1876), was exceptionally popular and influential in the intellectual scene. This first translation was completed in 1859, but printed three years later in 1862. In the period between its manuscript form and its publication, however, *Terceme-i Telemak* was an integral part of the reading material of the capital's artistic and intellectual scene and circulated in manuscript form in Ottoman *salons*. Because of its success the work was reprinted only six months after its first publication as well as in 1867 and 1870.

The second translation, made by another distinguished figure in the political and cultural arena, Ahmed Vefik Paşa (1823-1891), in 1869, yet printed in 1880, was also popular and was reprinted more than once. Yet, it was Yusuf Kamil Paşa's *Terceme-i Telemak* that stirred up a lively interest for ancient Greek history and mythology and triggered translations of works on ancient history into Ottoman Turkish. Actually, *Terceme-i Telemak* was an introduction to classical mythology and to Homer in Ottoman-Turkish. Ottoman readers considered the work as the continuation of Homer's *Odyssey*.

We may say that the penetration of Homeric poems into the Ottoman literature was closely connected with translations of European literature that was highly inspired by the art and culture of ancient Rome and Greek. By the 1880s Ottoman interest in Homer, the *Iliad* and the *Odyssey* increased and Homer became more and more a point of reference for Ottoman intellectuals.

HOMER AND TROY IN NEW OTTOMAN TURKISH LITERATURE

As noted above, the first Ottoman Turkish attempt to translate the *Iliad* into Ottoman Turkish is the translation of Na'im Fraşeri (1846-1900) in 1885 or 1886 (1303). Fraşeri served as a member and chairman of the Committee of Inspection and Examination (*Encümeni Teftiş ve Muayene*) affiliated to the Ministry of Public Instruction and responsible for checking and censoring books and magazines before printing.

In the 15-page preface to his prose translation, altogether a booklet of 43 pages, Na'im Fraşeri emphasizes his pioneering position (see his quote above). However, the former Minister of Education and leading figure of the humanist politics of the 1930s and 1940s in Turkey, Hasan Ali Yücel (1897-1961), maintains that it is the Ottoman diplomat Sadullah Paşa (1839-1890) who actually deserves to be called the first translator of the *Iliad* into Turkish. Sadullah Paşa's translation contained 10 couplets of two rhyming verses and a part in prose. Yücel incorporated the 10 couplets in his publication. Sadullah Paşa's translation had not been published, however, which makes a correct statement on this subject impossible. Na'im Fraşeri's printed work is for this reason regarded as the first translation of Homer's *Iliad*.

An essay published on 2 February 1885 in the periodical *Kevkebü'l Ulum* confirms this. The anonymous author states that hopefully soon the *Iliad* and the *Odyssey* 'will be translated into Turkish, so that we will not have to go without Homer's work any longer'. Before publication of the first translation of the Iliad, Ottoman Turkish readers had the opportunity to broaden their knowledge of Homer through essays in periodicals. Between December 1884 and March 1885, for instance, three extensive articles, including a biography of Homer, an introduction to his poems and a summary of the books of the Iliad, appeared in the periodical *Kevkebü'l Ulum*.

Almost a decade earlier a play inspired by the *Odyssey* was produced by Ali Haydar (1836-1914). The verse comedy,

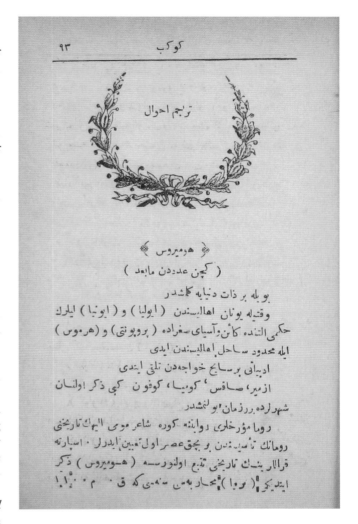

Before the publication of the first translation of the *Iliad*, Ottoman Turkish readers were able to extend their knowledge of Homer through magazines. Three extensive articles appeared for example between December 1884 and March 1885 in the magazine *Kevkebü'l Ulum*, including a biography of Homer, an introduction to his works and a summary of the *Iliad*. *Kevkebü'l Ulum* 3 January 1885, page 93.

Rüya Oyunu, published in 1876/1877, was about a dream of Bey (Lord) about the nymph Calypso. Bey believed himself to be in love with Calypso. The nymph, on the other hand, deeply in love with Odysseus, was waiting for his return. She told Bey that Odysseus had sailed away with Mentes and Telemachus. Although she was in a position to stop Odysseus, her love prevented her from doing so. At the end of the play, Bey awakes and writes down the contents of his dream to send to an interpreter.

Homer and the *Iliad* also received appropriate attention in a treatise on Troy that appeared in the third volume of *Kamus ül-Alâm* (1891), or *Dictionnaire Universel d'Histoire et de Géographie*, written by Na'im Fraşeri's brother Şemseddin Sami Fraşeri (1850-1904). The massive six-volume encyclopaedia, published between 1889 and 1899, dealing with important Ottoman and Islamic subjects, figures and countries and, at the same time, with Western history and geography, is a work of exceptional calibre. *Kamus ül-Alâm* brought western and eastern history and geography together. The essay dealing with Troy outlined the contemporary knowledge of Troy in the Ottoman Empire. A history of Troy, a chronological list of Trojan rulers, the Trojan War, and the archaeological developments in the region were included in the article. Special attention was given to the location of the site on Ottoman soil: 'Truva or Troya, situated in the north-western part of Asia Minor, nowadays within the Province of Biga', 'at the western foot of Mount Ida (that is to say Kaz) and along the river Xanti (that is to say Menderes)'.

A second translation of the first song of the *Iliad* into Ottoman Turkish from the Greek, written by Selanikli Hilmi, appeared in 1898 or 1899: *İlyas yahud şâir-i şehîr Omiros* (The *Iliad* or the celebrated poet Homer). Little is known about the author; yet, according to the text on the title page, the translator was a member of the Committee of Inspection and Examination (*Encümeni Teftiş ve Muayene*), and consequently like Na'im Fraşeri an Ottoman bureaucrat. Hilmi's translation of 61 pages includes an introduction of 15 pages (in the Ottoman alphabet) and the first book of the *Iliad* in two chapters. The first chapter (26 pages) is called 'Wrath! Violence!' and the second (20 pages) 'Departure!'.

Hilmi's translation had a great effect on significant literary figures. The leading intellectual of the time, Yahya Kemal Beyatlı (1884-1958), who, together with his contemporary Yakub Kadri Karaosmanoglu (1889-1974), initiated the neo-Hellenist movement in the early 20th century, expressed his high appreciation of Selanikli Hilmi's translation by saying that he had been tremendously touched by this work.

ADMIRATION FOR 'THE PRINCE OF POETS'

The aforementioned writer [Homer] and the great works the Iliad and the Odyssey are most excessively recited by respectful learned literary figures. This is why Homer is correctly remembered by his nickname the Prince of Poets.
(*Kevkebü'l Ulum*, 19th December 1884 (1 Rebi'ül-evvel 1302))

The two writings in verse, the Iliad and the Odyssey are the oldest and most respected, and the most famous and well-received works of the old Greeks.
(Na'im Fraşeri, 1885/1886 (1303))

Homer and the *Iliad* were accorded their appropriate place in the third part of *Kamus ül-Alâm* (1891). This encyclopaedia in six substantial parts, published between 1889 and 1899, is an exceptional work on significant Ottoman and Islamic themes, personalities and countries, and in addition on Western history and geography. The essay on Troy provides a summary of contemporary knowledge of Troy in the Ottoman Empire: a history of Troy, a chronological list of rulers, the Trojan War and archaeological developments in the region. Special attention is paid to the location of Troy on Ottoman soil.

I am translating a poem in verse renowned as the Iliad, a literary work written by Homer, a powerful genius whose knowledge has been a guide and who is given the honour of being the originator of poetry in ancient Greek literature.
(Selanikli Hilmi, 1898/99 (1316))

The Ottoman intellectuals evidently recognized the importance of Homer and, above all, they were aware of the extraordinary position of the *Iliad* and the *Odyssey* in the history of literature. With this in mind, Fraşeri, in his preface to his translation, emphasizes Homer's exceptional influence on later literary figures of various backgrounds. He informs his Ottoman Turkish readers that the works of Homer were a 'breeding ground' not

Frontispiece of Selanikli Hilmi, *İlyas yahud şâir-i şehîr Omiros* (*The Iliad, or the celebrated poet Homer*), Istanbul 1898 or 1899. Hilmi did the second Ottoman Turkish translation of the first book of the *Iliad*. Little is known about the translator, but according to the frontispiece he was a civil servant at the Education Ministry, much like Na'im Fraşeri. Hilmi's translation runs to 61 pages and includes an introduction of 15 pages and the First Book of the *Iliad* in two chapters.

only for ancient Greeks, but also for Romans and subsequent European writers and poets as well. 'Famous poets such as Hesiod, Aeschylus, Euripides, Sophocles and the writer of comedies Aristophanes', he continues, 'were all guided by Homer and tragedians in particular quoted the *Iliad* and the *Odyssey* intensively'. With respect to the Romans, he states that they 'followed the Greeks in all fields, and therefore in literature as well'. 'Virgil deserves to be called the Homer of the Romans. His work the Aeneid is like a continuation of the *Iliad* and the *Odyssey*,' Fraşeri says. Subsequently, he draws attention to literary figures such as 'Horace, Tasso, Dante, Milton and the rest of old and new European poets forming a caravan by following the preceding.' And according to Fraşeri, 'the leader of the caravan is Homer'.

Selanikli Hilmi's account of Homeric reception is even more sumptuous. He pays glowing tribute to Homer as a poet 'who nourished the creation of art' and praises the *Iliad* as a source of inspiration 'for poets with the most venerable minds'. To emphasize the respect of esteemed literary figures for the Iliad, he quotes Shakespeare and Rousseau but he also pays attention to the vast Homeric appreciation of ancient philosophers, such as Aristotle.

Both Fraşeri and Selanikli Hilmi draw explicit attention to the high regard of Alexander the Great for Homer. The Alexander or Iskender Legends are well-known in the Muslim World, and, moreover, Alexander the Great had an exceptional position in Ottoman culture as well. Presumably as a result of the Ottoman appropriation of Alexander, Fraşeri underlines explicitly that Alexander the Great was not a Greek, 'but a foreigner' to the Greeks. Subsequently, stressing the attraction of the *Iliad* for the great ruler, he states that although he was 'not a Greek national, he committed the *Iliad* to memory from beginning to end'.

After discussing Alexander's devotion to Homer at length, both translators pay due attention to *The Adventures of Telemachus*. In view of the popularity of the story among the Ottoman Turks, however, this is not surprising. Fraşeri points out that 'Fenelon's book the Adventures of Telemachus is an addendum to the *Odyssey*'. Selanikli Hilmi praises Homer and suggests that his Ottoman Turkish readers compare 'the celebrated story "Telemachus" of Fenelon with the Iliad'. He emphasizes that Homer's poems are the reference against which the contents of Telemachus could be tested. The relation between the *Odyssey* and *the Adventures of Telemachus* was also strongly emphasized in the periodical *Kevkebü'l Ulum*. Assuming that Ottoman Turks were acquainted with Telemachus, readers were informed that many of the episodes of Telemachus had their origins in the *Odyssey*.

According to Fraşeri, 'until now no other poet in the world has reached the level of Homer. He will always be the father of the poetry and the leader of the poets and the *Iliad* and the *Odyssey* will always be distinguished among the rest of the verses'. And what's more, according to *Kevkebü'l Ulum*, no poet has ever been able to match him.

PREFERENCE FOR THE *ILIAD*

Troy was situated near Çanakkale. Although in the past Troy and both its siege and the war were considered to exist only in the imagination, the excavations in the surroundings have confirmed and strengthened the contents of the Iliad.
(Na'im Fraşeri, Istanbul 1885/86 (1303))

The city of Troy or Ilion, with strong and solid city walls, strengthened with many citadels on the Asian shore (must be in the direction of the province of Izmir. Although history has not yet settled this issue, the natural requirements of the region have confirmed our idea).
(Selanikli Hilmi, Istanbul 1898/99 (1316))

The first Ottoman translation activities of Homeric literature concentrated on the *Iliad*. The excavations in Troy and the public attention drawn to these activities must have strengthened this preference. Hence, both Fraşeri and Hilmi pay attention to geographical locations of Troy. Fraşeri, moreover, gives brief information on the results of the archaeological research at the site. From the 1890s onwards, newspapers and periodicals paid increasing attention to the archaeological activities at Troy that, according to an article published on 8 March 1893 in the periodical *İkdam*, 'had become famous thanks to Homer's epic'.

As is noticeable in articles, for instance in periodicals such as *İkdam* and *Servet-i Fünun*, the Ottoman reading public had been informed about the history of the excavations at Troy, yet also about issues such as the dispute between scholars about the correct site (Ballıdağ or Hisarlık), the prominent role of Frank Calvert and the most current archaeological research and results of the time. Next to these informative texts, the press also reported on visitors at the site and their origins. This shows a close involvement with and interest in the actual site of Troy in this era.

Besides a preference for the *Iliad* and a deep admiration for Homer, biographical notes on Homer were also incorporated in literary texts, with a distinct connection between the famous poet and the city of Izmir within the territories of the Empire.

IZMIR, HOMER'S HOMETOWN

'Like many famous figures of antiquity, Homer, too, was an illegitimate child. Because Cretheis the daughter of Melanopus gave birth to him on the banks of the river Meles in the vicinity of Izmir, she named him Melesigenes, which means child of the river Meles'.
(*Kevkebü'l Ulum*, 19th December 1884 (1 Rebi'ül-evvel 1302))

'Although his nationality, his time and his life story are veiled in mystery and ambiguity, there is a strong possibility that he was born ten centuries before Christ and two centuries after the Trojan war. His birthplace is the city of Izmir, his mother's name is Cretheis and his father is unknown. He got his nickname Son of Meles because he was born on the banks of the river Meles, which at that time ran near Izmir'.
(Na'im Fraşeri, Istanbul 1885/1886 (1303))

The location of Homer's birthplace is much disputed. Seven cities claim to be his place of birth: Smyrna, Chios, Colophon, Salamis, Rhodes, Argos and Athens. The outcomes of 19th century archaeological research, however, strengthened the possibility of Smyrna (Modern Izmir) as Homer's birthplace. The biographical information in *Kevkebü'l Ulum* and Fraşeri's preface both explicitly emphasize this possibility by referring to the legend that Homer's name was Melesigenes. In fact, they seem quite convinced that their eminent city of Izmir is the place where Homer came into the world. In all probability, the writers based their knowledge on various Homeric biographies, in particular on the *Life of Homer* of Pseudo-Herodotus, which declares Smyrna to be the birthplace of Homer and places Homer's birth date as 168 years after the Trojan War.

The biography of Homer given in the essay in the *Kevkebü'l Ulum* is quite detailed and pays comprehensive attention to geographical aspects. On the other hand, it is generally known that Ottoman intellectuals knew antique Greek geography very well. In their translations of ancient works and other literary productions, they usually marked the antique places within the Ottoman Empire.

The author of the essay in the *Kevkebü'l Ulum* tells his readers about Homer's childhood, his teacher's prediction of a bright future, Mentes' (chief of the Taphians in the *Odyssey*) invitation to travel along with him on the sea, his long journeys and visits to various places (locations in the *Odyssey*), how he did research during his journey and composed poems based on his observations, how he went blind in Colophon, Mentor's care for him and how he got the name Homer in Cyme (north-west Turkey). On this point the author states that the blind Melesigenes went to Cyme to work as a bard and after a while became remarks that he had a pleasant life in Chios and that eventually he was much loved everywhere in Greece. Finally Homer fell ill during a journey from Samos to Athens near Ios, where he stayed a while and finally died.

Fraşeri then again emphasizes that, although the life story and the conditions of the poet of the *Iliad* and the *Odyssey* may be veiled, his existence could never be denied. Moreover, he concludes that 'it is not the name of Homer that gave the above-mentioned famous works their reputation and fame; quite the reverse, the works made the author famous. Therefore, Homer is the *Iliad* and the *Odyssey*'.

Although the existence of an interest in Homer and appreciation of Homeric literature at the end of the 19th century is obvious, Homeric translations into Ottoman Turkish, conversely, were clearly not numerous. In fact, Homeric literary production consisted of no more than a few attempts. Not one complete Turkish version of Homeric literature was produced in the Ottoman Empire. As a result of the clash between mythology and Ottoman norms, Muslim intellectuals of the late Ottoman Empire were inexperienced with mythology and hesitated to utilize it as a source. Although very ambitious and enthusiastic at the start, neither Fraşeri nor Selanikli Hilmi finished their work. In fact, both walked on untrodden ground. While Fraşeri chose to fill the gap and introduced, discussed and explained in detail the pagan gods, their actions and characteristics and their role in Homeric literature, Hilmi decided to ignore or veil mythological figures and events.

The fall of the Ottoman Empire in 1922 and the institution of the Turkish republic in 1923 would change this course of events. The following political, social and cultural reforms of Atatürk and his circle of Kemalists, were based on Wwestern principles of governance. The creation of a new Turkish identity, a fusion of various linguistic, religious and ethnic identities, were dominant in the intensive programme of remodelling the nation. Actually, the Kemalist nationalist reinterpretation of history, the 'Turkish Historical thesis', transformed Asia Minor into a Turkish region from earliest antiquity. According to this narrative, the Turkish subjects of the new republic were descendants of all the civilizations of Anatolia. From this point of view, Trojans became proto-Turks. Furthermore, Trojan heritage and Homeric texts were absorbed into history textbooks, the Ionians were given a Turkish background, Homer received a regular Turkish name Omer, and Troy was called Turova. After the foundational period of the secular young republic, the cultural policy from 1938 until 1950 was characterized by humanist ideas. During this period and also after 1950, when the instrumental use of Homeric heritage for identity claims by the Turkish government became less intense and constructed, various complete translations of the *Iliad* and the *Odyssey* were produced.

Portrait of Sultan Mehmed II (1432-1481), in miniature against a background of gold leaf, painted by Professor A. Süheyl Ünver (1898-1986) in 1943. Süheyl Ünver, doctor, historian, scientist and artist, is one of the most prominent and versatile figures in Turkish cultural history. The painting is inspired by the medallions of the medallist and painter Costanzo da Ferrara (1450-1524), who went to Istanbul to produce medallions at Mehmed's invitation.

renowned in the city. The senate was advised to take care of the blind poet, because he could bring great fame to the city with his songs. Yet, one of the administrators objected and said according to the article : 'If we are going to give every blind man we meet a salary, soon we will carry a convoy of blind men on our shoulders'. 'From then on,' the author resumes, 'the name Melesigenes disappeared and Homer, which means blind, replaced it.Subsequently, the blind poet cursed Cyme and left for Phocaea (Foça, north-west Turkey). There, too, he was dogged by misfortune'.

The article then goes on to discuss Homer's struggle with Thestorides, who recorded Homer's poems in exchange for bed and board and left for Chios. He made people believe that the poems were his own and became famous on the island. Homer followed the 'thief' to Chios, but Thestorides 'ran off. On Homer's last years the author of the article in *Kevkebü'l Ulum*

NEO-HELLENISM IN TURKEY

BEŞIR AYVAZOĞLU

'Neo-Hellenism' is a term that is often chiefly associated with Western, European thinkers and artists. However, and perhaps paradoxically, the movement also made an impact in Turkey. This brief contribution presents a number of important Turkish poets, writers and politicians, all of whom borrowed significantly from the Homeric heroic past.

One of the more prominent of these was Yahya Kemal (1884-1958), a leading Turkish poet, author and politician. He was deeply influenced by Jean Moréas (1856-1910), a poet, essayist and art critic of Greek origin, whom he probably met in Café Vachette in Paris where he lived for ten years. After about two years, he returned to Istanbul as a Neo-Hellenist and a member of the École Romane (a literary genre founded by Moréas that forsook symbolism and reverted to classical forms as of 1890). The idea of the "Greek Miracle" was prominently in his mind, and Homeric lines bringing Neo-Hellenistic breath to Turkish poetry enriched his vocabulary. Yahya Kemal highlighted the beauty of the Turkish language by comparing it favourably to the "immaculate and pure" Greek art of those days, and by adopting and even embracing European culture. In some respects, the tendency to appreciate European culture had already been prevalent in the Ottoman realm since after the so-called *Tanzimat Period*, a period of reformation and modernisation between 1839 and 1876. Yahya Kemal went even further; for him, learning more about Ancient Greek culture was the only way of understanding European culture.

Yakup Kadri (1889-1974) was a young author who became interested in Ancient Greek and Latin literature after Yahya Kemal, shortly after his arrival in Istanbul, introduced him to *Sur la Pierre Blanche* by Anatole France. Despite their differences, the two men soon became close friends. Impressed with the sonnets, especially in *Les Trophées* by Hérédia, Yahya Kemal repositioned himself within the École Romane movement, focusing on the "transition from Persian culture to Greek". This was fresh subject matter for Turkish intelligentsia in those days, but he heavily influenced Yakup Kadri with his new interests. They attempted to spread their ideas of a 'Mediterranean Civilization Basin' by founding a new journal, *Havza* (Basin) However, this attempt faltered. Kadri's and Kemal's failure was especially the result of opposition by Cenab Şahabeddin (1870-1934), a major poet of the Servet-i Fünun literary school. Indeed, the protagonist Tevfik Fikret (1867-1915) later stated that, had it not

been for Şahabeddin, *Havza* would almost certainly have been launched.

Having failed with *Havza*, Yahya Kemal and Yakup Kadri published their ideas in the newspaper *Peyam* in November 1913. Yahya Kemal's "Reflections under the Pinewood" articles, which were published in the literary supplement of *Peyam*, are a further testimony to the author's central position in Turkish Neo-Hellenism. His review article entitled "A Book of Myth" of *Esâtîr-i Yunaniyan* (*The Greek Myths*) (1909-1913) by Mehmed Tevfik Pasha (1855-1915), in particular, can be regarded as the manifesto of Neo-Hellenism. Mehmed Tevfik Pasha had given his book to Yahya Kemal himself. The Ottoman politician Mehmed Tevfik Pasha had, like many retired officers, politicians and philosophers in Europe, devoted himself to the study of Classical mythology after his retirement. His book clearly made an impression on Yahya Kemal, for upon receiving the tome, he is said to have exclaimed: "I wonder whether, while the light of barbarians in the East goes out, the Gods will awake from their slumbers in the mountains of Lydia, as Yakup Kadri has foreseen?" For Yahya Kemal, Mehmed Tevfik Pasha's book was the starting point of an era of Anatolian rebirth (like the Renaissance had been in Italy).

Considering the times (with especially the negative impact of the Balkan Wars on Turkish popular sentiment), it was almost inevitable that both Yahya Kemal and Yakup Kadri clashed with Turkish nationalists. Both Yahya Kemal and Yakup Kadri were especially critical of the work of Celal Sâhir (1883-1935), an important nationalist thinker of the period. However, they themselves were in turn also attacked in various publications – especially because of their seemingly positive approach towards things 'Greek'. In fact, Ömer Seyfeddin made fun of the Neo-Hellenism movement and symbolically characterized Yahya Kemal and Yakup Kadri as traitors working for the Greeks in his story "The Enemy of Boycott" published in the newspaper *Tanin*.

Such criticism, as well as the closing of *Peyam* in those turbulent days, seems to have caused Yahya Kemal to relapse into silence and revert to a more traditional stance. After a gap in his writings of three years, Yahya Kemal reappeared as a "traditional" Ottomanist. Unlike his old friend, Yakup Kadri defended his ideas of Neo-Hellenism till the end, as is evident from his preface to the translation of the *Odyssey* by Ahmet Cevat

This cartoon of Yahya Kemal (1884-1958) in ancient costume, drawn by Sedat Nuri, appeared in the literary supplement *Peyam-ı Edebi* of the newspaper *Peyam* on 26 January 1914. Two acknowledged intellectuals, Yahya Kemal and Yakup Kadri (1889-1974), launched the Turkish neo-Hellenist movement in 1912. The movement's members published articles on their great admiration for Classical Antiquity in a range of newspapers and magazines and regarded the classics as providing an example for Turkish literature and culture. There was also criticism of neo-Hellenist ideas, spurred on in particular by the Balkan Wars of 1912 and 1913. According to the critical text accompanying the cartoon, Yahya Kemal is 'a neo-Hellenist poet, his work is unpublished, just like Homer he declaims...'.

Esâtîr-i Yunaniyan (*Greek Mythology*) by Mehmed Tevfik Pasha (1855-1915), published in 1913. Greek mythology is treated very extensively in this book. Publication of this book of 762 pages belongs to the zeitgeist of the progressive late Ottoman period in which Homer and Greek mythology gained an increasing place in the Ottoman-Turkish intellectual world.

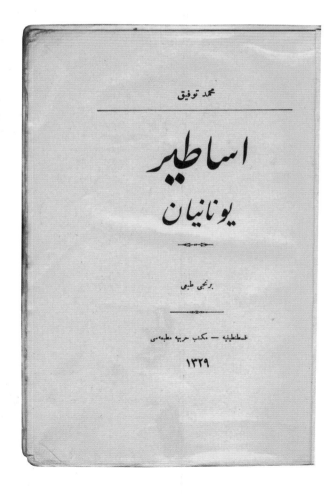

Emre (1876-1961): "While I am writing for the first translation of Homeric work into our beautiful language, my hands keep trembling and I am unable to pick up the pen. I simply feel myself close to the first source of unique truth and I tingle as if a unique wisdom, called beauty, and freshness sprung from a divine fountain runs through my veins."

يونانستان

ايشوئيد
ئاوليه
دوريه
آخاييه

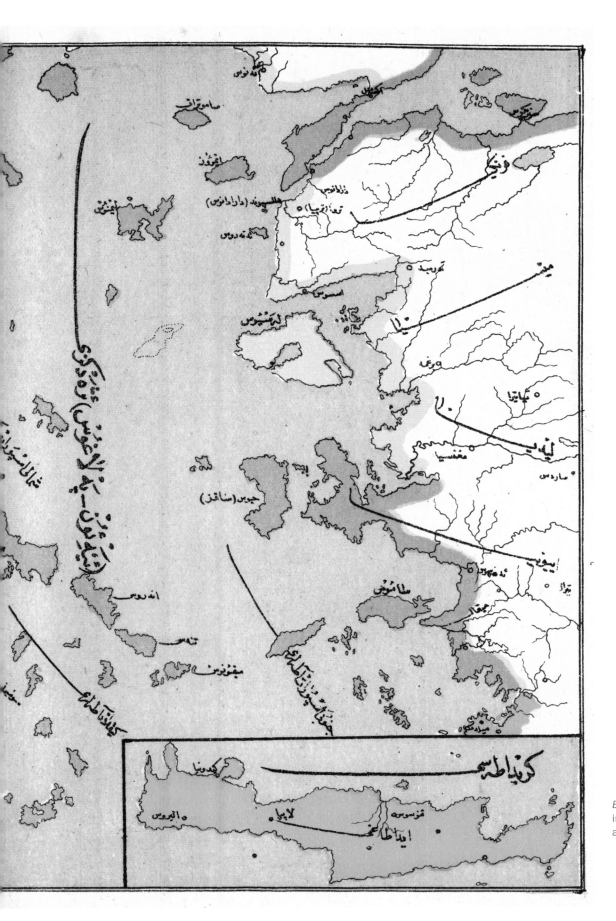

Esâtîr-i Yunaniyan
includes maps showing
ancient civilisations.

INTEREST IN MYTHOLOGY

Although Neo-Hellenism never became a mainstream movement in Turkey, its presence in Turkish cultural life did not go unnoticed. This is evident in an interview by the Turkish diplomat Ruşen Eşref (1892-1959) of the influential poet Ahmet Haşim (1884-1933). Especially Haşim's description of Yahya Kemal is remarkable:

"Yahya Kemal is watching the blueness of the Mediterranean from between ruined white marble columns, lying under the shadow of an olive tree with silver leaves on the Lesbos beaches. It is as if this poet has wrestled with centaurs near the Meander River and talked and made fun with the echo fairies in the bulrushes. He has the same role in our literature as an old hero scattering the clouds of Birds in the Stymphalian swamps. His arrows dispersed the birds that are hindering our poetry, and he killed the Nemean lion of our literature."

The slight irony in his words means that Ahmet Haşim did not take Neo-Hellenist ideas too seriously, although this does not necessarily indicate that he had no interest in Greek civilization and mythology whatsoever. In effect, it was impossible not to be influenced by prevalent ideas about the Greek Miracle and the origins of Western civilisation, and not to develop an interest in mythology when dealing with contemporary French literature. And so there are indications that Ahmet Haşim, despite his apparent scepticism, also took an active interest in mythology. Like Yahya Kemal, he was clearly inspired by especially French thought on the importance of the Greek past and culture, even preferring French pronunciations for Greek proper names. One of his students at the Academy of Fine Arts asserted that Ahmet Haşim knew the ancient Greek and Roman gods like he knew the members of his own family and that it was mythology that empowered his imagination.

Salih Zeki (1864-1921), an admirer and close friend of Ahmet Haşim, is the first Turkish poet totally inspired by Greek mythology. All the poems in his books *Persefon* (1930), *Asya Şarkıları* (1933), *Pınar* (1936), *Rüzgâr* (1939), *Titan* (1966) and *Laton* trilogy (1964-67-68) are either about mythology or inspired by mythology. His passion became the subject of humour, even attracting severe criticism from Ahmet Haşim himself.

The influence of the interest in Greek mythology – that started in the Tanzimat Period- on Turkish literature was limited. It did, however, motivate Turkish nationalists to revive Turkish mythology and epics belonging to the times when the Turks had not yet adopted Islam. Yet even nationalists did not entirely ignore Greek mythology. Hüseyinzâde Ali (1864-1940), who was among the first Turkish nationalists, advocated focusing on

Greek and Latin sources, advice that was heeded by Abdullah Cevdet (1869-1932) and Ziya Gökalp (1876-1924). According to Ziya Gökalp "all classics started with Homer and Virgil". He argued that Turkish literature should not focus on romanticism or other literary genres before adopting all aesthetic aspects of these Greek and Roman Classics, especially in view of the need to create a national literature praising and encouraging ideals and heroism.

Limited though it was, Hellenism gradually gained some influence on the development of Turkish literature and nationalist thought. Although Ömer Seyfettin (1864-1920) seriously attacked Yahya Kemal's and Yakup Kadri's Neo-Hellenism in his "The Enemy of Boycott", he did advise the youth to read Homer as a lesson; as a sacred book. In his article entitled "European Literature and Greek Classics", which was published in *Turkish Women Journal* of 9 January 1919, he again argued for the importance of Homer, and summed up and translated the *İliad* (from a French version by Lecomte de Lisle: *Iliad, The Epic of the Oldest Greek Poet Homer*). He was not alone in this. Ali Cânib, another early nationalist, published a book entitled *Epopée* (1927) in which he mentioned the Iliad, the *Odyssey* and Kalevala frequently. Some went even further and appropriated the past: Rıza Nur (1879-1942) claimed that Greek mythology derived from Turkish mythology; a thesis that was adopted by Nurettin Mustafa in Egypt and Yusuf Ziya Bey in Turkey in his book *Turkish History* (in the chapter on Turkish mythology).

Similarly, Yusuf Ziya (Özer) Bey in his book *Turkish Civilization Before Ancient Greece* (1928) stated that names of non-Greek pedigree in the history and geography of Ancient Greece must be Turkish. He followed up on this assertion by arguing that Turkish communities came to Greece in ancient times and founded a great civilization. The traces of Turkish language in the modern Greek language, he argued, were the result of later, Greek, migrations to a hitherto highly civilized 'Turkish' Greece. In a similar vein, Yusuf Ziya Bey analysed numerous words of Turkish origin in almost all fields of study (ranging from law to philosophy, from agriculture to art and ancient Greek mythology).

In sum, Ancient Greek and Latin culture did not attract much attention during the first years of the republic (during the "Single-Party Period"). However, later on in Turkish political history, especially between 1939 and 1945, the classics were at the centre of Turkish cultural policies, with Turkish intellectuals falling in love with Homer and classical mythology. One of the results of this renewed interest was the so-called *Mavi Anadolucular* (Blue Anatolians) movement, and a distinct turn of interest towards the Mediterranean.

ATATÜRK IN TROY

RÜSTEM ASLAN – MITHAT ATABAY

From Antiquity onwards the Trojan War has been regarded as a clash between the West and the East, as the archetypical conflict between Asia and Europe. Indeed, virtually all the important figures in European and Near Eastern history interpreted the war in this manner. For instance, while Persian king Xerxes was crossing the Hellespont with his strong army to invade the Greek lands in 480 BC, he visited the fortress of Priam and sacrificed 1,000 head of cattle to Athena of Ilion. Vice versa, when Alexander the Great invaded the Persian Empire in 334 BC, he sacrificed an animal on the tomb of Achilles and complained that there was nobody like Homer with him to sing of his exploits. His successor Lysimachus (361-281 BC) rebuilt Ilion and erected the magnificent Temple of Athena, of which the remains are visible to this day. Even after Antiquity, the Trojan War was considered as the origin of conflict between Europe and Anatolia and, potentially, as a *casus belli*. After Mehmed the Conqueror took control of Istanbul, he visited Troy in 1462 and said, "We avenged the Trojans by conquering Istanbul." Mehmed's visit to Troy represents the first Ottoman interest in that site and the first attempt to appropriate Trojan history. After Mehmed, however, the site remained deserted and Ottoman interest in Troy seems to have waned. Following Schliemann's excavations and particularly after "Priam's Treasure" had been on display in Athens in 1874-1875, certain Ottoman intellectuals in Istanbul started to show a renewed interest in Troy. The revival of interest in the site and its history, limited though it was to a small group of intellectuals, probably had much to do with the appointment of Osman Hamdi Bey as director of the Imperial Museum. Although public interest in Troy dwindled after the publication of W. Dörpfeld's excavation results in 1893, Troy gained a wider importance with the visit of Mustafa Kemal (later to be known as Atatürk) to the region during the Balkan Wars.

MUSTAFA KEMAL'S DEPARTURE FOR MILITARY INVESTIGATIONS AND HIS VISIT TO TROY ON THE TRAIL OF ALEXANDER THE GREAT

Although Troy's ruins had been identified and widely discussed at the beginning of the 20th century, the name of Troy is not recorded even once in the memories of Captain Selahattin, who stayed in a Turkish village named Çıplak near the ruins of Troy in 1912 for almost six months. This notable absence demonstrates the lack of general interest in Troy in this early period. This, however, was about to change.

Although Mustafa Kemal was stationed in Tripoli (in Cyrenaica) when the Balkan War broke out, he left that city on 24 October 1912 and arrived in Istanbul via Egypt, Trieste and Romania. At this point, virtually all of Rumelia had been invaded, while the Bulgarian army now approached Çatalca (Chataldja). Upon arriving at Istanbul, Mustafa Kemal was posted to the Ministry of War on 21 November. During his short-lived commission at the Ministry, Kemal stressed the importance of the Bolayır isthmus, arguing that it "is the entrance to the region and controls all traffic from the Black Sea to the Mediterranean." Moreover, any army stationed in this region could counterattack the Bulgarian army near Çatalca. Subsequently, the Ottoman War Ministry established a reorganized army corps at the Bolayır isthmus. Command of these "Reorganized Forces for the Mediterranean Strait" (as they were called) was given to Fahri Pasha, with Major Ali Fethi (Okyar) as his Chief of Staff and Mustafa Kemal as Chief of Staff Operations. He was appointed to this position on 25 November 1912 with the objective of defending the Dardanelles and Gallipoli against enemy attack, be it sea-borne or overland (from Bolayır).

The trenches of Gallipoli were, in a way, the foundation of the later Turkish state, for it united Ali Fethi and Mustafa Kemal, and Dr Tevfik Rüştü (Aras), a friend of Mustafa Kemal's and a leading member of the Party of Union and Progress in Istanbul. Before taking up his new position at Gallipoli, Mustafa Kemal met with Rüştü in Istanbul and offered him a position at Çanakkale (on the Dardanelles). Rüştü, as a member of the Association of Schools of Medicine and General Health, was nominated as chief physician of the Red Crescent Hospital at Çanakkale. It was the beginning of a Turkish 'triumvirate' that lasted into the Republican period: Mustafa Kemal became the first president of Turkish Republic and remained in that position until his death, whilst Ali Fethi became the first president of the assembly after the proclamation of the republic and then served as prime minister. Dr Tevfik Rüştü acted as head of the population exchange commission at first, and served as the minister of foreign affairs from 1925 to 1938.

When Mustafa Kemal was appointed to Gallipoli, Istanbul was being shelled by Bulgarian artillery around Lake Terkos.

Presidential decree to despatch the 512 coins found during excavations at Troy in 1932 to the United States through the American embassy in Turkey, under condition that they would be returned the following excavation season. The coins were sent to the US for cleaning and research. The request for temporary despatch originated with the Education Ministry. The decree was signed by the president of the Republic of Turkey, Gazi Mustafa Kemal (Atatürk), and the commission responsible on 19 July 1932.

Presidential decree granting the archaeologist Carl Blegen permission to conduct excavations at Troy in 1934. The decree is signed by Gazi Mustafa Kemal (Atatürk), first president of the Republic of Turkey, and the commission responsible on 5 November 1933.

Large crowds of immigrants from Balkans fled to the City, while the Ottoman lines crumbled. In politics, too, the realm had become dangerously instable. On 3 December 1912, the Ottoman Empire signed the Çatalca (Chataldja) Armistice with the Balkan states excluding Greece, followed by peace negotiations in London on 13 December. Meanwhile, the war with Greece lingered on. The situation from an Ottoman perspective was rather depressing. While the historical capital Edirne had been regained, virtually all of Thrace was now under Bulgarian sway.

Faced with this situation, Mustafa Kemal initiated a military investigation on 26 March, reviewing the threat of potential enemy attacks on Gallipoli. Kemal and his adjutant departed from Bolayır, arriving in Karainbeyli, Kumköy, Yalova, Akbaş and Sestor via Ortaköy and Tayfur. En route he visited the Sestos-Abydos region where the Persian King Xerxes shipped his army to Anatolia using 674 pontoons, taking notes. After

a lunch at Bigalı Castle he went to Kilia Bay and Maydos, surveying Kilitbahir Castle, the condition of the Namazgâh and Hamidiye bastions, and then progressed towards Krithia, where he spent the night.

The following day, Mustafa Kemal went to Seddülbahir Castle and crossed to the Anatolian side by boat. Following the path of Alexander the Great, he visited the Orhaniye Bastion. He later arrived in Yenişehir and examined the geographical situation at this point of the Dardanelles at the site known as the Tomb of Achilles. He strolled about the ruins of Troy and drew some sketches in his notebook. As a result of these investigations Mustafa Kemal made a historical evaluation and decided that the defence of the Anatolian coast should not be problematic; the main defensive lines had to be deployed along the European coast.

THE PERCEPTION OF TROY ON THE TURKISH FRONT DURING THE DARDANELLES BATTLE AND MUSTAFA KEMAL

As we have seen, the Ottoman Empire had already been significantly weakened by the Balkan wars in particular. While the Ottoman alliance with the German Empire in the First World War resulted in even more problems, and the acute threat of an invasion in Western Anatolia, it also meant an influx of German military expertise into the Ottoman army. At the same time, the strategic importance of the Troad also resulted in a renewed interest in Troy and, amongst soldiers of both the Allied and Ottoman-German side, a sense of treading in the footsteps of Homer's heroes.

The threat of an Allied invasion of the Troad (with the ultimate aim of capturing Istanbul and opening the sea routes to the Black Sea) became a reality on 25 April 1915, when Allied troops landed on Trojan shores. To their surprise, they were

A Turkish officer among the ruins of Troy during the Gallipoli Campaign, also known as the Dardanelles Campaign in 1915. Standing on lookout, he observes the British fleet sailing into the Dardanelles. It cannot be seen from the photograph, but ironically one of the British warships was called HMS Agamemnon.

met by a resolute Ottoman defence.. Despite the notorious conditions at Gallipoli, entries in the diaries of soldiers indicate an awareness of the Troad's heroic history and of the symbolism of this new "Trojan War". Paul Schweider's book entitled *In the General Headquarters of the Turks during the Dardanelles Battle* is an example of these sentiments. Schweider made numerous comparisons between the present and the heroic past in his diary, and many of these comparisons, such as this passage, were later used for his book:

And Mount Ida, divine residence of the Father of the Gods, just behind Troy is rising to the sky. In the coming days, while standing on the castle of Priam I will longingly and curiously look at the two great hills where Achilles and Patroclus were buried. I understand from one of the military escorts that these two hills had not only historical but also particularly strategic importance during the Dardanelles bombardment. More than 3,000 years after Achilles dragged Hector's dead body around Troy before he himself died through an arrow in his heel, naval officers were now standing on the hills where the two Homeric heroes were buried, and watching through artillery glasses a war of nations which was much bigger than those that had previously been waged for Ilion.

Schweider was certainly not alone in comparing Gallipoli with the Trojan War as various of his fellow German officers made similar remarks in their diaries. The same applies to the Allied side.

Troy's more recent archaeological past also played a part in the war at Gallipoli, for the farmhouse of Frank Calvert, situated nearly four kilometres southeast of Troy, was used as military quarters by German and Turkish soldiers. Haydar Mehmed Alganer, the Chief of Staff in the Anafartalar region, who had taken the famous picture of Mustafa Kemal at the Arıburnu Front, stayed in the farmhouse for a while. Whilst Alganer mentions the ruins of Troy and the Calvert family, he does not make any historical comment on the matter. There was, however, a library in the farmhouse as Major Alganer described: "I stay on my own during spare time. I regret not bringing a sofa from Istanbul. I got a German book on Troy but I cannot find time to read. It is not of much interestto me anyway. Now I look forward to receiving letters from home." Evidently, Alganer was not particularly interested in Troy from a cultural perspective. On the other hand, Mustafa Kemal does speak of Troy and the Trojan War when referring to the hard-fought battles in Gallipoli. In his memoires touching upon the Battle of the Dardanelles, he mentions Troy and his visits to the site quite frequently.

The German politician Ernst Jackh, who visited Mustafa Kemal twice during the war, recalls Kemal's memories from the Dardanelles Campaign:

The report I sent to Zeki Pasha, the head adjutant of Sultan, at the end of September 1915 consisted of these subjects: When I was welcomed by Liman Von Sanders (the German officer in charge of the coastal defence), I mostly spent time with Fevzi and Mustafa Kemal. They saw me investigating defence fronts in the front line stretching towards the Karamenderes Valley and Troy on the Dardanelles Strait, and from the northern corner of the Anafarta Group to the end of the Gallipoli peninsula. Once we were watching the British warships over the hills where Achilles and Patroclus were buried. I cannot imagine a victory of greater historical value than that won by the soldiers on the Dardanelles Strait. On the one hand there was artillery – a symbol of the enormous progress of Western technology in the 20th century – while there were carts on the other hand – the most primitive transportation vehicles drawn by oxen, carrying modern ammunition to Turkish soldiers.

These impressions suggest that Mustafa Kemal talked with German officers about the Trojan War and historical comparisons with contemporary events. Mustafa Kemal's remark after the Dumlupınar Victory, "Now we have taken revenge for Hector," attributed to him by Sabahattin Eyüboğlu, should perhaps be seen in that light.

The interest of Mustafa Kemal Atatürk in Troy continued after the foundation of the Republican regime. Atatürk founded the Turkish Historical Society and, in 1931, this Society published a history in four volumes for secondary schools: the Trojan War was included in the first volume. In the same year the cabinet gathered under the presidency of Mustafa Kemal for the purpose of granting an excavation permit in Troy to the American archaeologist Carl Blegen. Troy thus returned to the hands of archaeologists.

Lieutenant-Colonel Mustafa Kemal Atatürk (left) during the Gallipoli Campaign in 1915. Atatürk is here standing on the Dardanelles in the vicinity of Troy in a photograph taken by Major Haydar Alganer. The photograph is part of the collection of the Çanakkale Deniz Museum and the camera used is in the Çimenlik Kalesi Museum.

THE BLUE ANATOLIANS

ÖMER FARUK ŞERIFOĞLU

The interest in Hellenic (Ancient Greek) and Latin cultures, which had gradually increased during the late Ottoman and early Republican period, gained further momentum in Turkey in the period 1939 to 1945, when İsmet İnönü served as Turkey's second President. The most notable result of this interest in European culture was a large number of translations of Western classics, produced under the supervision of Hasan Âlî Yücel (1897-1961), as Minister of Education best known because of his reformation of the Turkish educational system. The Translation Bureau was established, with the specific intent of Westernizing Turkey and promoting humanism.

HUMANIST CULTURAL POLITICS

This bureau in many ways served as the headquarters of a humanist movement, promoting its mission through its journal *Tercüme* (Translation). While the drive towards humanism and Western culture was – in part, at least – politically motivated, an interest in Western and, specifically, classical culture, was now something that was shared by a wider segment of the country's (intellectual) elite. Various leading thinkers of the Republican period, such as Nurullah Ataç (1898-1957), Sabahattin Eyüboğlu (1908-1973), Sabahattin Ali (1907-1948), Bedrettin Tuncel (1910-1980) and Nusret Hızır (1899-1980) were linked to the journal.

Tercüme's mission was to create a new culture based on Hellenistic-Latin culture, as opposed to a Turkish culture with Islamic values. This is evident in various contributions to the journal. In his foreword to a special edition of *Tercüme*, which focused on Hellenistic culture, Hasan Âlî Yücel noted that 'we need to recognize the Ancient Greeks with their grammar, social lives and all their works in order to know ourselves'. It is at this time that some humanist men of letters, like Nurullah Ataç and Suat Yakup Baydur (1912-1953), while defending the purity of the Turkish language, argued that Greek and Latin languages should become part of the Turkish curriculum. And indeed, Istanbul University opened its Greek and Latin Language and Literature Departments in 1942-1943, while Latin was taught in some high schools in Istanbul and Ankara from that same year on.

Soon the impact of Humanist cultural policies and the related translation activities became evident, as many poets and authors included or referred to classical mythology in their works. Ahmet Hamdi Tanpınar (1901-1962) and Ahmet Haşim (1884-

Halikarnas Balıkçısı, Bedri Rahmi Eyüboğlu and Azra Erhat, prominent figures in the humanist intellectual circle known as the Blue Anatolians, during one of their many 'Blue Cruises'. The circle embraced humanist ideas and its members were well versed in the classics. They aimed at an Anatolian alternative to Greek culture in their writings. The 'blue' in the name refers to the Aegean Sea that links Anatolia to Aegean culture. The 'Greek Miracle' (the rise of classical Greek culture between the 8th and 5th centuries BC) was for them less a specifically Greek than rather an Aegean or Ionian miracle – and thus of Anatolian origin. Homer is seen as an Anatolian and the *Iliad* as an Anatolian epic.

1933) are prime examples of this new movement. Both authors frequently alluded to mythology in their articles and novels. In his poem entitled İnsanlar Arasında (*Among Humankind*) for instance, Tanpınar likens Zeus to a human being.

AN ANATOLIAN ALTERNATIVE

Governmental policies to further humanism and interest in European classics had other side effects. The circle of the Blue Anatolians (*Mavi Anadolucular*) is perhaps the most interesting of these. While the members of this circle (or movement) embraced humanistic thought and were well-read in European Classics, they focused on an Anatolian alternative to Hellenistic culture in their writings. The name of their movement refers to

One of the last champions of the Blue Anatolians was probably Turgut Özal, the eighth president of the Republic of Turkey and author of the book *La Turquie en Europe* (published in French in 1988 and in English in 1991).

Turkish translation of Turgut Özal's well known book *La Turquie en Europe*, a romanticised history of Anatolian culture drawing together several historical periods.

this position, focusing both on Anatolia, and on Aegean culture (i.e. the blue colour of the Aegean Sea).

For one of the first of these Blue Anatolians, Cevat Şakir Kabaağaçlı (1890-1973), the Greek Miracle (the rise of Classical Greek culture in the 8th to 5th centuries BC) was not so much a Greek thing, but rather an Aegean or Ionian miracle – and thus of Anatolian pedigree. Embracing the ancient name of Bodrum (where he lived in exile) and using the pseudonym The Fisherman of Halicarnassus, Kabaağaçlı considered Anatolian culture to be superior to Hellenistic culture. This also affected his view on the origins of perhaps the greatest classical author of them all, for Kabaağaçlı argued that Homer, too, was an Anatolian rather than a Greek. As a consequence, he considered the *Iliad* to be an Anatolian epic. By combining humanist ideas and theories from the early days of the Turkish Republic with aspects of the Turkish humanism of the 1940s, the ideas of The Fisherman of Halicarnassus clearly indicate the future course of Blue Anatolianism. In his writings, Kabaağaçlı's initial interest in Classical Greek culture and mythology became something much more, and developed into a real passion for the Classics – albeit in an Anatolian-Aegean setting.

Sabahattin Eyüboğlu (1908-1973), the second major figure of the Blue Anatolians, had more or less the same opinions. In his article "The *Iliad* and Anatolia", he argues with an unbelievable naivety that the *Iliad* is a way to liberation. The *Iliad* (available in Turkish translations by A. Kadir (1917-1985) and Azra Erhat (1915-1982)), he suggests, can lead the reader to a Mediterranean morning full of hope, verging on a veritable Renaissance. He continues by asserting that Turkey:

is our country not due to the fact that we conquered it, but because we are an inseparable part of it. Even if there were a majority of other peoples in the land, all of these will unite. It is us, the conqueror as well as the conquered, the melting of peoples and cultures... The East and the West band together... We are another kind of Turk, another kind of Muslim. The dominant essence of our being is Anatolia, the cradle of civilization.

Though the Blue Anatolians' discourse was distinct from contemporary official (state) ideology in its attitude to "others" (by way of adopting the multi-cultural heritage of Anatolia), the movement's overall ideology was clearly fervently nationalist. As such, it has been criticized by various intellectuals, most notably Murat Belge, a well-known left-liberal thinker, academic and civil rights activist.

One of the last protagonists of Blue Anatolianism was arguably Turgut Özal (1927-1993), the eighth president of Turkish Republic and author (though it is rumoured to have been penned by someone else) of the book "La Turquie en Europe" (published in French in 1988 and in English in 1991). It is a fictionalized account of Anatolian culture, bringing different historical ages under the same roof through the recurrent use of the word "we". With its moderate approach to Islam and strong humanistic emphasis above nationalist feelings, this Anatolian way of thinking reappears in every corner of history when Turkish identity is made to be combined with the West.

HOMER AND ISMIR

ŞÜKRÜ TÜL

It suffices to look at the image on a pot found in Thebes (see page 83 and 164) in order to understand the effect of Homer on his period. According to Joachim Latacz, Homer wrote the *Iliad* around the 750s BC and the *Odyssey* in 725 BC. The Theban pot, which shows the abduction of Helen by Paris is dated around 730 BC (although some have argued for an alternative interpretation). Homer's poems clearly had a major impact on Greek society, but little is known about the man. Who was Homer? Where did he come from? These questions were already hotly debated in ancient times.

A range of Roman texts indicate that Smyrna (modern Izmir) was – in Roman times – considered to be the birthplace of Homer. Yet another text, describing the contest of Hesiod and Homer, indicates that many cities wanted to embrace Homer. A reference to "Melesigenes" (born of Meles), Homer's name at birth, suggests that he was born in Smyrna, which was indeed one of the cities that later claimed to be his city of birth. Meles was the river that flowed through Smyrna, and in some legends, Homer is reported to have been the child of the Meles River and the nymph Cretheis. Alternatively, Pseudo-Herodotus reports that a young girl named Cretheis was sent to Smyrna from her hometown Cyme, because she had become pregnant. At Smyrna, she gave birth to a baby to be called Melesigenes on the banks of the river Meles. Pseudo-Plutarch writes several times that Cretheis was descended from Cyme and was forced to marry a teacher from Smyrna named Phemius in order to hide her pregnancy. She then delivered a baby on the banks of river Meles. Pindar (referred to in the Vita Scorialensis II), notes that both Smyrna and Chios could have been Homer's birthplace. Proclus has a similar approach, evaluating the claims that Homer was born in Colophon, Chios and Smyrna. He also states that Homer first saw light on the banks of river Meles. Hesychios of Miletus also discussed the origins of the great poet and, pointing especially to the name Melesigenes, considered Smyrna to be the most likely candidate. Hesychios was not alone in preferring Smyrna as Homer's birthplace: in the Vita Romana by Stesimbrotos of Thasos, Smyrna is named as the poet's hometown. Smyrna is again mentioned in the "Vita Scorialensis", although other sites, such as Colophon and Chios are included as plausible candidates. This text again dwells on Homer's parentage: his father was the river god Meles. The relation between Homer and the River Meles, at any rate, seems to have been important to all ancient authors: Colophon, Smyrna and Chios were all situated relatively close to that river, and consequently were considered to be plausible candidates. Despite this (or perhaps because of it), consensus was never reached, and the question remains hotly debated to this day. Nowadays, the poet's very existence is sometimes questioned. with some arguing that Homer was not a single person, but rather a group of poets, following the same poetic tradition. This group is then referred to as the Homeridai.

In a way, Homer's language (with strong Ionian links, and various – older- Aeolian influences) suggest that there was, indeed, a link with Smyrna. Both archaeology and ancient sources (Herodotus, *Historiae*, I, 150; Strabo, *Geographica*, XIV 4-634) indicate that Aeolian Greeks had settled the region around Smyrna during the so-called Dark Age, around 1000 BC. At a somewhat later point, Ionian Greeks settled in the region and Smyrna quickly became a major centre of the Ionian Greek world.

Through archaeology, much is known about the Smyrna of Homer's time. The site of Homer's Smyrna today is known as Tepekule. Archaeologically speaking, Homer's time corresponds to the Early and Middle Geometrical period (875-750 BC) and Late Geometrical period (750-700 BC), and settlement remains belonging to these periods have been found at Smyrna during excavations headed by Professor Ekrem Akurgal. During these excavation, city walls made of mud brick (with an average width of 3.5 meters and dating to ca. 850 BC), houses and a wheat silo (*tholos*) were uncovered, indicating that Smyrna had been a well-fortified and important city during Homer's lifetime. In strata dating to the Late Geometric period (ca. 725 BC), remains of a temple and a processional road have been found. Amongst the finds was vase with a representation of a seven stringed lyre, which may indicate the poetic way of life at the site. Yet another image of a lyre on a chimney pot is dated slightly later, about 670 BC.

Although these early pictorial references to poetic activity at Smyrna do not explicitly refer to Homer, it is clear that the inhabitants of classical Smyrna considered the great poet a fellow Smyrnaean. Strabo (*Geographica*, XIV, 37-646) writes that the inhabitants of Pagos – the Hellenistic settlement overlooking the old town of Smyrna, and known today as Kadifekale – considered the poet as such. To stress their Homeric heritage, they

minted a type of bronze coin that they called Homereion. On these coins, the poet was displayed. In this, the Smyrnaeans were not alone, for the city of Colophon issued similar coins.

The competition between the cities of Smyrna and Colophon over the Homeric past was expressed in more ways than one. In addition to Smyrna's Homeric coins, the city included a building known as the Homereion, which was surrounded by stoas (*tetrastoon*). Inside the Homereion stood a wooden statue of Homer. A somewhat similar situation could be found at Clarus, a major sanctuary of Apollo some 13 km from Colophon (which controlled the temple), where a large sculpture of a poet (quite possibly Homer) was erected. The sculpture was discovered in 1952 by Louis Robert, who was head of Turkish-French excavations in the 1950s. The archaeological finds at Clarus may tally with the numismatic evidence (where Homer is often shown on one side of the coin, with Apollo on the other side) and a reference by Pseudo-Plutarch to an inscription at the bottom of a statue (Pseudo-Plutarch, *De vita poesi Homeri*, 1, 4.5) which reads: "Homer, the son of Meles, you enlivened your hometown Colophon and the whole of Hellas (Greece)!".

With this inscription, the inhabitants of Colophon asserted their claim to Homer. Yet even the inscription indicates that the river Meles was the birthplace of Homer. Since this river, as Strabo asserts, ran right beside the city walls of Smyrna (*Geographica*, Book XIV, 646-37), Smyrna seemed to have the better cards. However, Strabo also pointed out that neither Smyrna nor the river Meles are mentioned in Homer's epics (*Geographica*, XII, 554-27).

There is an additional problem, for the identity of the river Meles was lost. Since the 17th century various attempts have been made to identify one of the smaller streams near Izmir as the old Meles. The most likely candidate now appears to be the Halkapınar lagoon and the small stream running into it.

Homer Monument in Izmir, erected in 2002 by the Turkish sculptor Professor Ferit Özşen. The monument consists of two marble components with figures taken from the *Iliad*. The legend is a quote attributed to Homer in which he says: 'I was born in the lap of Izmir, where the Meles joins the sea.' By means of this monument, Izmir aims to show that Homer came from the city.

A bust of Homer erected in 2003 in the garden of the Faculty of Letters of the Dokuz Eylül University in Izmir.

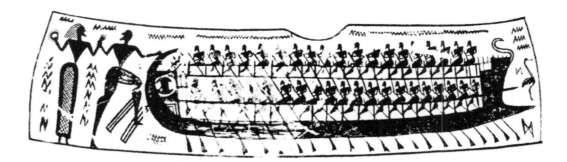

A marble tablet with an inscription referring to the Meles from Halkapınar (but now at the Bornova Merkez mosque), seems to strengthen this identification.

From at least the 18th century onwards, Smyrna figured prominently in the European collective mind as the birthplace of Homer. Various sites in and near the city (such as a grotto which was identified as 'Homer's cavern') were readily associated with the great poet, although there really was very little to no evidence whatsoever to support these associations. It did, however, further tourism.

Meanwhile, the inhabitants of Izmir remembered the poet by means of a journal called *Omiros*, which is published by the "United Education Association", a Rum (Greek) society between the years 1873 and 1878. In addition to this, the name Omirion was given to one of the girls' schools in the French

Drawing of an illustration on a krater (mixing vase for wine and water) from ca. 730 BC (see also page 83), perhaps showing the moment at which the Trojan Prince Paris leads Helen, the wife of King Menelaus, aboard his ship to sail away to Troy. There is no clear evidence for this kind of mythological interpretation of this scene. The way he 'takes her by the arm' could also be a leaving gesture.

district of the city in 1881. Even more recently, in 2002, a monument to Homer (by the sculptor Professor Ferit Özşen) was erected in the Yeşildere delta (which is often – but mistakenly – seen as the river Meles). Lastly, a bust of Homer was erected in the courtyard of the Faculty of Science and Letters of the Dokuz Eylül University in May 2003.

Before Homer set down the orally transmitted stories about the Trojan War, the stories were recited by rhapsodes accompanying themselves on a lyre. Rhapsodes were bards of a kind, except that they did not extemporise, but rather stuck fairly closely to their script. A lyre – appropriately – is shown on this shard found in Smyrna (Izmir), perhaps from the time that Homer lived there.

This statue of Homer, presumably from the 4th century, is in the Izmir Museum for History and the Arts. The lower part was excavated in Clarus near Colophon, one of the 12 Ionian cities in Western Turkey, in 1950, and subsequently taken to the Archaeological Museum in Izmir. The top of the same statue was found 30 years later at the same site and added to the collection of the Archaeological Museum in Selçuk (Ephesus). The two museums competed for the complete statue over the years between 1992 and 2004, Izmir demanding the head and Selçuk the lower part. The head finally went to Izmir, the city with a claim to being Homer's birthplace.

9 ETERNAL TROY

THE EXCAVATIONS IN TROY FROM PAST TO PRESENT: THE DISCOVERIES, DISCUSSIONS AND RESULTS

RÜSTEM ASLAN

The ruins of Troy are located at the western edge of Anatolia, near the southern entrance to the Dardanelles Strait. The region was known as the Troas during the classical period (which is often anglicised as 'the Troad' in scholarly literature), but is known as the Biga Peninsula today. Situated between the Aegean and the Sea of Marmara, between Asia and Europe, Troy lies on the outskirts of a limestone plateau between the rivers Karamenderes (Scamander in the *Iliad*) and Dümrek (Semois). Today it lies six kilometres from the Aegean coast and 4.5 kilometres from the Dardanelles Strait. Because of its geographical position, it always had a strategic importance to whomever ruled the area.

Troy and its surroundings stand at the centre of the *Iliad*, a work which is believed to have been written down by Homer in the 730s BC The poet, or those who informed him, must have carefully surveyed the Karamenderes Valley, the now-lost port on the Aegean coast, and Tenedos, Imbros, Samothrace and Mount Ida – all of which can clearly be seen from Troy today, since many geographic details in the *Iliad* match the region's geography.

In the 19th and the beginning of the 20th centuries, numerous classical philologists carried out critical studies suggesting that the content of the epic is no more than fiction and not based on true events. In fact, some researchers doubted whether Homer and Troy had existed at all.. But despite these views, Homer was increasingly read and admired and, from the 17th century onwards, numerous travellers visited the region in pursuit of Homer.

The Dardanelles Strait, islands, mountains and even some streams mentioned in the epic can be easily discovered. Most of the travellers who visited the region, expressed opinions about the location of Priam's Citadel. Though the region was always known as Troy/Ilios in Greek and Roman times, the city's precise location within the Troad appears to have been forgotten during (at the latest) the 11th century.

Aerial photograph of the ruins of Troy. In the background the plains of Troy, the Dardanelles, Gallipoli and the islands of the Aegean.

Map of Troy and the Troad drawn by Jean-Baptiste Lechevalier in 1786. Between 1785 and 1787 he conducted an extensive investigation along the southern edge of the plain where he believed Troy had lain. In 1791 he published his theory that he had discovered the city on the Pınarbaşı Ballıdağ hill. His ideas were to dominate the debate over Troy for almost a century.

TRAVELLERS IN PURSUIT OF TROY

During the Middle Ages, those travellers that visited the region with the aim of locating Homer's Troy, usually presumed that settlements such as Alexandria Troas or Siegon – the remains of which could still be seen along the Aegean coasts – were the site of the legendary Troy. But by the 17th century, such assumptions were increasingly criticised. George Sandys (1610) and George Wheeler (1675) were among the first to critically examine the possible location of Troy. These two travellers argued that Troy should not be sought along the coast, but more inland. The precise location of the ancient city remained, however a matter of conjecture. Various possibilities were put forward by travellers such as Richard Pococke (in 1740), but in the absence of any maps, we cannot be sure where exactly these early travellers thought to have located Troy. The first to pinpoint Troy was Alexander Pope, who attached an imaginary map to his 1716 translation of the *Iliad*. Although the map showed no clear reference to the contemporary geography of the Troad, it proved an incentive for Robert Wood, a British explorer who is

mostly known through his publications of his visits to Baalbek and Palmyra, to look for the famous city in the Troad on behalf of the Society of Dilettanti in 1750.

Wood suggested a mountainous place in the inner region for the site of Troy, but most contemporary researchers did not think much of this suggestion. Various surveys in the region conducted by Comte de Choiseul-Gouffier, the ambassador of France in Istanbul, provide basic geographical data for the site of Troy for the first time. His surveys, which were conducted within the framework of a wider effort to map and document the North-Eastern Aegean, started in 1784, when Comte de Choiseul-Gouffier was appointed ambassador, and continued partly until 1820, when de Choiseul-Gouffier was removed from his position. Jean-Baptiste Lechevalier, the personal assistant of the Comte de Choiseul-Gouffier, examined the southern edge of the Troy valley intensively between the years 1785 and 1787 and claimed that he had found the location of Troy at the hill known as Pınarbaşı Ballıdağ. This site was in many ways an interesting option. A defensive circuit could be observed on this hill, it overlooked the valley of Troy, and it was situated next to the River Menderes. Moreover, there were four tumuli in its vicinity. Apart from the defensive circuit, various remains suggested the existence of a lower city. A vast number of springs were present at the site which made the identification of the site all the more plausible. A citadel, a lower city, burial mounds of heroes, the nearby rivers Scamander and Semois and

The Pınarbaşı Ballıdağ hill shown in a watercolour by W. Gell, 1801. The hill looks out over the Trojan plain and the Karamenderes (Scamander) River. Lechevalier discovered a defensive wall and several tumuli. This lent great credibility to his theory that Troy might have lain here.

various springs... It all seemed to add up. Lechevalier published his discovery and theories in 1791. His ideas dominated the debate on Troy for almost a century.

Lechevalier's work is interesting for more than one reason. For around the same time, Hisarlık – the site that is now accepted as Troy- was mentioned as a possible contender for the first time by Franz Kauffer, another assistant of Comte de Choiseul-Gouffier. Kauffer visited the Troas region in order to test and approve Lechevalier's thesis. In 1803, however, Kauffer suggested that Hisarlık might have been Ilion, the site once considered as a new capital city by the Roman Emperor Constantine. This claim soon turned into a more concrete theory. Edward Daniel Clarke visited the Troad in 1801 and noted several classical coins from Ilion, leading him to point to Hisarlık as the site of Greek and Roman Ilion. At the site he found various inscriptions that confirmed his hunch. However, the identification of Hisarlık as the site of classical Ilion did not necessarily conflict with the identification of Pınarbaşı-Ballıdağ as pre-classical Troy, especially since Lechevalier's finds so clearly fit Homer's description of Troy. That classical Troy did not stand on the spot of Homer's city was also apparent in Strabo, who described these sites as different settlements in his famous book (XIII).

Despite all that, the identification of Pınarbaşı-Ballıdağ as Troy gradually became less attractive – especially since no more data confirming the site as Homer's Troy were forthcoming. In addition, it was increasingly felt that the site's considerable distance to the sea, and the fact that its springs were cold (and not hot as in Homer), made this site less compelling as Homer's city.

The turning point in the search for Troy was the article published in the *Edinburgh Magazine* in April 1820, on the topography of Troy by Charles MacLaren (who, incidentally, had before publication never visited the region). Two years later MacLaren expanded this article into a book of 270 pages. After visiting Hisarlık in 1863, he revised and published the book again in the same year. Maclaren scrutinized all former publications about the topography of Troy and determined that Lechevalier had mistakenly identified two rivers. In the *Iliad*, the Scamander is the largest river of the region, converging with the River Semois in front of Troy, and then flowing into Hellespont. This is not the case at Pınarbaşı: as MacLaren pointed out, only Hisarlık possibly matches the Homeric description. He concluded that the river Karamenderes was the ancient Scamander, and Dümrek the ancient river Semois.

BACKGROUND TO THE EXCAVATION

Maclaren's 1863 book drew the attention of Frank Calvert, a British citizen living in Çanakkale. He started two small scale excavations on his own land at Hisarlık in 1863 and 1865. Although Calvert was soon convinced that he had uncovered the remains of Troy, the small scale of his excavations and his modest means to pursue his interest further meant that he drew only limited attention.

Heinrich Schliemann was not aware of Maclaren's Hisarlık/Troy identification when he first visited the region. He dug at Pınarbaşı-Ballıdağ for a few weeks, where the results of his excavation did not convince him that the site was indeed Troy. When he missed the ship for Athens, he was obliged to stay for another two days at Çanakkale. This is how he met Calvert. Calvert told Schliemann about Hisarlık and his excavations, referring to Maclaren's thesis on Troy. Although Schliemann neither visited the site at that point, nor bothered to read Maclaren's thesis, he was convinced by Calvert's identification of Troy at Hisarlık. He presented the report on his journey through Greece and Troy as a doctoral thesis to Rostock University in Germany in 1869, claiming that he himself had discovered Troy at Hisarlık. The thesis was approved. A year after his trip to Troy, Schliemann came back as a doctor of history and archaeology, with the aim of excavating the site. This, however, was easier said than done, and official permission was not forthcoming. (Complaints about Schliemann

In 1803 Franz Kauffer put forward the theory for the first time that Hisarlık had perhaps been Ilion, or Troy. This initial sketch of Hisarlık was published in 1822.

by a local landowner did not help.) He finally obtained permission in 1871 and started his excavations in that same year. He would continue, with interruptions, until 1890 (1871-73; 1878-79; 1882; 1890), uncovering in 1873 Priam's Treasure; the hoard that brought Schliemann instant fame. He smuggled the treasure first to Athens and later to Germany. Following the Second World War, most of the Treasure was taken to Russia as spoils of war, where it is now exhibited in the Pushkin Museum in Moscow. Schliemann's excavations caused tremendous damage to the site; his ambition led him to ruthlessly dig through various architectural remains (some of these turned out to be from the Late Bronze Age) in order to find the city of Homer's *Iliad*.

After Schliemann's death, excavations at Troy were continued by his friend, the German architect Wilhelm Dörpfeld (1853-1940), who dug at the site between 1893 and 1894. Dörpfeld identified various additional layers of Trojan settlement, and corrected many mistakes made by his old friend. After a long break, the American archaeologist Carl W. Blegen (1887-1917) reinitiated excavations at Troy in the years 1893-1894. Blegen's excavations at Troy laid the foundation of modern Mediterranean (Aegean) archaeology; his later publications still stand out in terms quality and thoroughness. After a 50-year break, new excavations started under the supervision of Manfred Osman Korfmann of Tübingen University. He was director of these excavations until his death in 2005. The excavations of Korfmann resulted in numerous new insights. One of these was that Troy during the late Bronze Age had been a characteristically Anatolian town and that it possessed a fortified lower city.

The results of over a century of excavations at Troy are, in part, reviewed in chapter 2. Through the work of numerous archaeologists and other specialists at Hisarlık, we can now distinguish nine major settlement layers at Troy, and we know more of Troy's place in the Troad and its position on the international stage.

Excavations at Troy by the German archaeologist Wilhelm Dörpfeld in 1893. Dörpfeld identified several layers of settlement in Troy, correcting many of Schliemann's errors.

The excavations at Troy under the direction of Manfred Osman Korfmann yielded a large number of fresh insights. One of these was that Late Bronze Age Troy had been a typical Anatolian port with a fortified lower city, as shown in this reconstruction diagram.

IS IT TROIA, TRUVA OR TROY?

The toponym Troy is written and pronounced differently in various languages: "Troie" in French, "Troy" in English, "Troje" in Dutch, "Troia" in Italian and "Troja" in German. As for Turkish, it is pronounced and written in at least seven different ways: Troya, Truva, Torova, Turova, Turoya, Toruya, Toruva. In international (especially German) academic circles, "Troia" is usually preferred, since it comes closest to the Homeric spelling of the placename.

The origins of and variations in the toponym have been discussed in various scholarly works, most notably by the eminent scholar Joachim Latacz, in his book *Homer – The First Poet of the West* (*Homer Der erste Dichter des Abendlands*). The preference for "Troia" (rather than any of the other options mentioned above) in academic circles is a relatively recent development, probably due to the scientific impact of the Tübingen excavation reports (starting in 1988), where "Troia" is used almost exclusively. Korfmann and his colleagues were, however, not the first to prefer this variant of the toponym, for several world-known Turkish archaeologists (such as Prof. Ekrem Akurgal and Prof. Cevdet Bayburtluoğlu) had used the word "Troia" already many years earlier. Likewise, the Çanakkale Archaeological Museum also preferred the name Troia before the Tübingen excavations started in 1988. While academia nowadays seems relatively united in referring to the Homeric site as "Troia", one wonders why the name of this specific North-Western Anatolian site has so many variations, in so many different languages – although especially in Turkish (which includes, as noted above, no less than seven variants). In fact, the variations in writing and pronunciation are based on the efforts of intellectuals in Istanbul, seeking a Turkish equivalent to French words and concepts which were very popular in the 19th century. For that reason, the French word "Troie" pronounced as "Truva" became common from that time on. After the alphabet revolution and with the use of Latin letters instead of Arabic, many different versions of Truva appeared in the course of time.

As has been argued above, "Troia" is nowadays preferred in international academic circles. In Turkey, "Troya" (*Troy in English*) is also frequently used in popular editions because there is no difference in the pronunciation of Troya and Troia. In addition to that, it accords to Turkish grammar rules to use the letter "y" instead of "i" as in Troya too. As noted, academics prefer "Troia" as a scientific term. However, Blue Anatolians like Azra Erhat and Sabahattin Eyüboğlu, emphasizing the importance of Anatolian heritage, preferred the name "Troya". This can also be observed in the works of contemporary Turkish men of letters such as *Troya'da Ölüm Vardı* (*Death in Troy*) by Bilge Karasu and the translation of *The Trojan Women* (*Troyalı Kadınlar*) by Euripides.

TROY AS DISPLAYED IN MUSEUMS

LAURIEN DE GELDER

From the time that the ancient remains of the city of Troy were exposed by archaeologists artefacts were despatched to be exhibited in many different locations all over the world. We are able to see the points of view about ancient Troy in these exhibitions.

Following an intensive excavation campaign that took place between 1871 and 1873 under the direction of the German archaeologist Heinrich Schliemann (see 7.1), the finds were initially displayed in the South Kensington Museum (now the Victoria and Albert Museum). Schliemann expected to become famous for his excavations at Troy, the city where East and West had battled each other, but once in Europe he did not receive the enthusiastic reception he had hoped for.

While the larger museums of Western Europe showed only limited interest in the collection, the finds were on display to the public in London in 23 glass display cases and cabinets for a period of two years. In 1880 Schliemann decided to transfer the collection to the Museum für Völkerkunde in Berlin and – in 1881 – to donate it to the German people. The collection, which included Priam's Treasure, fell under the control of the Prussian authorities and remained in Berlin, where they were initially exhibited temporarily in the Kunstgewerbemuseum, the current Martin-Gropius-Bau. In around 1885 the collection was moved to the Neues Museum. In 1921 the collection, by then supplemented by artefacts from Schliemann's estate and with new finds from Troy uncovered by his successor Dörpfeld, was housed in the Staatliche Museum für Vor- und Frühgeschichte (State Museum for Pre-History and Early History). Here items from Priam's Treasure are currently to be seen in the permanent exhibition in the Schliemann Room, although as copies.

During the Second World War a large part of the collection of the Museum für Vor- und Frühgeschichte was taken for 'safe' storage to a bunker near the Berlin Zoo, although at the end of the war many of the artefacts turned out to have disappeared. During the post-war years an increasing amount of pottery was restored to Berlin by the Soviet Union, where the archaeological collection was now divided between East and West. Priam's Treasure remained missing.

EXHIBITIONS

One of the first exhibitions following the subdivision of the archaeological collection between East and West Berlin was

The finds made at Troy were first displayed in London. Heinrich Schliemann is shown in this 1877 illustration from *The Illustrated London News* giving a lecture to The Society of Antiquarians in London.

Het goud der Thraciërs. Troje-Thracië exhibiting archaeological treasures from museums in East Germany and Bulgaria. It went on display in the Boijmans van Beuningen Museum in Rotterdam in 1984. This was the first exhibition on Troy in Western Europe that put artefacts from East Germany on display.

This exhibition had as theme the culture of Troy in the Early and Late Bronze Age, which would have been identical to that of the Thracians of the same period, displaying next to each other comparable artefacts from the two regions.

Before the fall of the Berlin Wall in 1989, it was difficult to organise an exhibition containing artefacts from both East and West Berlin. German reunification ensured that the Schliemann collection in Berlin was united once more. There are at least 11,886 artefacts involved. The exhibition *Schliemann's Troia* was organised in 1991 to mark this reunification, opening in the Ruhrlandmuseum, now the Ruhr Museum, in Essen and moving subsequently to Krefeld and Munich. This exhibition was on show in the Rijksmuseum van Oudheden (National Museum of Antiquities) in Leiden at the end of 1991.

The museum world was hit by a bombshell when the Russian authorities finally acknowledged in September 1993 that Priam's Treasure had been lying hidden all those years in Moscow' Pushkin Museum. East and West confronted each other in the battle for Schliemann's gold. Both Germany and Turkey laid claim to the treasure, but the Russians justified their possession of the treasure by describing it as restitution for the suffering caused by the Germans during the Second World War. The Pushkin Museum has since 1996 put on display 259 artefacts from the treasure excavated by Schliemann.

Perhaps the largest and most talked-about exhibition on Troy to date was *Troia - Traum und Wirklichkeit (Troy – Dream and Reality)* that drew almost a million visitors in 2001 and 2002. The exhibition travelled throughout Germany from Stuttgart via Braunschweig to the former West German capital of Bonn. One half of the exhibition, *Traum*, translated Homer's *Iliad* into representative art, while the other half, *Wirklichkeit*, showed the results of more than 20 years of excavation at Troy under the direction of the German archaeologist Manfred Korfmann. His findings caused controversy in both the media and the academic world. Korfmann and his colleague Frank Kolb found themselves on diametrically opposite sides and conducted a scientific feud in public. In the exhibition, Korfmann strove again – after a long interval – to make a link between Homer's *Iliad* and the archaeological site of Troy. Kolb accused him of a lack of scientific thoroughness in making the link and compared Korfmann unfavourably to the famous Schliemann.

Another important exhibition was put on in 2002-2003 in the Yapı Kredi Vedat Nedim Tör Museum in Istanbul: *Troya: Efsane ile Gerçek Arası Bir Kente Yolculuk (Troy: journey to a city between legend and reality)*. This exhibition focused much more on the archaeology of Troy, bringing together artefacts from various Turkish collections, primarily from Istanbul and Çanakkale. The exhibition made a huge contribution to the awareness of Troy among the Turkish public.

The toponym Troy is written and pronounced differently in various languages. This Turkish postage stamp with the Wooden Horse of Troy was printed in Vienna in 1956. The German translation is shown under the Turkish name of the city.

In 2006 the successful and notable exhibition *Mythos Troja* was held in the Antikensammlungen (Antiquities Collections) and the Glyptothek in Munich, comprising artefacts from both collections. The exhibition centred on the myth surrounding Troy. The same year the Museum für Vor- und Frühgeschichte in Berlin organised a Troy exhibition focusing on Schliemann together with the archaeological museum in Warsaw. Another angle of approach to the subject was illuminated in 2008 with the exhibition *Homer – Der Mythos von Troia in Dichtung und Kunst (Homer – The Myth of Troy in Poetry and Art)* in Basel, which was primarily about the poet.

The exhibition *Troje. Stad, Homerus en Turkije (Troy. City, Homer and Turkey)* in Amsterdam's Allard Pierson Museum in 2012-2013 is displaying many of the artefacts seen in the Turkish exhibition of 2002-2003. It delves in greater depth into the way in which Troy has been appropriated down the years than previous exhibitions. For the Greeks the story was part of their culture; Rome laid claim to Troy with the story of Aeneas, and Turkey is the country where the history was played out. The key figures are Homer, as progenitor of the story, the Roman Emperor Augustus, who used his cultural policy to disseminate the idea that the Romans were descended from the Trojans, Heinrich Schliemann, who linked the *Iliad* to the site of Troy, and Atatürk, who compared the Battle of Gallipoli in the First World War – where the Ottoman Empire held off an attempt by the British and French to take Istanbul – to the Trojan War.

TROY AS COMIC STRIP

HERBERT VERRETH

The Trojan War, along with its previous history and aftermath, is dealt with by many authors of Antiquity, sometimes extensively and sometimes in the form of passing reference. Small wonder that these dozens of authors, who attempted to recount the story in both Greek and Latin over a period of more than a thousand years, each created their own Troy. It is thus far from easy to rework all these versions and variations into an internally coherent whole. Nevertheless this is precisely what Eric Shanower has been attempting to do since 1998 with his series of comics entitled *Age of Bronze*, that now runs to 32 issues, or more than 750 extremely detailed pages in black-and-white. Literally all the variations of the narrative material are accorded their rightful historical and psychological place in his magisterial epic, as Shanower strives to draw as many objects and buildings as accurate copies of real archaeological examples. The drawings are beautiful and the story is gripping. In his version, the Greeks have just landed at Troy, and so it is impossible to estimate the hundreds, or even thousands, of pages he will need to complete the story.

Homer's *Iliad* has been turned into a comic strip several times before, but rarely in such convincing manner. Within the *Illustrated Classics* series, which seeks to offer a kind of *Reader's Digest* overview of comics of world literature masterpieces, we find *The Iliad* (1950) and *The Rage of Achilles* (1975). The short story *The Iliad* (1956) by Cuvelier appeared in the magzine *Tintin*, and the black-and-white *The Iliad* in the magazine *Ohee* (1966) by Sels and Renaerts. Follet and Stoquart wrote their own Iliad in two parts in 1974; the drawings are good, but the story is unfortunately poorly reworked. The beautifully illustrated book *The Iliad and the Odyssey* (1996) by Marcia Williams is on the borderline between comic and children's book. There are also numerous other comic book versions of the *Iliad*.

Many comic book artists have interpreted the Trojan War in their own way. *Questor* by Jean-Luc Sala drawn by Saviori & Bassini is a recent example. The main character says in this drawing: 'A primitive wooden vehicle spelled the demise of a city hewn from granite, marble and porphyry.'

Troy also often turns up in the many *Odyssey* comics as the city where Odysseus started out on his 10-year voyage. Consider for example the slightly erotic album *Ulysse* by Pichard (1974-1975), *The Wanderings of Odysseus* (1975) or the children's comic *Goofy, 6. Odysseus* (1981). The adventures of the hero Aeneas also start out in this city, as related by the *Aeneid* in the series *Illustrated classics* (1963) and the Latin comic book *Illa res Troiana* by Blandford and Hill (1968).

On occasion cartoonists let their own imaginations rip on the traditional stories. For example in *Deux contre Troie* (*Two against Troy*, 1962), two children end up at the time of the Trojan War with 'the history guide', a story in which there is no lack of amusing anachronism. In *Thor. The Trojan War* (1981) the Norse god takes sides with some Trojans and goes a round with his Greek counterparts. In an episode in *Les grandes amours contrariées* (*Famous Unhappy Couples*, 1982), King Menelaus fights a war against the Trojans precisely to get rid of his irritating wife Helen. In the extremely successful *Le dernier Troyen. Le cheval de Troie* (*The Last Trojan. The Trojan Horse*, 2004), the story of the Fall of Troy is transported to an intergalactic war in the distant future. The new series *Questor. Ménage à Troie* (*Questor. Trouble in Troy*, 2011), and *Troie. Le peuple de la mer* (*Troy. The People from the Sea*, 2012) are more fantasy than history. Over the last few years, there has apparently been an enormous increase in the number of French comics on Antiquity, including many on the Trojan cycle, but most remain untranslated as yet.

References to Troy also occur in dozens of comics about the late Greek and the Roman worlds, revealing how significant Homer's tales continued to be throughout Antiquity. Alexander the Great's fascination with the Greek hero Achilles, whose grave he visited at Troy, is well known – a detail that is frequently referred to in comics.

Each cartoonist creates their own Troy. Some try to stick to the ancient sources as closely as possible, while others make use of the well known stories to create a point of departure for their own ideas. Some attempt to reconstruct the arms and architecture of the Late Bronze Age as accurately as possible, while others are content to portray an anachronistic city filled with 'classical' Greek temples. There is also the problem of how to visually distinguish the Trojans from the Greeks, especially because there is so little archaeological material available on the Trojan civilisation. As in the film *Troy* (2004) directed by Wolfgang Petersen, Troy is often presented in comics as a city with Minoan, Hittite or loosely 'oriental' characteristics. This decision may be justified to a certain extent, but it remains a purely hypothetical reconstruction.

THE *ILIAD* IN THE 20TH CENTURY

JACQUELINE KLOOSTER

Where does Troy lie? The question that has exercised the minds of archaeologists and historians since Calvert and Schliemann is the following: is Hisarlik in fact the steep holy Troy of Homer? And what remains of Troy? Regardless of what the archaeologists may think-- for many others Troy is more than a location: it is a symbol, as for instance the words of the Bulgarian-French-American author Rachel Bespaloff in her 1940 essay on the *Iliad* illustrate:

> *The city may have been burned to the ground, no stone left on top of another, but it lives on in the epic as living witness to the real or imaginary conflict of which it was the object.*
> (Rachel Bespaloff, *de l'Iliade*)

Troy's significance lies within the *Iliad*, and is thus present wherever this epic is read. Is there still good reason to read a poem about a lost city that is almost 3,000 years old? Yes; for it remains a masterful, wise and ambivalent poem about war, the eternal theme par excellence.

The *Iliad* depicts war as a ghastly yet splendid affair. At times the epic is a eulogy to the heroic martial code, the bloody intoxication of war and the immortal renown (*kleos*) that battle bestows on the youthful warrior. But it is also a lament on the appalling, senseless loss of the young lives of those warriors, the prospect of inevitable *collateral damage*: death, rape and slavery. Remarkably the conflict between Greeks and *Trojans* is never presented as a conflict of 'our heroes' versus 'the barbarians'. If one did not know any better, one could easily think that

Homer was a Trojan, as the French philosopher Simone Weil remarked in her essay on the *Iliad*, also published in 1940.

Even the immortal gods, by turns amused and tormented, observing the spectacle from the Olympian heights of their own perpetual invulnerability, ultimately do not have a decisive say in the course of events. Moira, Fate – a higher and faceless power – has decreed that Troy will fall. The heroes on the battlefield can only play out their roles, gain their eternal glory, and die their horrible deaths. There is no reason.

This fact was grasped by the Alexandrian poet Cavafy, who, in his poem Trojans published in 1905, turned the eternal losers into a metaphor for all useless human striving, without however providing any clue what that striving could be for or why it is doomed:

> *Our efforts are those of the unfortunate;*
> *our efforts are like those of the Trojans*
>
> *(...)*
> *Nevertheless, our fall is certain. Above,*
> *on the walls, the mourning has already begun.*
> *The memories and the sentiments of our days weep.*
> *Bitterly Priam and Hecuba weep for us.*
> (In: C.P. Cavafy, *Poems*)

That a fickle and indescribably beautiful woman is the cause of this war dovetails superbly with the notion of war as the capricious will of the Fates. Moreover, *Helen* is of course the 'obscure object of desire' par excellence. Little wonder then that later versions of the myth locate Helen as a dream figment in Troy, while in reality she remains behind in Egypt, as in Euripides' Helen. She is ultimately, as perhaps every war objective, a mirage as desirable as it is intangible, a fata morgana. In his poem *Helen and Menelaus* published in 1908, the English poet Rupert Brooke sees in Helen – almost prophetically – both the poetic symbol of a beauty *to die for* and the banal reality, the slipperiness of martial ideology:

> *(...)*
> *I*
> *High sat white Helen, lonely and serene.*
> *He [Menelaus] had not remembered that she was so fair,*
> *And that her neck curved down in such a way (...)*
> *II*
> *So far the poet. How should he behold*
> *That journey home, the long connubial years?*
> *He does not tell you how white Helen bears*
> *Child upon legitimate child, becomes a scold*
> *(...)*

> *Often he wonders why on earth he went*
> *Troyward, or why poor Paris ever came.*
> *(...)*
> (Rupert Brooke, *Helen and Menelaus*)

SARPEDON IN THE TRENCHES

It is scarcely surprising that the *Iliad* resonated especially and in various ways in a 20th century plagued by world wars of unrivalled ferocity. The famous *noblesse oblige* speech spoken by Sarpedon, fighting on the side of the Trojans, to his comrade in arms Glaucus proved particularly to inculcate a yearning for honour and glory in schoolboys:

> *"Glaucus, why in Lycia do we receive especial honour as regards our place at table? Why are the choicest portions served us and our cups kept brimming, and why do men look up to us as though we were gods? Moreover we hold a large estate by the banks of the river Xanthus, fair with orchard lawns and wheat-growing land; it becomes us, therefore, to take our stand at the head of all the Lycians and bear the brunt of the fight, that one may say to another, Our princes in Lycia eat the fat of the land and drink best of wine, but they are fine fellows; they fight well and are ever at the front in battle.' My good friend, if, when we were once out of this fight, we could escape old age and death thenceforward and for ever, I should neither press forward myself nor bid you do so, but death in ten thousand shapes hangs ever over our heads, and no man can elude him; therefore let us go forward and either win glory for ourselves, or yield it to another."*
> (*Iliad*, 12.310-328, translated by Samuel Butler)

The nine million largely anonymous deaths on the battlefields of the First World War – the result of gas attack, machine gun, landmine, bombing or simply the ghastly bayonet charge through the muddy trenches – rapidly made clear that this military code of heroic man-to-man combat, with its eternal glory set down in verse, had come to an end once and for all. And with it ended a period in Western civilisation in which Sarpedon's exhortation, along with Hector's celebrated words that whoever fell in battle for his country and died a hero's death (*Iliad* 15.494-499; *Dulce et decorum pro patria mori* in the notorious version of Horace's *Ode* 3.2), could be held up as an example to young men. See for example Wilfred Owen's 1917 poem describing in gruesome detail the agony of a comrade following a gas attack and concluding with the lines:

My friend, you would not tell with such high zest
to children ardent for some desperate glory,
The old Lie; Dulce et Decorum est
Pro patria mori.
(Wilfred Owen, *Dulce et decorum est*)

The Wooden Horse at the visitors' entrance to the excavations at Troy. The Wooden Horse is not mentioned in the *Iliad*. Nevertheless, it has become the key icon of Homer's story of the city's fall.

Lewis Milestone's 1930 film about the First World War, *All Quiet on the Western Front* – based on Erich Maria Remarque's novel, *Im Westen nichts neues* – provides another excellent illustration of this. In it a classics teacher deploys his pedantic stupidity to despatch an entire class of 18-year-olds to futile death at the front using misconstrued quotes torn from their classical contexts, among them Sarpedon's lines. While the lines themselves are not in the novel, the film version has the teacher quoting Sarpedon and Horace.

SIMONE WEIL AND RACHEL BESPALOFF

The heroic code might have disappeared, then, but certainly not the urge to make war. In 1940, at the start of Europa's second great 'cataclysm', Simone Weil's impressive essay *L' Iliade, ou le poème de la force* was published. Weil, a brilliant young philosopher, teacher and socialist of Jewish origin, wrote this anguished reflection on the *Iliad* as France was falling. Her central thesis is contained in the opening sentence of her argument: 'The real hero, the real theme, the core of the *Iliad* is force.' Weil then defines 'force' as 'the x that turns anyone subjected to it into a thing'. Not only those made to suffer *force* are turned into objects, but those who make use of *force* are turned to stone, dehumanised. For Weil the *Iliad* is consequently 'le plus beau, le plus pur des miroirs' – the purest and most beautiful mirror – in the light of the fact that she continues to see the effects of *force* manifesting themselves everywhere around her. The nations of Europe trampled underfoot are the new Troy.

Weil admires the *Iliad* for the boundless compassion with which it depicts this ineluctable dynamic of human suffering, and for the wisdom of the poet, who perceives that the victors could at any moment find themselves the vanquished. It is precisely this dynamic that ensures that in war we will always want to continue the fight – to rebalance the scales, to avenge the suffering caused us. It is for Patroclus that Achilles ultimately kills again, not for Helen or for Agamemnon.

Weil's interpretation a desperate one; however much love she may see in the *Iliad* – between Andromache and Hector, Thetis and Achilles, Achilles and Patroclus – it is always a doomed love, a love that makes us yearn for an end to *force*, for the peace that is occasionally mentioned in passing, as in the description of the springs 'where in the time of peace before the coming of the Achaeans the wives and fair daughters of the Trojans used to wash their clothes' (*Iliad* 22.147-156). These are the springs that Achilles and Hector run past in deadly pursuit.

Despite the great subtlety of her interpretation, Weil loses sight of one significant detail: the *Iliad* also takes a grim pleasure in war. And Weil also appears to be unable or unwilling to accord full value to the brilliant end, the temporary breathing space in this world of *force*, the compassion that Achilles shows the father of the slain Hector in returning his son to him.

Interestingly enough, another essay on the *Iliad* by another French philosopher of Jewish origin, Rachel Bespaloff, appeared at virtually the same time. She appears to have been setting her thoughts down on the significance of the *Iliad* during times of war when Weil's ground-breaking essay appeared. Bespaloff's nuanced essay pays greater attention to the ambivalence of war in Homer's work, but somehow lacks the monolithic power of Weil's essay. Bespaloff realises that Homer and Tolstoy, with whose *War and Peace* she compares the *Iliad*, share a 'virile love for war and a virile abhorrence of it'. It is impossible to separate these two sides of war in Homer's poetry. In the *Iliad* war is above all an ineluctable given that holds up a mirror to human fate with its changing fortunes, suffering and glory, friendship and treachery, cruelty and compassion. Bespaloff does not allow pacifist preoccupations to condition her interpretation of Homer to the extent that Weil does. Her true hero is thus Hector, because he fights for a reason, for Troy, his threatened country: 'As Apollo's protégé, Ilion's protector, defender of a city, a wife, a child, Hector is the protector of transient joys.'

Taken together these two essays form a penetrating illustration of what the *Iliad* has to say to readers in times of duress: both recognise elements of their own merciless reality in Hom-

er's hymn to Troy, even if is an open question whether this offers them any consolation. The last sad parallel between these two keen-eyed readers of Homer is their decision to end their own war-ravaged lives.

ETERNAL TROY

We have in the meantime left innumerable wars behind us. Images and stories turn up in the news that cause anyone who knows the *Iliad* to shudder with recognition, for example the filming of the bodies of the US soldiers as they were dragged in delirious triumph behind jeeps through the streets of Mogadishu:

> *The dust rose from Hector as he was being dragged along, his dark hair flew all abroad, and his head once so comely was laid low on earth, for Jove had now delivered him into the hands of his foes to do him outrage in his own land.*
> (*Iliad* 22.401-4, translated by Samuel Butler)

Or take the hooded Iraqis humiliated and tortured by US soldiers seeking revenge for their slain comrades on anyone who comes to hand. Like Achilles slitting the throats of a dozen youths on Patroclus' grave 'like another would cut a bunch of flowers', to quote Weil.

Troy fell, long ago, possibly somewhere in Asia Minor, at a spot now called Hisarlik. The *Iliad* merely predicts that fall, symbolically and implicitly, with the death of Hector, the city's hero and protector. But Troy is laid siege to daily with the same grisly joy, for the same immortal Helen, and with the same inconsolable women and children left behind. The *Iliad* is everywhere.

'In Trojan fields the poppies blow.' Troy has been a region of constant military significance. During the First World War the city was once more in the frontline when Allied troops landed on the nearly shores. Many of these soldiers were well aware of the historical aspect of this landing, and some of them wrote poems about it that were at times fatalist.

BIBLIOGRAPHY

INTRODUCTIONS

Numerous books have been written about Troy, the Trojan War, and about the question whether the works of Homer have a basis in history. One of the best introductory publications is *Troia und Homer; Der Weg zur Lösung eines alten Rätsels* (2001) by the great scholar on Homer, Joachim Latacz. This book was updated and translated into English in 2004: *Troy and Homer; Towards a Solution of an old Mystery* (Oxford 2004). Latacz has also written about Homer and his World, for example *Homer. His Art and His World* (1996). Michael Wood's *In Search of the Trojan War* (London 1985) is still a good introduction on the historicity and the history of research about Troy and the Trojan War. Short introductions on Homer, the archaeology of Troy the Trojan legends can be found in the exhibition catalogue *Troia. Traum und Wirklichkeit* (2001), edited by Barbara Theune-Grosskopf. The latest research on Troy's archaeological site are published in the series *Studia Troica*.

1. For ancient ideas on Homer, see B. Graziosi, *Inventing Homer. The Early Reception of Epic* (Cambridge 2002). For an overview of the debate on the oral origin of the Homeric epics, see S. Reece, 'Homer's *Iliad* and *Odyssey*: From Oral Performance to Written Text' in M.C. Amodio (ed.), *New Directions in Oral Theory* (Tempe 2005), 43-89. Defending the thesis that Homer has never existed is M. West, 'The Invention of Homer' in *The Classical Quarterly* 49 (1999), 346-382. The art of poetry in Homer is described by A. Ford, *Homer. The Poetry of the Past* (Ithaca, New York and London 2002), and I.J.F. de Jong, 'The Homeric Narrator and his own *kleos*', *Mnemosyne* 59 (2006), 188-207. Invaluable is the *Homer Encyclopedia* in three volumes, edited by M. Finkelberg. On the relationship between the oral and epic traditions in the Near East and the Greek world, see W.F.M. Henkelman, *Iter ad Paradisum. Terug naar Gilgameš, en verder, Lampas* 42 (2009), 31-55, and H. Vanstiphout, *Het epos van Gilgamesh* (Nijmegen 2002).

2. Hundreds of books have been published on the archaeology of Troy. As a rule, especially the recent publications by Korfmann and members of his team (including Joachim Latacz) give the best introductions and refer to older publications that are still relevant to this field. The series *Studia Troica* has to be singled out especially. In this series, Korfmann and his team have published the latest research and views on this historic city. A good introduction is M. Korfmann (ed.), *Troia. Archäologie eines Siedlunghügels und seiner Landschaft* (Mainz am Rhein 2006). A slightly more popular book, with many beautiful illustrations, was published by N. Fields, D. Spedaliere en S. Sulemsohn: *Troy. 1700-1250 BC* (Oxford 2004).

3. The best handbook on the history of the Hittites is written by Trevor Bryce, *Kingdom of the Hittites* (Oxford 2005). Bryce has also published an excellent book about the contacts between the Great Kings in the ancient Near East, including the relations between the Hittites and Ahhiyawa: *Letters of the Great Kings of the Ancient Near East: The Royal Correspondence of the Late Bronze Age* (London 2003). Together with Eric Cline en Gary Beckman, Bryce has translated all Hittite texts on Ahhiyawa with a commentary in *The Ahhiyawa Texts* (Atlanta 2011). In recent years a number of handbooks have been published on the Mycenaean world. A thorough, albeit somewhat conservative, overview can be found in L. Schofield, *The Mycenaeans* (Los Angeles 2007). The political structures of Greece (and the question whether there was a united Mycenaean Greece) are dealt with by J. Kelder, *The Kingdom of Mycenae; a Great Kingdom in the Late Bronze Age Aegean* (Bethesda 2010). For Lineair B and the fascinating story of the deciphering of this ancient script, see Andrew Robson, *The Man who Deciphered Linear B; The story of Michael Ventris* (London/New York 2002).

4. An introduction to the controversy about Troy's lower city can be found in D.F. Easton, J. D. Hawkins, A. G. Sherratt en E. S. Sherratt, 'Troy in Recent Perspective', in *Anatolian Studies* 52 (2002), 75-109. The literature on Homer and the world he has described in his epics is vast and generally good. Readers of this book are especially referred to J.N. Coldstream, *Geometric Greece. 900-700 BC* (London en New York 2003), as well as the above mentioned *Troia. Traum und Wirklichkeit*. For the literary quality of the epics, see *Homer on Life and Death* by Jasper Griffin (Oxford 1980). The Dutch scholar Irene de Jong has given great impetus to the study of Homer by her many publications on Homer's narrative techniques, for example *Narrators and Focalizers. The Presentation of the Story in the Iliad* (Bristol 2004). De Jong and Latacz also contribute to the *Gesamtkommentar* on the *Ilias*, that has seen several volumes published since 2000.

5. A well-documented overview of the theme of the Trojan War in the archaic and classical Greek literature is given by H. Pallantza, *Der troische Krieg in der nachhomerischen Literatur* (2005). Suzan Woodford, *The Trojan War in Ancient Art* (Londen 1993) documents the images around the subject of the Trojan War. Anthony Snodgrass, *Homer and the Artists* (Cambridge 1998) is a thorough publication on the early images relating to Homer. John Boardman published *The Archaeology of Nostalgia, how the Greeks re-created their mythical past* (Londen 2002) on the Greeks of later ages and their use of their mythical past. For Troy and the epics of Homer in Roman times, see, among others, F. Castagnoli, 'Troiani nel Lazio' in *Enciclopedia Virgiliana* (Rome 1990), 289-90, P. Schrijvers (on Julius Caesar in Troy) and H. Smolenaars (on Troy in Vergil's *Aeneid*) in *Hermeneus* 74.4 (2002). For the Game of Troy see K.-W. Weeber, '*Troiae lusus*: Alter und Entstehung eines Reiterspiels' in *Ancient Society* 5 (1974), 171-96. The *Nachleben* of Troy in the Byzantine era comes to life in *Polemos tis Troados*, an edition of the Greek text with a lengthy introduction by M. Papathomopoulos and E.M. Jeffreys (Athens 1996). Katherine Callen King, *Achilles. Paradigms of the War Hero from Homer to the Middle Ages* (Berkeley-Los Angeles-Oxford 1987) has a broad overview and describes how the story of Troy was treated in

Byzantium (and Medieval Europe). For literary descriptions in the Byzantine era see W.J. Aerts, 'Das literarische Porträt in der byzantinischen literatur' in: *Groningen Colloquia on the Novel VII* (Groningen 1997), 151-195.

6. The best-known biography of sultan Mehmed II was written by Franz Babinger, *Mehmed der Eroberer und seine Zeit* (München 1953). The history of Mehmed II by Michael Critobulus was translated into English by C.T. Riggs, *History of Mehmed the Conqueror* (Princeton 1954). Cemal Kafadar, in his book *Between Two Worlds. The Construction of the Ottoman State* (Berkeley-Los Angeles-London 1995), writes about Mehmed II's visit to Troy. Klaus Kreiser writes on Homer in Turkey in his article 'Troia und die Homerischen Epen. Von Mehmet II. bis İsmet İnönü' in the above mentioned *Troia. Traum und Wirklichkeit*, 282-290. For Vondel, Troy and the *Aeneid*, see R. Th. van der Paardt, 'Vondels *Gijsbreght* en de *Aeneis*' in *Hermeneus* 59 (1987), 244-250. Troy and the Trojan heroes in Shakespeare's plays come into view in Ch. Martindale & M. Martindale, *Shakespeare and the Uses of Antiquity* (London 1990) and K. Palmer (ed.), *Troilus & Cressida* (London 1981). The concept *lieux de mémoire* is treated by P. Nora, *Les Lieux de mémoire* (Paris 1984-1992), and further by Pim den Boer in, among others, 'Loci memoriae-Lieux de mémoire' in A. Erll & A. Nünning (ed.), *Cultural memory studies: an international and interdisciplinary handbook* (Media and cultural memory, 8) (Berlin-New York 2008), 19-25. For the history of the epics of Homer in Europe see W. Helbig, *Das homerische Epos aus den Denkmälern erläutert* (Leipzig 1987), R. M. Ogilvie, *Latin and Greek. A History of the Influence of the Classics on English Life from 1600-1918* (London 1964) and N. Hepp, *Homère en France au XVIIe siècle* (Paris 1968).

7. Recently published, on Schliemann's life in the Netherlands: W. Arentze, *Schliemann en Nederland. Een leven vol verhalen* (Leiden 2012). Biographies of Schliemann include S. Schliemann (ed.), *Heinrich Schliemann Selbstbiographie bis zum Tode vervollständigt* (Leipzig 1936), L. E. Brodhaus, *Schliemann of Troy. The story of a gold seeker* (London 1931) en D.A. Traill, *Schliemann of Troy. Treasure and deceit* (London 1995). The role of Frank Calvert during the excavations in Troy and his relation to Schliemann is treated by S. Heuck Allen, *Finding the Walls of Troy. Frank Calvert and Heinrich Schliemann at Hisarlık* (Berkeley & Los Angeles 1999). The letters of Schliemann were published by E. Meyer (ed.), *Briefe von Heinrich Schliemann, gesammelt und mit einer Einleitung in Auswahl* (Berlin-Leipzig 1936), and E. Meyer (ed.), *Heinrich Schliemann. Briefwechsel* (Berlin 1953 en 1958). Schliemann published his own excavation reports in, among others, H. Schliemann, *Bericht über die Ausgrabungen in Troja im Jahre 1890* (Leipzig 1891) and H. Schliemann, *Troja, Ergebnisse meiner neusten Ausgrabungen auf der Baustelle von Troja, in den Heldengräbern, Bunarbaschi und andern Orten der Troas im Jahre 1882* (Leipzig 1884, Dortmund 1984/1987). The correspondences of the Ottoman government concerning Troy and Schliemann can be found in the Ottoman Archives of the Prime Minister in Istanbul. For the Ottoman-Turkish perspective of the excavations by Schliemann see R. Aslan, A. Sönmez and R. Körpe, 'Heinrich Schliemanns Ausgrabung in Troia nach Osmanischen Quellen' in *Studia Troica*, 18 (2009), 237-248, R. Aslan and A. Sönmez, 'Die Entdeckung und der Schmuggel des ›Priamos-Schatzes‹ von Hisarlık (Troia) nach Athen anhand osmanischer Quellen' in *Studia Troica*, 19 (to be published in 2012), G. Uslu, 'Ottoman Appreciation of Trojan Heritage, 1870–1875' in *Tijdschrift voor Mediterrane Archeologie*, 41 (2009), 4-10, U. Esin, '19. Yüzyıl Sonlarında Heinrich Schliemann'ın Troya Kazıları ve Osmanlılar'la İlişkileri' in Z. Rona (ed.), *Osman Hamdi Bey ve Dönemi Sempozyumu 1992* (Istanbul 1993), 179-191, D. A. Günay, 'İstanbul Arkeoloji Muzeleri Arşivinden Schliemann'nın Bir Mektubu' in *Light on Top of the Black Hill, Studies Presented to Halet Çambel – Karatepe'deki Işık, Halet Çambel'e Sunulan Yazılar* (Istanbul 1998), 57-69. A recently published handbook on archeology in the Ottoman Empire, including research of Ottoman sources is Z. Bahrani, Z. Çelik en E. Eldem (ed.), *Scramble for the Past: A Story of Archaeology in the Ottoman Empire 1753-1914* (Istanbul 2011). For developments in Ottoman-Turkish museums, see W.M.K. Shaw, *Possessors and Possessed. Museums, Archaeology, and the Visualization of History in the Late Ottoman Empire* (Berkeley & Los Angeles 2003).

8. The first Ottoman-Turkish translations of the *Iliad* book I were made by Na'im Fraşeri, Ilyada. *Eser-i Homer* (Istanbul 1303/1885 or 1886) and Selanikli Hilmi, *İlyas yahud şâir-i şehir Omiros* (Istanbul 1316/1898 or 1899). 19th-century Ottoman magazines that published on Homer are, among others, *Kevkebü'l Ulum* (between December 1884 and February 1885), *Ikdam* (8 March 1893 and 15 December 1897), *Servet-i Fünun* (7 April 1904). For history books in Turkish secondary schools in the 1930s, see *Tarih I-IV. Kemalist eğitimin tarih dersleri (1931-1941)* (Istanbul 2003), III-XIII. Cemal Kafadar writes about the classical sources for political ideas in the Ottoman Empre in 'Osmanlı Siyasal Düşüncesinin Kaynakları Üzerine Gözlemler' in *Modern Türkiye'de Siyasi Düşünce. Cumhuriyet'e Devreden Düşünce Mirası. Tanzimat ve Meşrutiyet'in Birikimi*, vol. 1 (Istanbul 2002), 23-37. An very important handbook on modern Turkish literature is I. Enginün, *Yeni Türk Edebiyatı (1839-1923)* (Istanbul 2010). The publication by O. Koçak, '1920'lerden 1970'lere Kültür Politikaları' in *Modern Türkiye'de Siyasi Düşünce: Kemalizm*, vol. 2 (Istanbul 2002), 370-419, describes Turkish cultural politics and the role of humanism. S. Yüksel writes about the role of Antiquity in Turkish literature in *Türk Edebiyatında Yunan Antikitesi (1860-1908)* (Sivas 2010). For neohellenism, see B. Ayvazoğlu, *Yahya Kemal, Eve Dönen Adam* in Kapı Yayınları (Istanbul 2008), Y.K. Karaosmanoğlu, *Gençlik ve Edebiyat Hatıraları* (Ankara 1969), M. Tevfik, *Esâtir-i Yunâniyan* (Kostantiniyye 1329) and S. Şemseddin, *Esatir-Dünya Mitolojisinden Örnekler* (Istanbul 2004). For more information on the Blue Anatolians see S. Eyüboğlu, *Mavi ve Kara* (Istanbul 1967), M. Belge, *Genesis, Büyük Ulusal Anlatı ve Türklerin Kökeni* (Istanbul 2008), S. Deren, 'Türk

Siyasal Düşüncesinde Anadolu İmgesi' in T. Bora en M. Gültekingil (ed.) *Modern Türkiye'de Siyasi Düşünce 4: Milliyetçilik* (Istanbul 2002), 533-540. Modern political varieties of Blue Anatolism are described by Turgut Özal in *Turkey in Europe and Europe in Turkey* (1991). For Izmir and Homer see H. Malay, 'Smyrna, Meles ve Halkapınar' in *Eren Akçiçek'e Armağan* (Izmir 2010), M. Akurgal, 'Hellenic Architecture in Smyrna 650-546 BC' in *Milesische Forschungen Band 5, Frühes Ionien: Eine Bestandaufnahme, Panionion Symposion Güzelçamlı* (26 September-1 October 1999), 123-136.

9. The publication *101 Soruda Troia* (Çanakkale 2011) by Rüstem Aslan is a very informative book on the various aspects of Troy, as well as the travel guide *Troia/Wilusa* written by Manfred O. Korfmann (2005). Information on comic strips and Antiquity can be found at http://bib.arts.kuleuven.be/bibliotheek/oudheidfilmstrip.cfm. Rachel Bespaloffs *de l'Iliade* (1940) was translated in 1945 by Mary McCarthy as *On the Iliad*. Simone Weil's essay *l'Iliade, ou le poème de la force* (1940) was published in English by P. Holoka in 2006: *Simone Weil's The Iliad or Poem of Force: A Critical Edition*. The collected poems of C.P. Cavafy were published with parallel Greek text by C.P. Cavafy, Anthony Hirst, Peter Mackridge and Evangelos Sachperoglou in 2007.

TEXT CREDITS

TEXTS

6.2 'Homer and Troy: from European to disputable *lieux de mémoire*' is an adaptation of Boer, P. den, 'Homer und Troja', in P. den Boer, H. Duchhardt, G. Kreis, W. Schmale (eds.), *Europäische Erinneringsorte* Volume 2 (Munich 2012), p. 189-200.

7.2 'Schliemann and the Ottoman Turks' is an adaptation of: Uslu, G., 'Ottoman Appreciation of Trojan Heritage 1870–1875', *Tijdschrift voor Mediterrane Archeologie* 41 (2009), 4-10.

DOCUMENTS

For this publication the following documents have been consulted:

7.2 Istanbul, Başbakanlık Osmanlı Arşivi

    I.HR. 250/14863: 10 Rebiülahir 1288 (29/06/1871)

    MF.MKT. 17/98: 23 Muharrem 1291 (12/03/1874)

    MF.MKT. 17/188: 11 Safer 1291 (30/03/1874)

    MF.MKT. 18/94: 19 Rebiülahir 1291 (05/06/1874)

    MF.MKT. 18/97: 23 Rebiülahir 1291 (09/06/1874)

    MF.MKT. 18/147: 09 Cemaziyelahir 1291 (24/07/1874)

    MF.MKT.. 26/153: 26 Safer 1292 (03/04/1875)

7.3 BOA MF.MKT., 18/147, 24 Temmuz 1874

8.3 Başbakanlık Cumhuriyet Arşivi (BCA), 030.0.18.01.02.40.78.019. (05/02/1933).

ILLUSTRATION CREDITS

Amsterdam, Allard Pierson Museum/Stephan van der Linden:
p. 12, 15 (left), 18 (donated by dr. Bierens de Haan), 27 (left),
41, 53 (below), 69, 73, 79, 80, 85, 86, 96, 108

Amsterdam, Bijzondere Collecties van de Universiteit van
Amsterdam/Stephan van der Linden: p. 114, 116, 119 (left),
128, 172, 174

Amsterdam, Tom Blau/Camera Press/Hollandse Hoogte:
p. 52 (left)

Amsterdam, Hollandse Hoogte: cover illustration

Amsterdam, De Nederlandse Opera: 126

Amsterdam, Peter F. van den Eijnde: p. 67 (above)

Amsterdam, Laurien de Gelder: p. 14, 27

Amsterdam, Günay Uslu: p. 145, 146, 147

Amsterdam, Willemijn Waal: p. 44

Argos, Archaeological Museum: p. 56

Athens, Thomas Loughlin: p. 17, 47, 57, 62-63, 131

Athene, Jonathan Tomlinson: p. 51

Belgium, Jean Housen: p. 53 (above)

Berlin, Deutsches archäologisches Institut
(www.hattuscha.de): p. 42

Berlin, Museum für Vor- und Frühgeschichte, Staatliche
Museen zu Berlin-Stiftung Preußischer Kulturbesitz: p. 26, 130

Berlin, Vorderasiatisches Museum, Staatliche Museen zu
Berlin-Stiftung Preußischer Kulturbesitz: p. 20

Brussels, Koninklijke Musea voor Kunst en Geschiedenis: p. 8

Çanakkale, Çimenlik Kalesi Museum: p. 158

Carlisle, PA, Dickinson College: p. 54

Dreamstime Stock Photography (www.dreamstime.com): p. 71

The Hague, Hoogsteder & Hoogsteder: p. 110, 113

Heemstede, René van Beek: p. 25 (below), 38, 70, 180

Florence, DeAgostini Picture Library/Scala: p. 89

Florence, Namur Archive/Scala: p. 102

Florence, Scala: p. 87, 108

Istanbul, Mithat Atabay Koleksiyon: p. 156

Istanbul, Eyüboğlu Familiearchief: p. 160

Istanbul, Istanbul Arkeoloji Müzeleri: p. 2, 45, 75

Istanbul, Gülbün Mesara Koleksiyon: p. 149

Istanbul, Ottoman Archives of the Prime Ministry:
p. 127 (above) (I.HR. 250/14863-1), 134 (I.HR. 250/14863-2),
135 (MF.MKT. 17/188), 136 (left) (MF.MKT. 18/97-1),
136 (right) (MF.MKT. 18/97-2)

Istanbul, Sevdet Serbest: p. 142

Istanbul, Ömer Faruk Şerifoğlu Koleksiyon: p. 151, 152-153, 160

Istanbul, Topkapı Sarayı Müzesi; p. 104, 107

Istanbul, Şükrü Tül: p. 163 (below), 164, 165

Izmir, Saffet Gözlükaya: p. 163 (above)

Leiden, Rijksmuseum van Oudheden: p. 15 (right), 38, 60, 84, 92

London, Bridgeman Art Liberary/Getty Images: p. 64

London, Tristram Kenton: p. 120

Londen, The British Library: p. 119 (right)

London, The National Portrait Gallery: p. 118

London, The Royal Opera House/Bill Cooper: p. 125

London, The Trustees of the British Museum: p. 83

Munich, Christoph Haußner: p. 22, 24, 25 (above)

New York, Herbert F. Johnson Museum of Art, Cornell
University: p. 76

Paris, RMN-Grand Palais (Musée du Louvre)/René-Gabriel
Ojéda: p. 78

Private collection: p. 90, 93, 115

Rotterdam, Museum Boijmans Van Beuningen/Studio Tromp,
Rotterdam: p. 111

Tilburg, Wim Hupperetz: p. 61 (right)

Troy, Projekt Troia, Dünya Kültür Mirası-World Heritage,
(Rüstem Aslan/ Murat Kıray): p. 5, 27 (rechts), 29, 30, 31, 32,
33, 34, 35, 36, 39, 61, 91, 138, 139, 140, 141, 166 (Hakan Öge),
167, 168, 169, 170, 171, 177, 179

Vatican City, Museo Gregorio Etrusco, Musei Vaticani: p. 65 (left)

Zoetermeer, Avision: p. 21, 49

PRODUCTION CREDITS

Publisher
wbooks
info@wbooks.com
www.wbooks.com
In collaboration with the Allard Pierson Museum
in Amsterdam (www.allardpiersonmuseum.nl)
and Sezer Tansuğ Sanat Vakfı in Istanbul.

Coordination
Paulien Retèl

Translations
Cem Yavuz and Kutse Altın (English-Turkish)
Rohan Minogue (Dutch-English)
Noctua Taal en tekst, Corinna Vermeulen
and Ilia Neudecker (English-Dutch)

Image editors
Paulien Retèl, Jorrit Kelder, Marissa van de Vrede

Editor text
Toon Vugts, Rohan Minogue

Design
Miriam Schlick (www.extrablond.nl)

Color separation
PRDigitaal

Printing
Printer Trento

Illustration
Cover Henri Paul Motte, engraving after *The Trojan Horse*.
Page 2 One of Troy's more spectacular finds, these pieces are
part of the the gold headdress found by Heinrich Schliemann
in the layers Troy II/III. They are dated to the Early Bronze
Age, 2600-300 BC.
pagina 5 The site of Troy today.
pagina 8 Pyxis (jewellery box) depicting the judgement
of Paris, 575-525 BC.

ISBN 978 90 400 0750 7 (Dutch edition)
ISBN 978 90 663 0001 9 (Turkish edition)
ISBN 978 90 400 0793 4 (English edition)
NUR 651

W BOOKS